HANDBOOKS

ARCHES & CANYONLANDS
NATIONAL PARKS

W. C. McRAE & JUDY JEWELL

SOUTHEASTERN UTAH

Black Ridge Canyons Wilderness Area

Westwater

Dolores River

Cisco

128

Colorado River

Castle Valley

128

Manti-La Sal National Forest

46

Summit Point

La Sal

191

Moab

Arches National Park

191

La Sal Junction

SAN JUAN

Thompson Springs

GRAND

191

313

Dead Horse Point State Park

Canyonlands National Park

Canyonlands National Park

Crescent Junction

6 191

70

Green River

Green River

Colorado River

Green River State Park

LOWER SAN RAFAEL RD

San Rafael River

Glen Canyon

National

Recreation

Area

191

6

WAYNE

70

EMERY

24

Dirty Devil River

6 191

70

Goblin Valley State Park

Hanksville

24

CANYONLANDS NATIONAL PARK

Dead Horse Point State Park

Labyrinth Canyon

VISITOR CENTER

313

MINERAL RD

MINERAL BOTTOM

LABYRINTH

DEAD HORSE POINT

DEAD HORSE POINT OVERLOOK

POTASH RD

SHAFER

SHAFER TRAIL RD

Canyonlands National Park

VISITOR CENTER

NECK SPRINGS

SHAFER CANYON OVERLOOK

Lathrop Trail

AIRPORT

River

Meander Canyon

Colorado

GOOSEBERRY

WHITE RIM OVERLOOK

WHITE RIM ROAD

Rim

GRAND VIEW POINT

GRAND VIEW TRAIL

MESA ARCH TRAIL

Aztec Butte

ISLAND IN THE SKY DISTRICT

Whale Rock

WILLOW FLAT

GREEN RIVER OVERLOOK

BUCK CANYON OVERLOOK

Murphy Point

Alcove Spring Trail

TAYLOR

Taylor Canyon

Taylor Trail

Syncline Trail

Upheaval Dome

UPHEAVAL DOME ROAD

CANDLESTICK

RIM RD

MURPHY HOGBACK

White

Green River

Stillwater Canyon

RIM

WHITE

HARDSCRABBLE

POTATO BOTTOM

Glen Canyon

National

Recreation

Area

MINERAL BOTTOM

GREAT GALLERY TRAIL

BLM

GREAT GALLERY PICTOGRAPHS

HORSESHOE CANYON UNIT

© AVALON TRAVEL

Canyonlands National Park

NEEDLES DISTRICT

MAZE DISTRICT

Beef Basin

Land of Standing Rocks

Colorado River

Lake Powell

HANS FLAT RANGER STATION

WHITE CRACK

COLORADO RIVER OVERLOOK

BIG SPRING CANYON OVERLOOK

CONFLUENCE OVERLOOK

Confluence

MAZE OVERLOOK

Elaterite Basin

North Canyon Trail

Orange Cliffs

BAGPIPE BUTTE OVERLOOK

FLINT SHEEP

FLINT TRAIL

SUNSET PASS

GOLDEN STAIRS

Waterhole Flat

Ernie's Country

The Fins

DOLL HOUSE

Spanish Bottom

Cataract Canyon

Lower Red

Lake Cyn Tr

DEVILS KITCHEN

Chesler Park

Elephant Canyon

Druid Arch

Squaw Canyon

Big Spring Cyn

Lost Canyon

Peekaboo Trail

Squaw Canyon

Elephant Canyon Scenic Drive

ELEPHANT HILL

POTHOLE POINT

SLICKROCK

Big Spring Canyon Scenic Drive

VISITOR CENTER

WOODEN SHOE OVERLOOK

SQUAW FLAT CAMPGROUND/TRAILHEAD

CAVE SPRING TRAIL

ROADSIDE RUIN

NEEDLES OUTPOST

Salt Creek Canyon

Horse Canyon

Castle Arch

Fortress Arch

Angel Arch

Bobbys Hole

2 mi

2 km

0

0

Contents

Discover Arches & Canyonlands

Southeastern Utah is so filled with staggering beauty, drama, and power that it seems like a place of myth. In this corner of Utah, two national parks, several national monuments and recreation areas, and multiple state parks are all within a day's drive of each other. The colorful canyons, arches, and mesas found within this high, dry area are surprisingly diverse, and each park has its own characteristic landscape. Nor are the riches here restricted to natural beauty: These rugged landscapes hold the remains of ancient Native American cultures, and the haunting beauty of their rock art is on display at hundreds of locations. The area's modern hub, and one of Utah's most vibrant communities, is Moab, a recreational mecca known for its mountain biking and comfortable, even sophisticated, dining and lodging.

The mystical beauty of Arches National Park, where delicate rock arches provide vast windows into the solid rock, is awe-inspiring and nearly magical. Short trails draw hikers into a dramatic landscape of slickrock promontories and stone bridges.

In Canyonlands National Park, the Colorado River carves through deep red sandstone. From the Island in the Sky unit, expansive vistas take in hundreds of miles of canyon country, while rafting the Colorado's Cataract Canyon is the wet and thrilling climax of many a vacation.

Beyond the national park boundaries, much of the land in

southeastern Utah is publicly owned, and in many cases it vies with the national parks in terms of beauty and grandeur. No trip to Island in the Sky should neglect a side trip to Dead Horse State Park, with its astonishing views into the Colorado River Canyon. Hikers looking for their own patch of wildlands should check out Fisher Towers, a Bureau of Land Management recreation area upriver from Moab. A bit off the beaten path, Hovenweep National Monument preserves a wondrous series of Anasazi villages perched on the edge of a cliff—and best of all, you'll often have the entire area to yourself.

Although many people first visit southeastern Utah as part of a grand tour of the Southwest, they often return here to further explore a smaller and distinctive corner of this vast landscape. After a small glimpse of the magnificence and variety, some latch on to one special place and return year after year, growing to know it intimately.

Planning Your Trip

▶ WHERE TO GO

Southeastern Utah encompasses some of the grandest landscapes on earth, including the first trenchings of the Colorado River's Grand Canyon, the improbably elegant stone bridges of Arches National Park, a wealth of ancient rock art, and hiking and biking paths renowned around the globe—all in an area roughly the size of West Virginia. Nearly all the sites in this guide are just a day's drive apart, so come with a week's vacation and catch an eyeful of astonishing natural beauty, explore ancient Native American culture, and partake of recreational high energy in such youthful hotbeds as Moab.

Arches National Park

Arches National Park, with its famous rock bridges, is a great family park: It's not too large, and there are lots of accessible hikes to explore. Unlike other Utah national parks, there's plenty to see even if you can't get out of the car and hike; the drive through the park is astonishing. But if you're up for it, take along comfortable shoes and hike the Windows Section, a series of arches and rock fins at the center of the park, and to Delicate Arch, overlooking the Colorado River. You'll need a permit (or better yet, join a ranger-led tour) and to be in good shape for the more challenging hikes into the remote and wonderful Fiery Furnace.

Canyonlands National Park

Canyonlands National Park comprises four sections: the River District, containing the canyons of the Colorado and Green Rivers;

IF YOU HAVE . . .

Hovenweep National Monument

- **A WEEKEND:** Stay in Moab and explore Arches National Park, the Island in the Sky District of Canyonlands, and Dead Horse Point State Park.
- **FIVE DAYS:** Add a trip to the Needles District of Canyonlands and a day of hiking

or biking around Moab.

- **A WEEK:** From Moab, head south to Blanding or Bluff (visit Hovenweep National Monument), west across Cedar Mesa, and north to Canyonlands' Horseshoe Canyon Unit and Goblin Valley State Park.

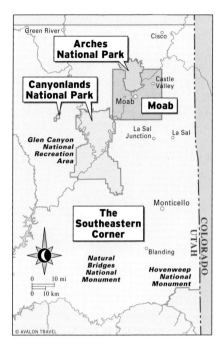

separate area, the Horseshoe Canyon Unit, lies to the west and contains a significant cache of prehistoric rock art.

Moab

At the heart of Utah's slickrock country, Moab is the recreation capital of southeastern Utah. Although mountain biking put Moab on the map, nowadays four-wheeling seems to be the extreme sport of choice. Arches National Park is just minutes from downtown, and Canyonlands' districts are an easy drive from Moab. But Moab is a destination in itself, a youthful high-energy town that offers good restaurants, brewpubs, and coffee shops.

The Southeastern Corner

Although Arches and Canyonlands parks get most of the attention from first-time visitors, veterans of the area know that southeastern Utah has abundant other wonders in national recreation areas, national monuments, and state parks. After you have explored the national parks, be sure to save time to visit such fascinating destinations as Natural Bridges National Monument, Hovenweep National Monument, Dead Horse Point State Park, and the lovely alpine glades of La Sal National Forest.

the Needles District, with hiking trails and backcountry roads through a standing-rock desert; the Maze District, a remote area filled with geologic curiosities and labyrinthine canyons; and the Island in the Sky District, a flat-topped mesa that overlooks all the rest. A

▶ WHEN TO GO

The parks are all open year-round, although spring (Apr.-early June) and early fall (Sept.-Oct.) are the most pleasant times to visit. They're also the busiest, and travelers may find that popular campgrounds and hotels are booked well in advance.

Spring rain can also dampen trails, and late winter and early spring storms can play havoc with backcountry roads.

Thunderstorms are fairly common in summer (late July-early Sept.) and bring the threat of flash flooding, especially in slot canyons. In Canyonlands, Arches, and Moab, summer temperatures can reach the 100s.

In Canyonlands and Arches, winter days tend to be bright and sunny, but nighttime temperatures can dip into the teens or lower. However, the lack of crowds and brilliant sunshine can make this a wonderful time to visit, if you don't mind layering your outer wear.

red rock formations in Canyonlands National Park

► BEFORE YOU GO

Although the national parks and public lands of southeast Utah are located in a geographically compact area, connecting the dots to visit each of them isn't always straightforward. The rugged topography of the area has made road building difficult, so visiting all of the areas we recommend requires planning ahead and making choices. Unpaved back roads can serve as shortcuts if you have a high-clearance vehicle, but check locally before setting out to determine current conditions: Rainstorms and snowmelt can render these roads impassable.

If you're planning on making the rounds of all of Utah's national parks, buy an America the Beautiful–National Parks and Federal Recreational Lands Pass ($80, good for one year) at your first stop to cover entrance to all national parks. If you plan to visit Hovenweep and Natural Bridges National Monuments as well as Arches and Canyonlands, pick up a Local Passport ($25, good for one year). Senior passes ($10 for a lifetime pass) and free passes for residents with permanent disabilities are also available.

What to Take

Unless you want to return from Utah looking like a leather handbag, remember to use lots of sunscreen. Prepare for wide variations in temperature; nights in the desert can be very chilly even when summer highs soar above 100°F.

There's no need to pack dressy clothes. Casual clothes are acceptable nearly everywhere, even in what passes for a classy restaurant.

Alcohol presents another issue. If you'll want to drink, especially away from Moab, pack your own, especially if you have discerning tastes. While many restaurants in the towns around the parks now offer a selection of alcoholic beverages, southeastern Utah does not have a drinking culture. Beer sold in grocery stores and most restaurants is 3.2 percent alcohol.

Bring your cell phone, but don't count on reception in the canyons of southern Utah.

Explore Arches & Canyonlands

Moab is an excellent hub for visiting Arches and Canyonlands, as it affords comfortable lodgings and very good dining in addition to a lively nightlife scene. But each of the parks also offers campgrounds, and the region also has a selection of guest ranches and B&Bs. In the southern part of the region, the tiny town of Bluff is a handsome destination with good hotels and restaurants and is a good center for visits to Hovenweep and Cedar Mesa.

▶ THE BEST OF ARCHES AND CANYONLANDS

If you're a hiker or biker, it's easy to spend a week exploring Southeast Utah—and if you're a fan of the backcountry, you could easily spend another week investigating such remote and otherworldly destinations as the Maze District and the Green River canyon.

Day 1

Drive into Moab and claim your hotel room (or campsite at Arches National Park). Take the rest of the day to explore this hip and youthful town with its obsessive regard for mountain biking and microbrews. It's not hard to find good food and convivial company, all with the splendid backdrop of red rock canyons.

Day 2

Explore Arches National Park, with a drive around the ring parkway and frequent stops for short hikes. Be sure to hike to the

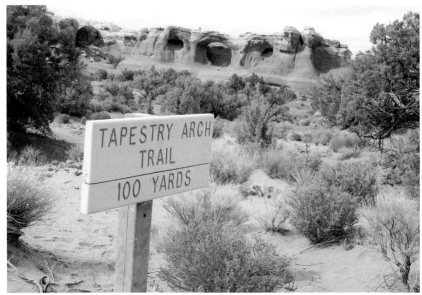

trail to Tapestry Arch, Arches National Park

dramatic Windows section and stand below these massive stone bridges. Save some time and energy to climb up the slickrock bluff to Delicate Arch, perhaps the park's most famed beauty spot.

Day 3

Get an early start on the day by joining a ranger-led hike of Arches' Fiery Furnace area (you'll need advance reservations for these popular and moderately strenuous tours), and then return to Moab to join a half-day raft trip that explores the canyons of the Colorado River.

Day 4

Check out the mesa-top vistas from Canyonlands' Island in the Sky District. On the way to the mother of all belvederes at Grand View Point, be sure to stop by Dead Horse Point State Park and take the short hike to cliff's edge or bike the park's Intrepid mountain bike trail system.

Day 5

Drive south from Moab to the Needles District of Canyonlands. On the way into the park, be sure to stop at Newspaper Rock, one of Utah's top caches of ancient Native American rock art. Plan to explore some of the Needles backcountry on hiking trails before driving south to Bluff to spend the night.

Day 6

From Bluff, drive east to Hovenweep National Monument, a very well preserved series of Anasazi stone-built villages at the edge of high-desert canyons. In the afternoon, return to Bluff and explore some of the many rock art panels in the area.

Day 7

From Bluff, drive back north to Highway 95, stopping to view the Anasazi ruins at Butler Wash, and detour into the wonder of Natural Bridges National Monument. Then, if you're visiting during summer, take Highway 276

Hanksville, north of Lake Powell

BEST DAY HIKES

hiking in the Fiery Furnace, Arches National Park

It's difficult to imagine more dramatic landscapes than those found in Southeastern Utah's national parks. These day hikes through epic canyons, arches, and needles of sandstone invite you to get out of your vehicle and explore.

CANYONLANDS

· **Horseshoe Canyon:** This hike takes you to phenomenal rock art at the **Great Gallery,** a near-mystical experience for many. The 6.5-mile trail requires negotiating a steep canyon wall, but experiencing the stunning petroglyphs in a verdant canyon is well worth the effort. The trailhead is 30 miles east of Highway 24 on gravel roads.

· **Neck Spring Trail:** In the **Island in the Sky District,** the landscape is nearly all vertical, and hiking trails explore the rock faces and canyon walls. This trail drops from the Island in the Sky road down to a series of springs in Taylor Canyon, a tiny oasis with songbirds and luxuriant plantlife, then loops back up the canyon wall to complete the delightful, not-too-arduous five-mile hike.

· **Confluence Overlook Trail:** Even though the Colorado River is responsible for trenching the incredible landscapes of Canyonlands, it's often difficult to see the river in its canyon. In the **Needles District,** this trail allows hikers to look down on the confluence of the Green and Colorado Rivers from 1,000-foot cliffs. This fairly easy 11-mile round-trip trail starts from the end of Big Spring Canyon Overlook Scenic Drive.

ARCHES

· **Delicate Arch:** This three-mile round-trip hike is a fantastic experience, a moderately demanding trail up a slickrock formation to the aptly named arch and transcendent views over the Colorado River Canyon.

· **Devils Garden:** If you'd prefer a trail without crowds, go to the end of the paved parkway and hike the 7.2-mile loop trail past eight arches and the weird formations in Fin Canyon. Crowds drop off after the first mile or so.

· **Fiery Furnace Trail:** Though this challenging backcountry trail is only two miles long, you can easily spend half a day or longer in this maze of narrow canyons. Access is restricted: You'll need a permit to hike on your own, or sign up in advance to join a ranger-led hike.

Lake Powell

south and cross the Colorado River's Lake Powell on the Halls Crossing-Bullfrog ferry service. Outside the ferry's season, you can continue on Highway 95 to cross the Colorado on the Hite Bridge, with no loss of scenic value. Once on the west side of the river, follow paved roads north to Hanksville and more Utah adventures.

▶ BEST BIKE RIDES

Moab is the center for some of the most noted mountain bike trails in the West. However, most of the trails here aren't for novices—you need to be proficient on your bike and ready for extreme weather before heading out on your two-wheeled steed. If you'd rather explore these backcountry routes with a guide, simply contact one of the many bike shops in Moab, and they can set you up with a tour.

Slickrock Bike Trail

This is the trail that started the mountain-bike craze in Moab, and it's a challenge even to strong riders. The aptly-named trail traverses steep, exposed slickrock faces on its nearly 10-mile length, passing a succession of canyon and mountain viewpoints.

Gemini Bridges

You'll find dramatic scenery along this 14-mile (one-way) trail that drops though the rock fins and arches of the Wingate Formation. The trick is getting to the trailhead, which is 12.5 miles uphill from Moab. The best answer is to hire a shuttle bus as transportation—from that point onward, this is one of the more moderate biking trails in the Moab area.

Monitor and Merrimac Trail

This 13.2-mile trail system north of Moab explores a varied series of desert landscapes, including the namesake Monitor and Merrimac mesas as well as Mill Canyon and its dinosaur fossil bed. This is a good training ride for the more challenging rides in the area.

MOAB Brand Trails

This new trail system joins four interconnecting routes that offer a total of 11 miles of cycling. The Bar-M trail is easy enough for families, while other trails include thrills and spills aplenty for more seasoned riders. Catch the trailhead north of Moab near the Bar M Chuckwagon.

▶ RIVER TRIPS

The Colorado River is the big name in river trips here, but there are certainly other options for those looking for more remote and challenging adventures. And even on the Colorado, you have a choice of white water, easy-going family tours, jet boats, and tours with light shows and meals—you'll find a plethora of outfitters in Moab ready to get you out on a river.

The Colorado River's Cataract Canyon

This is the most adventurous white-water trip in the Moab area, with lots of Class III and IV rapids through the Canyonlands and Glen Canyon area of the Colorado River. Most Cataract Canyon trips take four days to complete, although some outfitters offer motorized trips that conclude the trip in just two days.

The Colorado River's Westwater Canyon

Upstream from Moab, near the Colorado border, Westwater Canyon offers lots of white-water adventure in a day-long trip. If you're looking for an intense day of rafting but can't devote four days to Cataract Canyon, this is the trip for you.

The Colorado River's Fisher Towers Section

If you're an all-ages family group or not comfortable with white water, trips through the Fisher Towers section of the Colorado just upstream from Moab might be the answer. The rapids are fun without being frightening, and the scenery is top-notch. Full-day and half-day trips are available. This is also a trip that experienced rafters could easily negotiate on their own—just arrange to rent gear in Moab.

The Green River

For an easygoing backcountry experience, the Green River, which flows into the Colorado at Canyonlands National Park, offers stellar scenery and mild enough river conditions for canoeists. To make the full journey from the town of Green River to Mineral Bottom take five days.

The San Juan River

Board a raft in Bluff and paddle through some of the most remote canyons in the West. A three-day trip will get you to the town of Mexican Hat; add a few more days to navigate the meanders of the Goosenecks and pull out at Lake Powell.

Jet Boats and Tour Boats

If you're just looking for an easy way to get out on the Colorado River and experience its canyon landscapes, consider half-day or full-day jet-boat tours that explore the river on high-speed boats. Popular trips leave from Moab and race downriver to the boundary of Canyonlands National Park (jet boats aren't allowed in the park). Another option is the colorful sound-and-light tours provided by Canyonlands by Night (425/259-5261), which also offer the option of dinner cruises.

THE LEGACY OF ANCIENT ROCK ART

rock art at Sego Canyon, north of Moab

Southeastern Utah contains a rich tapestry of pictographs (drawings painted on rock using natural dyes) and petroglyphs (images carved into stone). Searching out rock-art panels can easily become an obsession, and it's a good one, since it will lead you far off the beaten path and deep into canyons that were once central for the area's ancient inhabitants.

- **Delicate Arch:** On this popular hiking trail in Arches is an often-overlooked panel of Ute Style rock-art images.

- **Great Gallery:** One of the most important rock-art sites in the United States is in Canyonlands' Horseshoe Canyon Unit.

- **Holly Ruins:** You'll find many petroglyphs at Hovenweep National Monument, one of Utah's best-preserved Anasazi villages.

- **Newspaper Rock:** Near Canyonlands' Needles District, this is another easily reached showcase of rock art.

- **Sego Canyon:** An hour north of Moab you'll find hundreds of etched images, starting with ghostly, shamanic-looking creatures right out of sci-fi movies.

- **Utah Scenic Byway 279:** Follow this highly scenic route roughly six west of Moab, where a series of petroglyphs appear at the base of 800-foot-high cliffs. Just look for the sign pointing to "Indian Writing."

ARCHES NATIONAL PARK

A concentration of rock arches of marvelous variety has formed within the maze of sandstone fins at Arches National Park, one of the most popular national parks in the United States. Balanced rocks and tall spires add to the splendor. Paved roads and short hiking trails provide easy access to some of the more than 1,500 arches in the park. If you're short on time, a drive through the Windows Section (23.5 miles round-trip) affords a look at some of the largest and most spectacular arches. To visit all the stops and hike a few short trails takes a full day.

Most of the early settlers and cowboys who passed through the Arches area paid little attention to the scenery. In 1923, however, a prospector by the name of Alexander Ringhoffer interested officials of the Rio Grande Railroad in the scenic attractions at what he called Devils Garden, now known as Klondike Bluffs. The railroad people liked the area and contacted Stephen Mather, the first director of the National Park Service. Mather started the political process that led to designating two small areas as a national monument in 1929, but Ringhoffer's Devils Garden wasn't included until later. The monument grew in size over the years and became Arches National Park in 1971. The park now comprises 76,519 acres—small enough to be appreciated in one day, yet large enough to warrant extensive exploration.

Thanks to unrelenting erosion, the arches

© JUDY JEWELL

HIGHLIGHTS

© AVALON TRAVEL

LOOK FOR (TO FIND RECOMMENDED SIGHTS, ACTIVITIES, DINING, AND LODGING.

(Balanced Rock: An unbelievable spire-upon-spire balancing act rising 128 feet from the desert, Balanced Rock is sure to give your camera a warm-up (page 25).

(Windows Section: Some of the park's largest arches are here—so are some of its largest crowds. But you have to go: Make it past the first arch and the crowds thin out (page 26).

(Delicate Arch Trail: Delicate Arch is beautiful when seen from the easily reached viewpoint. It's mystical when seen close up, after a tough 1.5-mile hike to its base. If you're not up to the hike, at least follow the trail across the Salt Wash footbridge and turn left to find a striking but often overlooked rock art panel, carved by Ute artists about 400 years ago (page 31).

(Fiery Furnace Trail: To reach this unusual wonderland of rock mazes, fins, and turrets, hikers should join a ranger-led tour. Hikes into this red-rock landscape are popular, so go online and book your tour in advance (page 31).

(Devils Garden Loop: This 7.2-mile loop trail, leading to eight named arches and through a landscape of bizarre rock fins, offers the park's best day hiking (page 32).

(Tower Arch Trail: This spire, with an arch at its base, is one of the park's most beautiful but neglected sights. The formation in Arches' backcountry is off-limits to the RV set—you'll need a high-clearance vehicle (page 34).

themselves are constantly changing. Every so often there's a dramatic change, as there was during the summer of 2008 when Wall Arch, a 71-foot span on the Devils Garden Trail, collapsed.

PLANNING YOUR TIME

If you only have part of the day to explore, drive the 18-mile length of the main park road with brief stops at Balanced Rock and the Delicate Arch viewpoint. At the road's end, set out on the Devils Garden Trail, but take only the trip to Tunnel and Pine Tree Arches. If you still

have some time, stop on the way back out of the park and take a stroll on the Park Avenue Trail.

A full day in the park allows plenty of time to stop at the visitors center and then hike the full Delicate Arch Trail and explore Devils Garden. Energetic hikers may want to do the entire 7.2-mile loop in Devils Garden; those who want less of a workout can walk the one-mile-long trail to Landscape Arch.

If you have more than one day to spend, plan ahead and register online for a ranger-led hike into the Fiery Furnace area of the park. This

ARCHES NATIONAL PARK

Long Valley

Yellow
Cat Flat

Eagle Park

Salt

Valley

Klondike Bluffs

TOWER ARCH
TRAIL

Primitive Trail

Dark Angel   Private Arch

Devils Garden

Double O Arch

Tower
Arch

Marching
Men

Landscape Arch

DEVILS
GARDEN LOOP

DEVILS GARDEN

Skyline Arch

Salt

Broken Arch

Valley

Wash

Sand Dune
Arch

4WD   RD

Arches

FIERY FURNACE
TRAIL

Salt Wash

Winter Camp Ridge

DELICATE
ARCH TRAIL

National

WOLFE RANCH

DELICATE ARCH
VIEWPOINT

To I-70

Park

PANORAMA POINT

Dry Mesa

Willow

Flats

Garden of
Eden

Double
Arch

Sevenmile Canyon

Courthouse

Rock
Pinnacles

BALANCED
ROCK

North/South
Window

WINDOWS
SECTION

Mat Martin Point

313

To Canyonlands
National Park
(Island in the
Sky District)

191

The Great Wall

Wash

Petrified Dunes

Sheep Rock

Courthouse
Towers Viewpoint/
The Organ

Three Gossips
Courthouse Towers

Colorado River

128

PARK AVENUE

VISITOR CENTER

Arths Pasture

0   2 mi

0   2 km

POTASH RD

279

191

Moab

© AVALON TRAVEL

EDWARD ABBEY: "RESIST MUCH, OBEY LITTLE"

Edward Abbey spent two summers in the late 1950s living in a trailer in Arches National Park. From this experience, he wrote *Desert Solitaire,* which, when it was published in 1968, introduced many readers to the beauties of Utah's slickrock country and to the need to preserve it. In the introduction to this book, he gives a word of caution to slickrock pilgrims:

> Do not jump into your automobile next June and rush out to the Canyon country hoping to see some of that which I have attempted to evoke in these pages. In the first place you can't see anything from a car; you've got to get out of the goddamned contraption and walk, better yet crawl, on hands and knees, over the sandstone and through the...cactus. When traces of blood begin to mark your trail you'll see something, maybe.

This sense of letting the outdoors affect you–right down to the bone–pervades Abbey's writing. He advocated responding to assaults on the environment in an equally raw, gutsy way. Convinced that the only way to confront rampant development in the American West was by preserving its wilderness, he was a pioneer of radical environmentalism, a "desert anarchist." Long before Earth First!, Abbey's fictional characters blew up dams and created a holy environmentalist ruckus in *The Monkey Wrench Gang.* Some of his ideas were radical, others reactionary, and he seemed deeply committed to raising a stir. Abbey's writing did a lot to change the way people think about the American West, its development, and staying true to values derived from the natural world.

Two biographies, *Edward Abbey: A Life,* by James M. Cahalan (Tucson: University of Arizona Press, 2001), and the less academic *Adventures with Ed,* by Abbey's good friend Jack Loeffler (Albuquerque: University of New Mexico Press, 2002), help readers see the person behind the icon.

takes about half a day; for the other half, head out via car or mountain bike to Tower Arch Trail.

Although Arches is known more for day hiking than backpacking, park rangers can help you put together a backpacking trip and issue the required backcountry permit.

Exploring the Park

The entrance to Arches National Park (435/719-2299, www.nps.gov/arch, $10 per vehicle, $5 bicyclists, motorcyclists, and pedestrians) is five miles north of downtown Moab on U.S. 191.

VISITORS CENTER

Located just past the park entrance booth, the expansive visitors center (7:30am-6:30pm daily Apr.-Oct., 8am-4:30pm daily Nov.-Mar.) provides a good introduction to what you can expect ahead. Exhibits identify the rock layers, describe the geologic and human history, and illustrate some of the wildlife and plants of the park. A large outdoor plaza is a good place to troll for information when the visitors center is closed.

A short slide program runs regularly, and staff members are available to answer your questions, issue backcountry permits, and check you in for a ranger-led tour in the Fiery Furnace area of the park. Look for the posted list of special activities; rangers host campfire programs and lead a wide variety of guided walks April-September. You'll also find checklists, pamphlets, books, maps, posters, postcards, and film for purchase. See the rangers for advice and the free backcountry permit required for overnight trips. The easy 0.2-mile **Desert Nature Trail** begins near the visitors center and identifies some of the native plants. Picnic areas are outside the visitors center and at Balanced Rock and Devils Garden.

Desert bighorn sheep frequent the area around the visitors center and can sometimes be seen from U.S. 191 just south of the park entrance. A sheep crossing about three miles north of the visitors center is also a good place to scan the steep talus slopes for these nimble animals.

A road guide to Arches National Park, available at the visitors center, has detailed descriptions that correspond to place-names along the main road. Be sure to stop only in parking lots and designated pullouts. Watch out for others who are sightseeing in this popular park. With less than 30 miles of paved road, the traffic can be surprisingly heavy in the summer high season.

If your plans include visiting Canyonlands National Park plus Hovenweep and Natural Bridges National Monuments, consider the so-called Local Passport ($25), which buys entry to all of these federal preserves. Purchase the pass at any of the park or national monument entrances.

MOAB FAULT

The park road begins a long but well-graded climb from the visitors center up the cliffs to the northeast. A pullout on the right after 1.1 miles offers a good view of Moab Canyon and its geology. The rock layers on this side of the canyon have slipped down more than 2,600 feet in relation to the other side. Movement took place about six million years ago along the Moab Fault, which follows the canyon floor. Rock layers at the top of the far cliffs are nearly the same age as those at the bottom on this side. If you could stack the rocks of this side on top of rocks on the other side, you'd have a complete stratigraphic column of the Moab area—more than 150 million years' worth.

PARK AVENUE

South Park Avenue overlook and trailhead are on the left 2.1 miles from the visitors center. Great sandstone slabs form a skyline on each side of this dry wash. A trail goes north one mile down the wash to the North Park Avenue trailhead (1.3 miles ahead by road). Arrange to be picked up there, or backtrack to your starting point. The large rock monoliths of Courthouse Towers rise north of Park Avenue. Only a few small arches exist now, although major arches may have formed there in the past.

◖ BALANCED ROCK

This gravity-defying formation is on the right, 8.5 miles from the visitors center. A boulder more than 55 feet high rests precariously atop a 73-foot pedestal. Chip Off the Old Block, a much smaller version of Balanced Rock, stood nearby until it collapsed in the winter of 1975-1976. For a closer look at Balanced Rock, take

© BILL MCRAE

The aptly named Balanced Rock only looks precarious.

The Windows Section is a good place for a short hike.

© JUDY JEWELL

the 0.3-mile trail encircling it. There's a picnic area across the road. Author Edward Abbey lived in a trailer near Balanced Rock for a season as a park ranger in the 1950s; his journal became the basis for the classic *Desert Solitaire.*

WINDOWS SECTION

The Windows Section of Arches is located 2.5 miles past Balanced Rock, on a paved road to the right. Short trails (0.25-1 mile one-way) lead from the road's end to some massive arches. Windows trailhead is the start for North Window (an opening 51 feet high and 93 feet wide), South Window (66 feet high and 105 feet wide), and Turret Arch (64 feet high and 39 feet wide). Double Arch, a short walk from a second trailhead, is an unusual pair of arches; the larger opening—105 feet high and 163 feet wide—is best appreciated by walking inside. The smaller opening is 61 feet high and 60 feet wide. Together, the two arches frame a large opening overhead.

Garden of Eden Viewpoint, on the way back to the main road, promises a good panorama of Salt Valley to the north. Under the valley, the massive body of salt and gypsum that's responsible for the arches comes close to the surface. Far-off Delicate Arch can be seen across the valley on a sandstone ridge. Early visitors to the Garden of Eden saw rock formations resembling Adam (with an apple) and Eve. Two other viewpoints of the Salt Valley area lie farther north on the main road.

DELICATE ARCH AND WOLFE RANCH

A bit of pioneer history survives at Wolfe Ranch, 2.5 miles north on the main road from the Windows junction (turn right and drive 1.8 miles to the parking area). John Wesley Wolfe came to this spot in 1888, hoping the desert climate would provide relief for health problems related to a Civil War injury. He found a good spring high in the rocks, grass for cattle, and water in Salt Wash to irrigate a garden. The ranch that he built provided a home

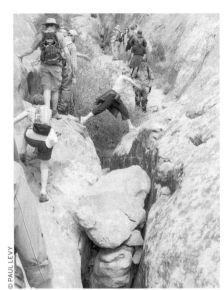

© PAUL LEVY

Sign up in advance for a ranger-led hike through the Fiery Furnace.

for him and some of his family for more than 20 years, and cattlemen later used it as a line ranch. Then sheepherders brought in their animals, which so overgrazed the range that the grass has yet to recover. A trail guide available at the entrance tells about the Wolfe family and the features of their ranch. The weather-beaten cabin built in 1906 still survives. A short trail leads to petroglyphs above Wolfe Ranch; figures of horses indicate that Ute people, rather than earlier inhabitants, did the artwork. Park staff can give directions to other rock-art sites; great care should be taken not to touch the fragile artwork.

Delicate Arch stands in a magnificent setting atop gracefully curving slickrock. Distant canyons and the La Sal Mountains lie beyond. The span is 45 feet high and 33 feet wide. A moderately strenuous three-mile round-trip hike leads to the arch. Another perspective on Delicate Arch can be obtained by driving 1.2 miles beyond Wolfe Ranch. Look for the small

arch high above. A short, steep trail (0.5 miles round-trip) climbs a hill for the best view.

FIERY FURNACE

The Fiery Furnace Viewpoint and trailhead are three miles from the Wolfe Ranch junction, on the right side of the main road. The Fiery Furnace gets its name from sandstone fins that turn flaming red on occasions when thin cloud cover at the horizon reflects the warm light of sunrise or sunset. The shady recesses beneath the fins provide a cool respite from the hot summer sun.

Closely packed sandstone fins form a maze of deep slots, with many arches and at least one natural bridge inside. Both for safety reasons and to reduce human impact on this sensitive area, which harbors several species of rare plants, hikers are encouraged to join a ranger-led hike. The hike is moderately strenuous and involves steep ledges, squeezing through narrow cracks, a couple of jumps, and hoisting yourself up off the ground. There is no turning back once the hike starts, so make sure you're physically prepared and properly equipped.

Rangers lead three-hour hikes (Mar.-Oct., $10 adults, $5 ages 5-12 and Interagency Senior Pass holders) into the Fiery Furnace twice each day. Unlike most ranger-led activities, a fee is charged for these hikes. Group size is limited to about 20 people, and it is not recommended for children under age five. Walks often fill weeks in advance. Make reservations online at www.recreation.gov or in person at the visitors center up to seven days in advance. To visit the Fiery Furnace without a ranger, visitors must obtain a permit ($5 pp) at the visitors center. A couple of Moab outfitters also lead hikes into the Fiery Furnace; these cost considerably more, but there's usually space available.

SKYLINE ARCH

This arch is on the right, one mile past the Sand Dune/Broken Arch trailhead. In desert climates, erosion can proceed imperceptibly for centuries

WHY ARE THERE ARCHES?

The park's distinctive arches are formed by an unusual combination of geologic forces. About 300 million years ago, evaporation of inland seas left behind a salt layer more than 3,000 feet thick in the Paradox Basin of this region. Sediments, including those that later became the arches, then covered the salt. Unequal pressures caused the salt to gradually flow upward in places, bending the overlying sediments as well. These upfolds, or anticlines, later collapsed when ground water dissolved the underlying salt.

The faults and joints caused by the uplift and collapse opened the way for erosion to carve hundreds of freestanding fins. Alternate freezing and thawing action and exfoliation (flaking caused by expansion when water or frost penetrates the rock) continued to peel away more rock until holes formed in some of the fins. Rockfalls within the holes helped enlarge the arches. Nearly all arches in the park eroded out of Entrada sandstone.

Eventually all the present arches will collapse, as Wall Arch did in 2008, but there should be plenty of new ones by the time that happens. The fins' uniform strength and hard upper surfaces have proved ideal for arch formation. Not every hole in the rock is an arch. To qualify, the opening must be at least three feet in one direction, and light must be able to pass through. Although the term *windows* often refers to openings in large walls of rock, windows and arches are really the same.

Water seeping through the sandstone from above has created a second type of arch—the pothole arch. You may also come across a few natural bridges cut from the rock by perennial water runoff.

A succession of rock layers is on display at Arches. The rocks on top of the salt beds—the rocks you actually see at Arches—are mostly Entrada sandstone, which is a pretty general category of rock. Within this Entrada Formation are three distinct types of sandstone. The formation's dark red base layer is known as the Dewey Bridge member. It's softer than the formation's other sandstones and erodes easily. Dewey Bridge rocks are topped by the pinkish orange Slick Rock member, the park's most visible rocks. The Slick Rock layer is much harder than the Dewey Bridge, and the combination of the two layers—softer rocks overlaid by harder—is responsible for the differential erosion that forms hoodoos and precariously balanced rocks. The thin top layer of Entrada sandstone, a white rock similar to Navajo sandstone, is called the Moab Tongue.

until a cataclysmic event happens. In 1940 a giant boulder fell from the opening of Skyline Arch, doubling the size of the arch in seconds. The hole is now 45 feet high and 69 feet wide. A short trail leads to the base of the arch.

DEVILS GARDEN

The Devils Garden trailhead, picnic area, and campground are all near the end of the main park road. Devils Garden offers fine scenery and more arches than any other section of the park. The hiking trail leads past large sandstone fins to Landscape and six other named arches. Carry water if the weather is hot or if you might want to continue past the one-mile point at Landscape Arch. Adventurous hikers could spend days exploring the maze of canyons among the fins.

KLONDIKE BLUFFS AND TOWER ARCH

Relatively few visitors come to the spires, high bluffs, and fine arch in this northwestern section of the park. A fair-weather dirt road turns off the main drive 1.3 miles before Devils Garden trailhead, winds down into Salt Valley, and heads northwest. After 7.5 miles, turn left on the road to Klondike Bluffs and proceed one mile to the Tower Arch trailhead. These roads may have washboards, but they are usually passable by cars in dry weather; don't drive on them if storms threaten. The trail to Tower

Arch winds past the Marching Men and other rock formations (3 miles round-trip). Alexander Ringhoffer, who discovered the arch in 1922, carved an inscription on the south column. The area can also be fun to explore off-trail with a map and compass or a GPS receiver. Those with 4WD vehicles can drive close to the arch on a separate jeep road. Tower Arch has an opening 34 feet high by 92 feet wide. A tall monolith nearby gave the arch its name.

4WD ROAD

A rough road near Tower Arch in the Klondike Bluffs turns southeast past **Eye of the Whale Arch** in Herdina Park to Balanced Rock on the main park road, 10.8 miles away. The road isn't particularly difficult for 4WD enthusiasts, although normal backcountry precautions should be taken. A steep sand hill north of Eye of the Whale Arch is difficult to climb for vehicles coming from Balanced Rock; it's better to drive from the Tower Arch area instead.

Recreation

Because of its great popularity and proximity to Moab, Arches sees a lot of visitors. Most are content, however, to drive the parkways and perhaps saunter to undemanding viewpoints. You can quickly leave the crowds behind by planning a hike to more outlying destinations. Arches' outback offers magnificent rewards for hikers willing to leave the pavement behind and get dusty on a backcountry trail.

HIKING

Established hiking trails lead to many fine arches and overlooks that can't be seen from the road. You're free to wander cross-country, too, but stay on rock or in washes to avoid damaging the fragile cryptobiotic soils. Wear good walking shoes with rubber soles for travel across slickrock. The summer sun can be especially harsh on the unprepared hiker—don't forget water, a hat, and sunscreen. The desert rule is to carry at least one gallon of water per person for an all-day hike. Take a map and compass or a map and GPS unit for off-trail hiking. Be cautious on the slickrock, as the soft sandstone can crumble easily. Also, remember that it's easier to go up a steep slickrock slope than it is to come back down.

You can reach almost any spot in the park on a day hike, although you'll also find some good overnight camping possibilities. Areas for longer trips include Courthouse Wash in the southern part of the park and Salt Wash in the eastern part. All backpacking is done off-trail. A backcountry permit must be obtained from a ranger before camping in the backcountry.

Backcountry regulations prohibit fires and pets, and they allow camping only out of sight of any road, at least one mile away, or trail, at least 0.5 miles away, and at least 300 feet from a recognizable archaeological site or nonflowing water source.

Park Avenue

- Distance: 1 mile one-way
- Duration: 1 hour round-trip
- Elevation change: 320 feet
- Effort: easy-moderate
- Trailheads: Park Avenue or North Park Avenue trailhead

Get an eyeful of massive stone formations and a feel for the natural history of the park on the easy-moderate Park Avenue trail. The Park Avenue trailhead, just past the crest of the switchbacks that climb up into the park, is the best place to start. The vistas from here are especially dramatic: Courthouse Towers, the Three Gossips, and other fanciful rock formations loom above a natural amphitheater. The trail

MORMON TEA

Although it's not the showiest wildflower in the desert, Mormon tea (*Ephedra viridis*) is widespread across southern Utah, and it's very common in Arches. This broom-like plant is remarkably well adapted to the desert, and many desert-dwelling humans have adapted themselves to enjoy drinking it as a tea.

The plant's branches contain chlorophyll and are able to conduct photosynthesis. The leaves are like tiny scales or bracts; their small size reduces the amount of moisture the plant loses to transpiration. Male and female flowers grow on separate plants.

Native Americans used this plant medicinally as a tea for stomach and bowel disorders as well as for colds, fever, and headaches. Some used it to control bleeding and as a poultice for burns.

Mormon tea is related to ma huang, a Chinese herb that is traditionally used to treat hay fever. All parts of the plant contain a small amount of ephedrine, a stimulant that in large concentrations can be quite harmful. Pioneers in southern Utah were mostly Mormons, who are forbidden to drink coffee or similar stimulants. When they learned that drinking the boiled stems of *Ephedra viridis* gave them a mild lift, they approached Brigham Young, the head of the Latter-Day Saints. Young gave the tea his stamp of approval, and the plant's common name grew out of its widespread use by Mormons. In Utah it's also sometimes called Brigham tea.

The tea itself is yellowish and, as one local puts it, tastes something like what she imagines boiled socks would taste like. To increase the tea's palatability, it's often mixed with mint, lemon, and sugar or honey. Pioneers liked to add strawberry jam to their Mormon tea.

If you are tempted to try this tea for yourself, make certain not to harvest plants in a national park. Women who are pregnant or nursing and people with high blood pressure, heart disease, diabetes, glaucoma, or other health problems should definitely avoid even the small amounts of ephedra present in Mormon tea.

drops into a narrow wash before traversing the park highway at the North Park Avenue trailhead. Hikers can be dropped off at one trailhead and picked up 30 minutes later at the other.

The Windows

- Distance: 1 mile round-trip
- Duration: 1 hour
- Elevation change: 140 feet
- Effort: easy
- Trailhead: end of Windows Road

Ten miles into the park, just past the impossible-to-miss Balanced Rock, follow signs and a paved road to the Windows Section. A one-mile round-trip loop along a sandy trail leads to the Windows—a cluster of enormous arches that are impossible to see from the road. Highlights include the **North** and **South Windows** and **Turret Arch.** Unmarked trails lead to vistas and scrambles along the stone faces that make up the ridge. If this easy loop leaves you eager for more exploration in the area, a second trail starts from just past the Windows parking area and goes to **Double Arch.** This 0.5-mile trail leads to two giant spans that are joined at one end. These easy trails are good for family groups because younger or more ambitious hikers can scramble to their hearts' content along rocky outcrops.

Delicate Arch Viewpoint

- Distance: 0.5 miles round-trip
- Duration: 15-30 minutes
- Elevation change: 100 feet
- Effort: easy-moderate
- Trailhead: 1 mile past Wolfe Ranch, at the end of Wolfe Ranch Road

If you don't have the time or the endurance for the relatively strenuous hike to Delicate Arch, you can view the astonishing arch from a distance at the Delicate Arch Viewpoint. From the

© PAUL LEVY

Delicate Arch is at the end of a 1.5-mile trail.

Horses didn't arrive in the area until the mid-1600s, so these petroglyphs are believed to be the work of the Ute people.

The first stretch of the main trail is broad, flat, and not especially scenic, except for a good display of spring wildflowers. After about half an hour of hiking, the trail climbs steeply up onto the slickrock and the views open up across the park to the La Sal Mountains in the distance.

Just before the end of the trail, walk up to the small, decidedly indelicate Frame Arch for a picture-perfect view of the final destination. The classic photo of Delicate Arch is taken late in the afternoon when the sandstone glows with golden hues. Standing at the base of Delicate Arch is a magical moment: The arch rises out of the barren, almost lunar, rock face, yet it seems ephemeral. Views from the arch over the Colorado River valley are amazing.

◖ Fiery Furnace Trail

- Distance: 2 miles round-trip
- Duration: 3 hours
- Elevation change: 250 feet
- Effort: moderate-strenuous
- Trailhead: Fiery Furnace viewpoint

The Fiery Furnace area is open only to hikers with permits ($5 pp) or to those joining a ranger-led hike. During summer, rangers offer two daily hikes (mid-Mar.-Oct., $10 adults, $5 ages 7-12 and Interagency Senior Pass holders) into this unique area; tickets are required. These hikes are popular and are often booked weeks in advance, so make reservations online at www.recreation.gov or in person at the visitors' center up to one week ahead.

Hiking in the Fiery Furnace is not along a trail; hikers navigate a maze of narrow sandstone canyons. The route through the area is sometimes challenging, requiring hands-and-knees scrambling up cracks and ledges. Navigation is difficult: Route-finding can be tricky because what look like obvious paths

viewing area, hikers can scramble up a steep trail to a rim with views across Cache Valley. Even though this is a short hike, it's a good place to wander around the slickrock for a while. It's especially nice to linger around sunset, when the arch captures the light and begins to glow. If you'd rather not scramble around on the slickrock, a short path leads about 100 yards from the parking area to a decent view of the arch.

◖ Delicate Arch Trail

- Distance: 3 miles round-trip
- Duration: 2 hours
- Elevation change: 500 feet
- Effort: moderate-strenuous
- Trailhead: Wolfe Ranch

For those who are able, the hike to the base of Delicate Arch is one of the park's highlights. Shortly after the trail's start at Wolfe Ranch, a spur trail leads to some petroglyphs depicting horses and their riders and a few bighorn sheep.

© PAUL LEVY

A little scrambling is required when exploring the Fiery Furnace.

often lead to dead ends. Drop-offs and ridges make straight-line travel impossible. It's easy to become disoriented. Even if you're an experienced hiker, the ranger-led hikes provide the best introduction to the Fiery Furnace.

If you're not able to get in on a ranger-led hike and aren't strapped for cash, several Moab outfitters, including **Canyonlands By Night** (1861 N. U.S. 191, Moab, 435/259-5361 or 800/394-9978, www.canyonlandsbynight, $81 adults) offer guided tours in the Fiery Furnace.

Broken and Sand Dune Arches

- Distance: 1 mile round-trip
- Duration: 45 minutes
- Elevation change: 140 feet
- Effort: easy
- Trailhead: on the right side of the road, 2.4 miles past the Fiery Furnace turnoff

A short sandy trail leads to small Sand Dune Arch (its opening is 8 feet high and 30 feet wide), tucked within fins. A longer trail (1 mile round-trip) crosses a field to Broken Arch, which you can also see from the road. The

opening in this arch is 43 feet high and 59 feet wide. Up close, you'll see that the arch isn't really broken. These arches can also be reached by a trail across from campsite 40 at Devils Garden Campground. Another beautiful arch, **Tapestry Arch,** requires a short detour off the trail between the campground and Broken Arch.

Look for low-growing Canyonlands biscuit root, found only in areas of Entrada sandstone, colonizing the sand dunes. Hikers can protect the habitat of the biscuit root and other fragile plants by keeping to washes or rock surfaces.

◖ Devils Garden Loop

- Distance: 7.2 miles round-trip
- Duration: 4 hours
- Elevation change: 350 feet
- Effort: strenuous
- Trailhead: Devils Garden

From the end of the paved park road, a full tour of Devils Garden leads to eight named arches and a vacation's worth of scenic wonders. This is one of the park's most popular areas, with several shorter versions of the full loop hike that

© PAUL LEVY

Broken Arch is not really broken – yet.

make the area accessible to nearly every hiker. Don't be shocked to find quite a crowd at the trailhead—it will most likely dissipate after the first two or three arches.

The first two arches are an easy walk from the trailhead and are accessed via a short side trail to the right. **Tunnel Arch** has a relatively symmetrical opening 22 feet high and 27 feet wide. The nearby **Pine Tree Arch** is named for a piñon pine that once grew inside; the arch has an opening 48 feet high and 46 feet wide.

Continue on the main trail to **Landscape Arch.** The trail narrows past Landscape Arch and continues to the remains of **Wall Arch,** which collapsed in August 2008. A short side trail branches off to the left beyond the stubs of Wall Arch to **Partition Arch** and **Navajo Arch.** Partition was so named because a piece of rock divides the main opening from a smaller hole. Navajo Arch is a rock-shelter type; prehistoric Native Americans may have camped here.

The main trail climbs up slickrock, offering great views of the La Sal mountains and Fin Canyon. At the Fin Canyon viewpoint, the trail curves left (watch for rock cairns) and continues

northwest, ending at **Double O Arch** (4 miles round-trip from the trailhead). Double O has a large oval-shaped opening (45 feet high and 71 feet wide) and a smaller hole underneath. **Dark Angel** is a distinctive rock pinnacle 0.25 miles northwest; cairns mark the way. Another primitive trail loops back to Landscape Arch via **Fin Canyon.** This route goes through a different part of Devils Garden but adds about one mile to your trip (3 miles back to the trailhead instead of two). Pay careful attention to the trail markers to avoid getting lost.

Landscape Arch

- Distance: 2 miles round-trip
- Duration: 1 hour
- Elevation change: 60 feet
- Effort: easy
- Trailhead: Devils Garden trailhead

Landscape Arch, with an incredible 306-foot span—six feet longer than a football field—is one of the longest unsupported rock spans in the world. It's also one of the park's more precarious arches to observe up close. The thin arch looks ready to collapse at any moment. Indeed, a spectacular rockfall from the arch on September 1, 1991, accelerated its disintegration, which is the eventual fate of every arch. Now the area directly underneath the arch is fenced off; when you look at the photos of the 1991 rockfall, you'll be happy to stand back a ways.

On the way to Landscape Arch, be sure to take the short side trails to Tunnel and Pine Tree Arches.

◖ Tower Arch Trail

- Distance: 3.4 miles round-trip
- Duration: 2.5 hours
- Elevation change: 450 feet
- Effort: moderate-strenuous
- Trailhead: Klondike Bluffs parking area
- Directions: From the main park road, take Salt Valley Road (a dirt road, but usually fine for passenger cars) west 7.7 miles to the Klondike Bluffs turnoff.

Most park visitors don't venture into this area of sandstone fins and big dunes. It's a bit like Devils Garden, but without the crowds.

After a short but steep climb, the trail levels out and opens up to views of Arches' distinctive sandstone fins and, in the distance, the La Sal and Abajo Mountains. The trail drops down to cross a couple of washes, then climbs onto the fin-studded slickrock Klondike Bluffs. Tower Arch is actually both an arch and a tower, and there's no mistaking the tower for just another big sandstone rock.

Because of the dirt-road access to this hike, it's best to skip it if there's been recent rain or if rain is threatening.

BIKING

Cyclists are required to keep to established roads in the park; there is no single-track or trail riding allowed. You'll also have to contend with heavy traffic on the narrow paved roads and dusty washboard surfaces on the dirt roads. Beware of deep sand on the 4WD roads, traffic on the main park road, and summertime heat wherever you ride.

One good, not-too-hard ride is along the Willow Springs Road. Allow 2-3 hours for an out-and-back, starting from the Balanced Rock parking area and heading west.

Perhaps the best bet for relatively fit mountain bikers is the 24-mile ride to Tower Arch and back. From the Devils Garden parking area, ride out the **Salt Valley Road,** which can be rough. After about 7.5 miles, turn left onto a jeep road that leads to the "back door" to Tower Arch.

Nearby, Bureau of Land Management and Canyonlands National Park areas offer world-class mountain biking.

CLIMBING

Rock climbers don't need a permit in Arches, although you should first discuss your plans with a ranger. All features named on U.S. Geological Survey maps are closed to climbing: That means any of the arches and many of the most distinctive towers are off limits. Slacklining is also prohibited in the park. There are still plenty of long-standing routes for advanced climbers to enjoy, although the rock in Arches is sandier and softer than in other areas around Moab.

Several additional climbing restrictions are in place. No new permanent climbing hardware may be installed in any fixed location. If an existing bolt or other hardware item is unsafe, it may be replaced. This effectively limits all technical climbing to existing routes or new routes not requiring placement of fixed anchors. Other restrictions are detailed on the park's website.

The most commonly climbed areas are along the sheer stone faces of **Park Avenue.** Another popular destination is **Owl Rock,** the owl-shaped small tower located in the Windows Section of the park. For more information on climbing in Arches, consult the bible of Moab-area climbing, *Desert Rock* by Eric Bjørnstad, or ask for advice at **Pagan Mountaineering** (59 S. Main St., Moab, 435/259-1117, www.paganclimber.

ARCHES NATIONAL PARK

© PAUL LEVY

Be sure to reserve ahead if you want to camp at Arches.

com), a climbing and outdoor-gear store that also offers a climbing guide service.

CAMPGROUNDS

Devils Garden Campground (elevation 5,355 feet, with water, year-round, $20) is near the end of the 18-mile scenic drive. It's an excellent place to camp, with some sites tucked under rock formations and others offering great views, but it's extremely popular. The well-organized traveler must plan accordingly and reserve a site in advance for March-October. Reservations (www.recreation.gov, $9 booking fee plus $20 camping fee) must be made no less than four days and no more than 240 days in advance. All campsites can be reserved, so during the busy spring, summer, and fall seasons, campers without reservations are pretty much out of luck. In winter, sites 1-24 are available as first-come, first-served. A camp host is on-site and firewood is available ($5), but there are no other services or amenities.

If you aren't able to score a coveted Arches campsite, all is not lost. There are many Bureau of Land Management (BLM) campsites within an easy drive of the park. Try the primitive BLM campgrounds on Highway 313, just west of U.S. 191 and on the way to Canyonlands National Park's Island in the Sky District. Another cluster of BLM campgrounds is along the Colorado River on Highway 128, which runs northeast from U.S. 191 at the north end of Moab.

CANYONLANDS NATIONAL PARK

The canyon country of southeastern Utah puts on its supreme performance in this vast park, which spreads across 527 square miles. The deeply entrenched Colorado and Green Rivers meet in its heart, and then continue south, as the mighty Colorado, through tumultuous Cataract Canyon Rapids. The park is divided into four districts and a separate noncontiguous unit. The Colorado and Green Rivers form the River District and divide Canyonlands National Park into three other regions. Island in the Sky is north, between the rivers; the Maze is to the west; and Needles is to the east. The Horseshoe Canyon Unit is farther to the west. This small parcel of land preserves a canyon on Barrier Creek, a tributary of the Green River, in which astounding petroglyphs and other ancient rock paintings are protected.

Each district has its own distinct character. No bridges or roads directly connect the three land districts and the Horseshoe Canyon Unit, so most visitors have to leave the park to go from one region to another. The huge park can be seen in many ways and on many levels. Paved roads reach a few areas, 4WD roads go to more places, and hiking trails reach still more, but much of the land shows no trace of human passage. To get the big picture, you can fly over this incredible complex of canyons on an air tour; however, only a river trip or a hike lets you experience the solitude and detail of the land.

The park can be visited in any season of the

HIGHLIGHTS

Great Gallery Trail

Mesa Arch Trail

Grand View Trail

White Rim Road

Land of Standing Rocks

Cave Spring Trail

Chesler Park

River-Running Through Cataract Canyon

BLM Newspaper Rock Historical Monument

Moab

Green River

Colorado River

0   10 mi

0   10 km

Blanding

© AVALON TRAVEL

LOOK FOR **(TO FIND RECOMMENDED SIGHTS, ACTIVITIES, DINING, AND LODGING.**

(White Rim Road: Take a few days to drive or bike this trail at the base of the Island in the Sky. Only high-clearance 4WD rigs or sturdy mountain bikes can make it on this scenic drive along the Colorado and Green Rivers (page 46).

(Mesa Arch Trail: This easy trail leads to a dramatic cliff-side arch. The sun rising through the arch is a sight to behold—if you have time and energy for just one hike in Canyonlands, this should be it (page 47).

(Grand View Trail: This short hike along slickrock cliffs captures the essence of the "Island in the Sky." A sheer mile below the trail,

the gorges of the Colorado and Green Rivers join to form Cataract Canyon, and in the distance, the odd promontories of the Needles District punctuate the skyline (page 49).

(BLM Newspaper Rock Historical Monument: This is one of Utah's foremost prehistoric rock-art sites and also one of the most easily accessible. The distinctive petroglyphs span 2,000 years of human history (page 51).

(Cave Spring Trail: The Cave Spring Trail in the Needles District introduces the geology and ecology of the park and passes an old cowboy line camp. It's also a good introduction to slickrock hiking; rock cairns mark the way and ladders assist hikers on the steep sections (page 53).

(Chesler Park: A lovely desert meadow contrasts with the characteristic red and white spires of the Needles District. The trail winds through sand and slickrock before ascending a small pass through the Needles to Chesler Park; the park itself is encircled by a loop trail (page 56).

(Land of Standing Rocks: Rock spires stand guard over myriad canyons in the Maze District. Land of Standing Rocks is a good place to camp, hike, and generally explore, but it's remote. Be sure to have a high-clearance 4WD vehicle, a compass, and some good maps (page 61).

(Great Gallery Trail: Ghostly life-size pictographs in the Great Gallery are in remote Horseshoe Canyon, just west of the main part of Canyonlands. The hike in to the Gallery offers pleasant scenery and spring wildflowers (page 64).

(River-Running Through Cataract Canyon: Downstream from its confluence with the Green River, the Colorado River enters Cataract Canyon and picks up speed. The rapids begin four miles downstream and extend for the next 14 miles to Lake Powell. Especially in spring, the 26 or more rapids give a wild ride equal to the best in the Grand Canyon (page 67).

CANYONLANDS

CANYONLANDS

CANYONLANDS NATIONAL PARK

To Moab

279

Potash

POTASH PLANT

To I-70 and Moab

Dead Horse Point State Park

313

VISITOR CENTER

DEAD HORSE POINT OVERLOOK

POTASH RD

DEAD HORSE POINT

SHAFER

Meander Canyon

River

Colorado

SHAFER TRAIL RD

SHAFER CANYON OVERLOOK

Lathrop

Trail

Lathrop Trail

AIRPORT

WHITE RIM ROAD

GOOSEBERRY

WHITE RIM OVERLOOK

Rim

Canyonlands National Park

VISITOR CENTER

NECK SPRINGS

MESA ARCH TRAIL

BUCK CANYON OVERLOOK

GRAND VIEW POINT

GRAND VIEW TRAIL

To I-70 and Green River

MINERAL RD

Labyrinth Canyon

TAYLOR

Taylor Canyon

Alcove Spring Trail

Whale Rock

Syncline Trail

Upheaval Dome

ISLAND IN THE SKY DISTRICT

Aztec Butte

WILLOW FLAT

GREEN RIVER OVERLOOK

Murphy Point

WHITE CRACK

UPHEAVAL DOME ROAD

CANDLESTICK

RIM RD

MURPHY HOGBACK

White

MINERAL BOTTOM

HARDSCRABBLE

POTATO BOTTOM

WHITE RIM ROAD

WHITE RIM RD

Stillwater Canyon

Green

River

LABYRINTH

Glen Canyon National Recreation Area

CANYONLANDS NATIONAL PARK

To I-70 and Green River

GREAT GALLERY TRAIL

HORSESHOE CANYON UNIT

BLM

GREAT GALLERY PICTOGRAPHS

HANS FLAT RANGER STATION

To Hwy 24

To Hwy 24

© AVALON TRAVEL

Lavender Canyon

Davis Canyon

To BLM NEWSPAPER ROCK
HISTORICAL MONUMENT,
Indian Creek, and Hwy 191

NEEDLES
OUTPOST

CAVE SPRING TRAIL

ROADSIDE RUIN

VISITOR
CENTER

WOODEN SHOE OVERLOOK

SQUAW FLAT
CAMPGROUND/TRAILHEAD

SLICKROCK

BIG SPRING
CANYON
SCENIC DRIVE

COLORADO RIVER OVERLOOK

BIG SPRING
CANYON OVERLOOK

POTHOLE
POINT

ELEPHANT
HILL

CONFLUENCE
OVERLOOK

Horse Canyon

Fortress Arch

Castle Arch

Angel Arch

Salt Creek Canyon

Peekaboo Trail

Lost Canyon

Squaw Canyon

Big Spring Cyn

Lake Cyn Tr.

Elephant Canyon

Drud Arch

CHESLER PARK

DEVILS KITCHEN

Confluence

Lower Red

Spanush Bottom

Cataract Canyon

RIVER-RUNNING
THROUGH CATARACT
CANYON

NEEDLES   DISTRICT

Bobby's Hole

B e e f   B a s i n

MAZE
DISTRICT

LAND OF
STANDING ROCKS

DOLL
HOUSE

Land of Standing Rocks

The Fins

Ernie's Country

MAZE
OVERLOOK

Colorado River

Canyonlands
National Park

Lake Powell

.5 mi

5 km

0

0

Elaterite Basin

North Canyon Trail

Orange Cliffs

FLINT TRAIL

GOLDEN
STAIRS

Waterhole Flat

BAGPIPE BUTTE
OVERLOOK

FLINT SHEEP

SUNSET PASS

year, with spring and autumn the best choices. Summer temperatures can climb over 100°F; carrying and drinking lots of water becomes critical then (bring at least one gallon per person per day). Arm yourself with insect repellent late spring-midsummer. Winter days tend to be bright and sunny, although nighttime temperatures can dip into the teens or even below zero Fahrenheit. Winter visitors should inquire about travel conditions, as snow and ice occasionally close roads and trails at higher elevations.

PLANNING YOUR TIME

Unless you have a great deal of time, you can't really "do" the entire park in one trip. It's best to pick one section and concentrate on it.

Island in the Sky District

The mesa-top Island in the Sky District has paved roads on its top to impressive belvederes such as Grand View Point and the strange Upheaval Dome. If you're short on time or don't want to make a rigorous backcountry trip, you'll find this district the best choice. It is easily visited as a day trip from Moab. The "Island," which is actually a large mesa, is much like nearby Dead Horse Point on a giant scale; a narrow neck of land connects the north side with the "mainland."

If you're really on a tight schedule, it's possible to spend a few hours exploring Arches National Park, then head to Island in the Sky for a drive to the scenic Grand View overlook and a brief hike to Mesa Arch or the Upheaval Dome viewpoint. A one-day visit should include these elements, plus a hike along the Neck Spring Trail. For a longer visit, hikers, mountain bikers, and those with suitable high-clearance 4WD vehicles can drop off the Island in the Sky and descend about 1,300 feet to White Rim Road, which follows the cliffs of the White Rim around most of the island. Plan to spend at least 2-3 days exploring this 100-mile-long road.

Needles District

Colorful rock spires prompted the name of the Needles District, which is easily accessed from Highway 211 and U.S. 191 south of Moab. Splendid canyons contain many arches, strange rock formations, and archaeological sites. Overlooks and short nature trails can be enjoyed from the paved scenic drive in the park; if you are only here for a day, hike the Cave Spring and Pothole Point Trails. On a longer visit, make a loop of the Big Spring and Squaw Canyon Trails, and hike to Chesler Park. A 10-mile round-trip hike will take you to the Confluence Overlook, a great view of the junction of the Green and Colorado Rivers.

Drivers with 4WD vehicles have their own challenging roads through canyons and other highly scenic areas.

Maze District

Few visitors make it over to the Maze District, which is some of the wildest country in the United States. Only the rivers and a handful of 4WD roads and hiking trails provide access. Experienced hikers can explore the maze of canyons on unmarked routes. Plan to spend at least 2-3 days in this area; even if you're only taking day hikes, it can take a long time to get to any destination here. That said, a hike from the Maze Overlook to the Harvest Scene pictographs is a good bet if you don't have a lot of time. If you have more than one day, head to the Land of Standing Rocks area and hike north to the Chocolate Drops.

Horseshoe Canyon Unit

Horseshoe Canyon Unit, a detached section of the park northwest of the Maze District, is equally remote. It protects the Great Gallery, a group of pictographs left by prehistoric Native Americans. This ancient artwork is reached at the end of a series of long unpaved roads and down a canyon on a moderately challenging hiking trail. Plan to spend a full day exploring this area.

River District

The River District includes long stretches of the Green and the Colorado Rivers. River-running is one of the best ways to experience the inner depths of the park. Boaters can obtain helpful literature and advice from park rangers. Groups planning their own trip through Cataract Canyon need a river-running permit. Flat-water permits are also required. River outfitters based in Moab offer trips ranging from half a day to several days in length.

Exploring the Park

There are four districts and a noncontiguous unit in Canyonlands National Park (www.nps.gov/cany, $10 per vehicle, $5 bicyclists, motorcyclists, and pedestrians, good for one week in all districts, no fee to enter Maze or Horseshoe Canyon), each affording great views, spectacular geology, a chance to see wildlife, and endless opportunities to explore. You won't find crowds or elaborate park facilities because most of Canyonlands remains a primitive backcountry park. If your plans include visiting Arches National Park plus Hovenweep and Natural Bridges National Monuments, consider the so-called Local Passport ($25), which allows entry to each of these federal preserves. Purchase the pass at any park or national monument entrance.

Front-country camping is allowed only in established campgrounds at Willow Flat (Island in the Sky) and Squaw Flat (Needles).

Rock climbing is allowed in the park, and permits are not required, unless the trip involves overnight camping; however, it's always a good idea to check in at district visitors centers for advice and information and to learn where climbing is restricted. Climbing is not allowed within 300 feet of cultural sites.

Pets aren't allowed on trails and must be leashed in campgrounds. No firewood collecting is permitted in the park; backpackers must use gas stoves for cooking. Vehicle and boat campers can bring in firewood but must use grills or fire pans.

The best maps for the park are a series of topographic maps by National Geographic/Trails Illustrated; these have the latest trail and road information. For most day hikes, the simple maps issued by park visitors centers will suffice.

VISITORS CENTERS

Since Canyonlands covers so much far-flung territory, separate visitors centers serve each district. One website (www.nps.gov/cany) serves the whole park and is a good source for current information and permit applications. There are visitors centers at the entrances to the **Island in the Sky District** (435/259-4712, 9am-4pm daily winter, longer hours daily spring-fall) and the **Needles District** (435/259-4711, 9am-4pm daily mid-Feb.-early Dec., longer hours mid-Feb.-Nov.). The **Hans Flat Ranger Station** (435/259-2652, 8am-4:30pm daily year-round) is on a remote plateau above the even more isolated canyons of the Maze District and the Horseshoe Canyon Unit. The River District is administered out of the **National Park Service Office** (2282 SW Resource Blvd., Moab, 435/719-2313, 8am-4pm Mon.-Fri.). This office can generally handle inquiries for all districts of the park. For backcountry information, or to make backcountry reservations, call 435/259-4351. Handouts from the ranger offices describe natural history, travel, and other aspects of the park.

If you are in Moab, it is most convenient to stop at the **Moab Information Center** (Main St. and Center St., 435/259-8825 or 800/635-6622), where a national park ranger is often on duty. All visitors centers have brochures,

EARLY EXPLORATION OF THE COLORADO RIVER CANYON

The Dominguez-Escalante Expedition skirted the east edge of the Colorado River Canyon in 1776 in an unsuccessful attempt to find a route west to California. Retreating back to New Mexico, the Spanish explorers encountered great difficulties in the canyons of southern Utah before finding a safe ford across the Colorado River. This spot, known as the "Crossing of the Fathers," now lies under Lake Powell. Later explorers established the Old Spanish Trail through Utah to connect New Mexico with California. The route crossed the Colorado River near present-day Moab and was used 1829-1848, when the United States acquired the western territories. Fur trappers also trav-

eled the canyons in search of beaver and other animals during the early 1800s; inscriptions carved into the sandstone record their passage.

Major John Wesley Powell led the first scientific expedition by boat through the Green River and lower Colorado River canyons in 1869, then repeated most of the journey in 1871-1872. Cowboys brought in cattle during the 1870s. Some of their camps, corrals, and inscriptions still survive, although grazing no longer takes place in the park. Uranium prospectors swarmed through the area with Geiger counters during the 1950s, staking thousands of claims and opening some mines. Most of the jeep roads in use today date from that time.

maps, and books, as well as someone to answer your questions.

TOURS

Rangers lead interpretive programs in the Island in the Sky and Needles Districts (Mar.-Oct.), and they guide hikers into Horseshoe Canyon (Sat.-Sun. spring and fall), weather permitting. Call the Hans Flat Ranger Station (435/259-2652) for details.

OUTFITTERS

Outfitters must be authorized by the National Park Service to operate in Canyonlands. Most guides concentrate on river trips, but some can take you on mountain bike trips, including vehicle-supported tours of the White Rim 4WD Trail. Most of the guides operating in Canyonlands are based in Moab. For a complete list of authorized outfitters, visit the park website (www.nps.gov/cany).

Biking

- **Escape Adventures** (at Moab Cyclery, 391 S. Main St., Moab, 435/259-7423 or 800/596-2953, www.escapeadventures.com)

- **Rim Tours** (1233 S. U.S. 191, Moab, 435/259-5223 or 800/626-7335, www.rimtours.com)
- **Western Spirit Cycling** (478 Mill Creek Dr., Moab, 435/259-8732 or 800/845-2453, www.westernspirit.com)

Rafting

- **Adrift Adventures** (378 N. Main St., Moab, 435/259-8594 or 800/874-4483, www.adrift.net)
- **Navtec Expeditions** (321 N. Main St., Moab, 435/259-7983 or 800/833-1278, www.navtec.com)
- **Sheri Griffith Expeditions** (503/259-8229 or 800/332-2439, www.griffithexp.com)
- **Tag-A-Long Expeditions** (452 N. Main St., Moab, 435/259-8946 or 800/453-3292, www.tagalong.com)
- **Western River Expeditions** (225 S. Main St., Moab, 435/259-7019 or 866/904-1163, www.westernriver.com)

BACKCOUNTRY EXPLORATION

A complex system of fees is charged for backcountry camping, 4WD exploration, and river rafting. Except for the main campgrounds at

Willow Flat (Island in the Sky) and Squaw Flat (Needles), you'll need a permit for backcountry camping. There is a $30 fee for a backpacking permit and, in the Needles District, a $10 day-use fee for a 4WD vehicle. Each of the three major districts has a different policy for backcountry vehicle camping, so it's a good idea to make sure that you understand the details. Backcountry permits are also needed for any trips with horses or stock; check with a ranger for details.

It's possible to reserve a backcountry permit in advance; for spring and fall travel to popular areas like Island in the Sky's White Rim Trail or the Needles backcountry, this is an extremely good idea. Find application forms on the Canyonlands website (www.nps.gov/cany). Forms should be completed and returned at least two weeks in advance of your planned trip. Telephone reservations are not accepted.

Back-road travel is a popular method of exploring the park. Canyonlands National Park offers hundreds of miles of exceptionally scenic jeep roads, favorites both with mountain bikers and 4WD enthusiasts. Park regulations require all motorized vehicles to have proper registration and licensing for highway use, and all-terrain vehicles are prohibited in the park; drivers must also be licensed. Normally you must have a vehicle with both 4WD and high clearance. It's essential for both motor vehicles and bicycles to stay on existing roads to prevent damage to the delicate desert vegetation. Carry tools, extra fuel, water, and food in case you break down in a remote area.

Before making a trip, drivers and cyclists should talk with a ranger to register and to check on current road conditions, which can change drastically from one day to the next. The rangers can also tell you where to seek help if you get stuck. Primitive campgrounds are provided on most of the roads, but you'll need a backcountry permit from a ranger. Books on backcountry exploration include Charles Wells's *Guide to Moab, UT Backroads & 4-Wheel Drive Trails,* which includes Canyonlands, and Damian Fagan and David Williams's *A Naturalist's Guide to the White Rim Trail.*

One more thing about backcountry travel in Canyonlands: You may need to pack your poop out of the backcountry. Because of the abundance of slickrock and the desert conditions, it's not always possible to dig a hole, and you can't just leave your waste on a rock until it decomposes (decomposition is a very slow process in these conditions). Check with the ranger when you pick up your backcountry permit for more information.

CANYONLANDS

Island in the Sky District

The main part of this district sits on a mesa high above the Colorado and Green Rivers. It is connected to points north by a narrow land bridge just wide enough for the road, known as "the neck," which forms the only vehicle access to the 40-square-mile Island in the Sky. Panoramic views from the "Island" can be enjoyed from any point along the rim; you'll see much of the park and southeastern Utah.

Short hiking trails lead to overlooks and to Mesa Arch, Aztec Butte, Whale Rock, Upheaval Dome, and other features. Longer trails make steep, strenuous descents from the Island to the White Rim Road below. Elevations on the Island average about 6,000 feet.

Although the massive cliffs in the area look to be perfect for rock climbing, in fact much of the rock is not suitable for climbing, and the remoteness of the area means that few routes have been explored. One exception is Taylor Canyon, in the extreme northwest corner of the park, which is reached by lengthy and rugged 4WD roads.

Bring water for all hiking, camping, and travel in Island in the Sky. Except for the

THE LIFE AND LANDSCAPE OF CANYONLANDS

GEOLOGY

Deep canyons of the Green and Colorado Rivers have sliced through rocks representing 150 million years of deposition. The Paradox Formation, exposed in Cataract Canyon, contains salt and other minerals responsible for some of the folded and faulted rock layers in the region. Under the immense pressure of overlying rocks, the Paradox flows plastically, forming domes where the rock layers are thinnest and causing cracks or faults as pressures rise and fall. Each of the overlying formations has a different color and texture; they're the products of ancient deserts, rivers, and seas that once covered this land. Views from any of the overlooks reveal that an immense quantity of rock has already been washed downriver toward California. Not so evident, however, is the 10,000 vertical feet of rock that geologists say once lay across the high mesas. The dry climate and sparse vegetation allow clear views of the remaining rock layers and the effects of erosion and deformation. You can read the geologic story at Canyonlands National Park in the 3,500 feet of strata that remain, from the bottom of **Cataract Canyon** to the upper reaches of **Salt Creek** in the **Needles District.**

FLORA AND FAUNA

Extremes of flash flood and drought, hot summers, and cold winters discourage all but the most hardy and adaptable life. Desert grasses, small flowering plants, cacti, and shrubs like blackbrush and saltbush survive on the mostly thin soils and meager 8-9 inches of annual precipitation. Trees either grow in cracks that concentrate rainfall and nutrients or rely on springs or canyon streams for moisture. Piñon pine and juniper prefer the higher elevations of the park, while cottonwoods live in the canyon bottoms that have permanent subsurface water. Tamarisk, an exotic and invasive streamside plant, and willows often form dense thickets on sandbars along the Green and Colorado Rivers. The hanging gardens of lush vegetation that surround cliff-side springs or seeps seem oblivious to the surrounding desert.

The fragile desert ecology can easily be upset, especially in the Needles District. Cattle, once overgrazed the grasslands and trampled cryptobiotic crusts and other vegetation. Increased erosion and growth of undesirable exotic plants like cheatgrass have been the result. Scars left by roads and mines during the uranium frenzy of the 1950s can still be seen, most commonly in the Island in the Sky District.

Fewer than 10 species of fish evolved in the canyons of the Colorado and the Green Rivers. These fish developed streamlined bodies and strange features, such as humped backs, to cope with the muddy and varying river waters. Species include Colorado pikeminnow, humpback chub, bonytail chub, and humpback sucker; most of these live nowhere else. All have suffered greatly reduced populations and restricted ranges as a result of dam building.

Of the approximately 65 mammal species living in the park, about one-third are rodents, and another third are bats. You're most likely to see chipmunks, antelope ground squirrels, and rock squirrels, which are often active during the day. Most other animals wait until evening to come out and feed; in the morning, look for tracks of mule deer, bighorn sheep, coyotes, gray foxes, badgers, porcupines, spotted skunks, beavers, black-tailed jackrabbits, wood rats, kangaroo rats, and many species of mice.

bottled water sold at the visitors center, there is no water available in this district of the park.

VISITORS CENTER

Stop here for information about Island in the Sky and to see exhibits on geology and history; books and maps are available for purchase. The visitors center (435/259-4712, 9am-4pm daily winter, longer hours spring-fall) is located just before the neck crosses to Island in the Sky. From Moab, go northwest 10 miles on U.S. 191, then turn left and drive 15 miles on Highway 313 to the junction for Dead Horse Point State Park. From here, continue straight for seven miles. Many of the park's plants grow and are identified outside the visitors center; look also at the display of pressed plants inside the center.

SHAFER CANYON OVERLOOK

Half a mile past the visitors center is the Shafer Canyon Overlook (on the left, just before crossing the neck). The overlook has good views east down the canyon and onto the incredibly twisting **Shafer Trail Road.** Cattlemen Frank and John Schafer built the trail in the early 1900s to move stock to additional pastures (the *c* in their name was later dropped by mapmakers). Uranium prospectors upgraded the trail to a 4WD road during the 1950s so that they could reach their claims at the base of the cliffs. Today, Shafer Trail Road connects the mesa top with White Rim Road and Potash Road, four miles and 1,200 vertical feet below. High-clearance vehicles should be used on the Shafer. It's also fun to ride this road on a mountain bike. Road conditions can vary considerably, so contact a ranger before starting. Shafer Trail Viewpoint, across the neck, provides another perspective 0.5 miles farther.

Back on top of the Island, the paved park road leads south from the neck six miles across Gray's Pasture to a junction. The Grand View Point Overlook road continues south while the road to Upheaval Dome turns west.

BUCK CANYON OVERLOOK

As the park road continues south, a series of incredible vistas over the canyons of the Green and Colorado Rivers peek into view. The first viewpoint is Buck Canyon Overlook, which looks east over the Colorado River Canyon. Two miles farther is the **Grand View Picnic Area,** a handy lunch stop.

GRAND VIEW POINT

At the end of the main road, one mile past the Grand View Picnic Area, is Grand View Point, perhaps the most spectacular panorama from Island in the Sky. Monument Basin lies directly

below, and countless canyons, the Colorado River, the Needles, and mountain ranges are in the distance. The easy 1.5-mile **Grand View Trail** continues past the end of the road for other vistas from the point.

Return to the main road to explore more overlooks and geological curiosities in the western portion of Island in the Sky.

GREEN RIVER OVERLOOK

The Green River Overlook is just west of the main junction on an unpaved road. From the overlook, Soda Springs Basin and a section of the Green River (deeply entrenched in Stillwater Canyon) can be seen below. Small Willow Flat Campground is on the way to the overlook.

UPHEAVAL DOME ROAD

At the end of the road, 5.3 miles northwest of the junction, is **Upheaval Dome.** This geologic oddity is a fantastically deformed pile of rock sprawled across a crater about three miles wide and 1,200 feet deep. For many years, Upheaval Dome has kept geologists busy trying to figure out its origins. They once assumed that salt of the Paradox Formation pushed the rock layers upward to form the dome. Now, however, strong evidence suggests that a meteorite impact created the structure. The surrounding ring depression, caused by collapse, and the convergence of rock layers upward toward the center correspond precisely to known impact structures. Shatter cones and microscopic analysis also indicate an impact origin. When the meteorite struck, sometime in the last 150 million years, it formed a crater up to five miles across. Erosion removed some of the overlying rock—perhaps as much as a vertical mile. The underlying salt may have played a role in uplifting the central section.

The easy **Crater View Trail** leads to overlooks on the rim of Upheaval Dome; the first viewpoint is 0.5 miles round-trip, and the second is one mile round-trip. There's also a small **picnic area** here.

◖ WHITE RIM ROAD

This driving adventure follows the White Rim below the sheer cliffs of Island in the Sky. A close look at the light-colored surface reveals ripple marks and cross beds laid down near an ancient coastline. The plateau's east side is about 800 feet above the Colorado River. On the west side, the plateau meets the bank of the Green River.

Travel along the winding road presents a constantly changing panorama of rock, canyons, river, and sky. Keep an eye out for desert bighorn sheep. You'll see all three levels of Island in the Sky District, from the high plateaus to the White Rim to the rivers.

Only 4WD vehicles with high clearance can make the trip. With the proper vehicle, driving is mostly easy but slow and winding; a few steep or rough sections have to be negotiated. The 100-mile trip takes 2-3 days. Allow an extra day to travel all the road spurs.

Mountain bikers find this a great trip too; most cyclists arrange an accompanying 4WD vehicle to carry water and camping gear. Primitive campgrounds along the way provide convenient stopping places. Both cyclists and 4WD drivers must obtain reservations and a backcountry permit ($30) for the White Rim campsites from the Island in the Sky visitors center. Find application forms on the Canyonlands website (www.nps.gov/cany); return the completed application at least two weeks in advance of your planned trip. Questions can be fielded via telephone (435/259-4351, 8am-12:30pm Mon.-Fri.), but no telephone reservations are accepted. Demand exceeds supply during the popular spring and autumn seasons, when you should make reservations as far in advance as possible. No services or developed water sources exist anywhere on the drive, so be sure to have plenty of fuel and water with some to spare. Access points are Shafer Trail Road (from near Island in the Sky) and Potash Road (Hwy. 279 from Moab) on the east and Mineral Bottom Road on the west. White Rim sandstone forms the distinctive plateau crossed on the drive.

HIKING
Neck Spring Trail

- Distance: 5.8-mile loop
- Duration: 3-4 hours
- Elevation change: 300 feet
- Effort: moderate
- Trailhead: Shafer Canyon Overlook

The trail begins near the Shafer Canyon Overlook and loops down Taylor Canyon to Neck and Cabin Springs, formerly used by ranchers (look for the remains of the old cowboy cabin near Cabin Springs), then climbs back to Island in the Sky Road at a second trailhead 0.5 miles south of the start. A brochure should be available at the trailhead. Water at the springs supports maidenhair fern and other plants. Also watch for birds and wildlife attracted to this spot. Bring water with you, as the springs are not potable.

Lathrop Trail

- Distance: 10.5 miles one-way to the Colorado River
- Duration: overnight
- Elevation change: 2,000 feet
- Effort: strenuous
- Trailhead: on the left, 1.3 miles past the neck

This is the only marked hiking route going all the way from Island in the Sky to the Colorado River. The first 2.5 miles cross Gray's Pasture to the rim, which affords fantastic vistas over the Colorado River. From here, the trail descends steeply, dropping 1,600 feet over the next 2.5 miles, to White Rim Road, a little less than seven miles from the trailhead. Part of this section follows an old mining road past several abandoned mines, all relics of the uranium boom. Don't enter the shafts; they're in danger of collapse and may contain poisonous gases. From the mining area, the route descends

FOUR-WHEELING IN CANYONLANDS

The 4WD White Rim Road snakes along the base of the Island in the Sky.

For people who think that just as a dog needs to run free every once in a while, sport-utility vehicles need to occasionally escape the home-to-work loop, Canyonlands is a tonic.

Each of the park's three main districts has a focal point for 4WD travel. In the Island in the Sky, it's the 100-mile-long White Rim Road. Four-wheelers in the Needles head to Elephant Rock for the challenging climb to a network of roads. The Maze's Flint Trail traverses clay slopes that are extremely slippery when wet. Though all of the park's 4WD roads are rugged, those in the Maze are especially challenging, and this area is by far the most remote.

Drivers should note that ATVs are not permitted in national parks. All vehicles must be street-legal. The most commonly used vehicles are jeeps. Four-wheel drivers should be prepared to make basic road or vehicle repairs and should carry the following items:

- at least one full-size spare tire
- extra gas
- extra water
- a shovel
- a high-lift jack
- chains for all four tires, especially October-April

Also note that towing from any backcountry area of Canyonlands is very expensive: It's not uncommon for bills to top $1,000.

Permits are required for overnight trips; camping is only in designated sites.

through a wash to White Rim Road, follows the road a short distance south, then goes down Lathrop Canyon Road to the Colorado River, another four miles and 500 vertical feet. The trail has little shade and can be very hot. Vehicular traffic may be encountered along the White Rim Road portion of the trail. For a long day hike (13.6 miles round-trip), turn around when you reach the White Rim Road and hike back up to the top of the mesa.

◖ Mesa Arch Trail

- Distance: 0.25 miles one-way
- Duration: 30 minutes
- Elevation change: 80 feet
- Effort: easy
- Trailhead: on the left, 5.5 miles from the neck

This easy trail leads to a spectacular arch on the rim of the mesa. On the way, the road crosses the grasslands and scattered juniper trees of

A short hike leads to the clifftop Mesa Arch.

© BILL MCRAE

Gray's Pasture. A trail brochure available at the start describes the ecology of the mesa. The sandstone arch frames views of rock formations below and the La Sal Mountains in the distance. Photographers come here to catch the sun rising through the arch.

Murphy Point

- Distance: 11-mile loop
- Duration: 5-7 hours
- Elevation change: 1,100 feet
- Effort: strenuous
- Trailhead: Murphy Point
- Directions: From the Upheaval Dome junction on the main park road, head three miles south. Turn right onto a rough dirt road and follow it 1.7 miles to Murphy Point.

Murphy Trail starts as a jaunt across the mesa, then drops steeply from the rim down to White Rim Road. This strenuous route forks partway down; one branch follows Murphy Hogback (a ridge) to Murphy Campground on the 4WD road, and the other follows a wash to the road one mile south of the campground.

White Rim Overlook Trail

- Distance: 0.75 miles one-way
- Duration: 1 hour
- Elevation change: 25 feet
- Effort: easy
- Trailhead: Grand View Picnic Area

Hike east along a peninsula to an overlook of Monument Basin and beyond. There are also good views of White Rim Road and potholes.

Gooseberry Trail

- Distance: 2.5 miles one-way
- Duration: 5 hours
- Elevation change: 1,400 feet
- Effort: strenuous
- Trailhead: Grand View Picnic Area

Gooseberry Trail drops off the mesa and makes an extremely steep descent to White Rim Road, just north of Gooseberry Campground. The La Sal Mountains are visible from the trail.

◖ Grand View Trail

- Distance: 1 mile one-way
- Duration: 2 hours
- Elevation change: 50 feet
- Effort: easy
- Trailhead: Grand View Point Overlook

At the overlook, Grand View Trail continues past the end of the road for other vistas from the point, which is the southernmost tip of Island in the Sky. This short hike across the slickrock will really give you a feel for the entire Canyonlands National Park. From the mesa-top trail, you'll see the gorges of the Colorado and Green Rivers come together; across the chasm is the Needles District. Look down to spot vehicles traveling along the White Rim Trail at the base of the mesa.

Aztec Butte Trail

- Distance: 1 mile one-way
- Duration: 1.5 hours
- Elevation change: 200 feet
- Effort: moderate
- Trailhead: Aztec Butte parking area, 1 mile north-west of road junction on Upheaval Dome Road

It's a bit of a haul up the slickrock to the top of this sandstone butte, but once you get here, you'll be rewarded with a good view of the Island and Taylor Canyon. Atop the butte a loop trail passes several Anasazi granaries. Aztec Butte is one of the few areas in Island in the Sky with Native American ruins; the shortage of water in this area prevented permanent settlement.

Whale Rock Trail

- Distance: 0.5 miles one-way
- Duration: 1 hour
- Elevation change: 100 feet
- Effort: easy-moderate
- Trailhead: Upheaval Dome Road, on the right, 4.4 miles northwest of the road junction

A relatively easy trail climbs Whale Rock, a

sandstone hump near the outer rim of Upheaval Dome. In a couple of places you'll have to do some scrambling up the slickrock, which is made easier and a bit less scary thanks to hand-rails. From the top of the rock, there are good views of the dome.

Upheaval Dome Viewpoint Trail

- Distance: 1 mile one-way
- Duration: 1.5 hours
- Elevation change: 150 feet
- Effort: easy
- Trailhead: Upheaval Dome parking area

The trail leads to Upheaval Dome overviews; it's about 0.5 miles to the first overlook and a mile to the second. The shorter trail leads to the rim with a view about 1,000 feet down into the jumble of rocks in the craterlike center of Upheaval Dome. The longer trail descends the slickrock and offers even better views. Energetic hikers can explore this formation in depth by circling it on the Syncline Loop Trail or from White Rim Road below.

Syncline Loop Trail

- Distance: 8-mile loop
- Duration: 5-7 hours
- Elevation change: 1,200 feet
- Effort: strenuous
- Trailhead: Upheaval Dome parking area

Syncline Loop Trail makes a circuit completely around Upheaval Dome. The trail crosses Upheaval Dome Canyon about halfway around from the overlook; walk east 1.5 miles up the canyon to enter the crater itself. This is the only nontechnical route into the center of the dome. A hike around Upheaval Dome with a side trip to the crater totals 11 miles, and it is best done as an overnight trip. Carry plenty of water for the entire trip; this dry country can be very hot in summer. The Green River is the only reliable source of water. An alternate approach is to start near Upheaval Campsite on White Rim Road; hike four miles southeast on through Upheaval Canyon to a junction with the Syncline Loop Trail, then another 1.5 miles into the crater. The elevation gain is about 600 feet.

Alcove Spring Trail

- Distance: 10 miles one-way
- Duration: overnight
- Elevation change: 1,500 feet
- Effort: strenuous
- Trailhead: 1.5 miles southeast of the Upheaval Dome parking area

Alcove Spring Trail connects with White Rim Road in Taylor Canyon. Five miles of the 10-mile distance is on the steep trail down through Trail Canyon and five miles is on a jeep road in Taylor Canyon. One downside of this trail is the 4WD traffic, which can be pretty heavy during the spring and fall. From the Taylor Canyon end of the trail, it is not far to the Upheaval Trail, which heads southeast to its junction with the Syncline Trail, which in turn leads to the Upheaval Dome parking area. Allow at least one overnight if you plan to hike this full loop. Day hikers should plan to turn around after the first five-mile section; this is still a very full day of hiking. Carry plenty of water—the trail is hot and dry.

CAMPGROUNDS

There is only one developed campground in the Island in the Sky District. **Willow Flat Campground** on Murphy Point Road has only 12 sites ($10), available on a first-come, first-served basis; sites tend to fill up in all seasons except winter. No water or services are available.

Camping is available outside the park at **Dead Horse Point State Park** (reservations 800/322-3770, www.reserveamerica.com, $20 plus $9 reservations fee), which is also very popular, so don't plan on getting a spot without reserving ahead. There are also primitive Bureau of Land Management (BLM) campsites along Highway 313.

Needles District

The Needles District, named for the area's distinctive sandstone spires, showcases some of the finest rock sculptures in Canyonlands National Park. Spires, arches, and monoliths appear in almost every direction. Prehistoric ruins and rock art exist in greater variety and quantity here than elsewhere in the park. Perennial springs and streams bring greenery to the desert.

While a scenic paved road leads to the district, this area of the park has only about a dozen miles of paved roads. Needles doesn't have a lot to offer travelers who are unwilling to get out of their vehicles and hike; however, it's the best section of the park for a wide variety of day hikes. Even a short hike opens up the landscape and leads to remarkable vistas and prehistoric sites.

To reach the Needles District, go 40 miles south from Moab (or 14 miles north of Monticello) on U.S. 191, turn west on Highway 211, and continue for 38 miles.

VISITORS CENTER

Stop at the visitors center (west end of Hwy. 211, 435/259-4711, 8am-4:30pm daily Nov.-Feb., longer hours Mar.-Oct.) for information on hiking, back roads, and other aspects of travel in the Needles, as well as backcountry permits, required for all overnight stays in the backcountry, and maps, brochures, and books. Take a moment to look at the little computer-animated slide show on the region's geology—its graphics make it all become clear. When the office isn't open, you'll find information posted outside on the bulletin board.

CANYONLANDS

Newspaper Rock preserves some of the richest, most fanciful prehistoric rock art in Utah.

◖ BLM NEWSPAPER ROCK HISTORICAL MONUMENT

Although not in the park itself, Newspaper Rock lies just 150 feet off Highway 211 on Bureau of Land Management (BLM) land on the way to the Needles District. At Newspaper Rock, a profusion of petroglyphs depict human figures, animals, birds, and abstract designs. These represent 2,000 years of human history during which prehistoric people and Anasazi, Fremont, Paiute, Navajo, and Anglo travelers passed through Indian Creek Canyon. The patterns on the smooth sandstone rock face stand out clearly, thanks to a coating of dark desert varnish. A short nature trail introduces you to the area's desert and riparian vegetation.

The cracks in the rock walls around **Indian Creek** offer world-class rock climbing; climbers should track down a copy of *Indian Creek: A Climbing Guide,* by David Bloom, for details and lots of pictures. **Moab Desert Adventures** (415 N. Main St., Moab, 435/260-2404 or 877/765-4273, www.moabdesertadventures. com) offers guided climbing at Indian Creek.

From U.S. 191 between Moab and Monticello, turn west on Highway 211 and travel 12 miles to Newspaper Rock. Indian Creek's climbing walls start about three miles west of Newspaper Rock.

NEEDLES AND ANTICLINE OVERLOOKS

Although outside the park, these viewpoints atop the high mesa east of Canyonlands National Park offer magnificent panoramas of the surrounding area. Part of the BLM's **Canyon Rims Recreation Area** (www.blm.gov), these easily accessed overlooks provide the kind of awe-inspiring vistas over the Needles District that would otherwise require a hike in the park. The turnoff for both overlooks is at milepost 93 on U.S. 191, which is 32 miles south of Moab and 7 miles north of Highway 211. There are also two campgrounds along the access road.

For the Needles Overlook, follow the paved road 22 miles west to its end (turn left at the junction 15 miles in). The BLM maintains a picnic area and interpretive exhibits here. A fence protects visitors from the sheer cliffs that drop off more than 1,000 feet. You can see much of Canyonlands National Park and southeastern Utah. Look south for the Six-shooter Peaks and the high country of the Abajo Mountains; southwest for the Needles (thousands of spires reaching for the sky); west for the confluence area of the Green and Colorado Rivers, the Maze District, the Orange Cliffs, and the Henry Mountains; northwest for the lazy bends of the Colorado River Canyon and the sheer-walled mesas of Island in the Sky and Dead Horse Point; north for the Book Cliffs; and northeast for the La Sal Mountains. The changing shadows and colors of the canyon country make for a continuous show throughout the day.

For the Anticline Overlook, continue straight north at the junction with the Needles road and drive 17 miles on a good gravel road to the fenced overlook at road's end. You'll be standing 1,600 feet above the Colorado River. The sweeping panorama over the canyons, the river, and the twisted rocks of the Kane Creek Anticline is nearly as spectacular as that from Dead Horse Point, only 5.5 miles west as the crow flies. Salt and other minerals of the Paradox Formation pushed up overlying rocks into the dome visible below. Down-cutting by the Colorado River has revealed the twisted rock layers. The Moab Salt Mine across the river to the north uses a solution technique to bring up potash from the Paradox Formation several thousand feet underground. Pumps then transfer the solution to the blue-tinted evaporation ponds. Look carefully at the northeast horizon to see an arch in the Windows Section of Arches National Park, 16 miles away.

The BLM operates two campgrounds in the Canyon Rims Recreational Area. **Hatch Point Campground** (10 sites, water early May-mid-Sept., $12) has a scenic mesa-top setting just off the road to the Anticline Overlook, about nine miles north of the road junction. Closer to the highway is **Windwhistle Campground** (water early May-late Sept., $12); it's six miles west of U.S. 191 on the Needles Overlook road.

NEEDLES OUTPOST

A general store just outside the park boundary offers a campground (435/979-4007, www.canyonlandsneedlesoutpost.com, mid-Mar.-late Oct., $20 tent or RV, no hookups), groceries, ice, gas, propane, a café, showers ($3 campers, $7 noncampers), and pretty much any camping supply you might have left at home. The campground is a great alternative to the park; sites have a fair amount of privacy and great views onto the park's spires. The turnoff from Highway 211 is one mile before the Needles visitors center.

BIG SPRING CANYON SCENIC DRIVE

The main paved park road continues 6.5 miles past the visitors center to Big Spring Canyon Overlook. On the way, you can stop at several nature trails or turn onto 4WD roads. The overlook takes in a view of slickrock-edged canyons dropping away toward the Colorado River.

HIKING

The Needles District includes about 60 miles of backcountry trails. Many interconnect to provide all sorts of day-hike and overnight opportunities. Cairns mark the trails, and signs point the way at junctions. You can normally find water in upper Elephant Canyon and canyons to the east in spring and early summer, although whatever remains is often stagnant by midsummer. Always ask the rangers about sources of water, and don't depend on its availability. Treat water from all sources, including springs, before drinking it. Chesler Park and other areas west of Elephant Canyon are very dry; you'll need to bring all your water. Mosquitoes, gnats, and deer flies can be pesky late spring-midsummer, especially in the wetter places, so be sure to bring insect repellent. To plan your trip, obtain the small hiking map available from the visitors center, the National

© BONYU CHU/FLICKR.COM

Cave Spring Trail

Geographic/Trails Illustrated's Needles District map, or USGS topographic maps. Overnight backcountry hiking requires a permit ($30 per group). Permits can be hard to get at the last minute during the busy spring hiking season, but you can apply for your permit any time after mid-July for the following spring. Find permit applications on the Canyonlands website (www.nps.gov/cany).

Roadside Ruin Trail

- Distance: 0.3 miles round-trip
- Duration: 20 minutes
- Elevation change: 20 feet
- Effort: easy
- Trailhead: on the left, 0.4 miles past the visitors center

This is one of two easy hikes near the visitors center. It passes near a well-preserved Anasazi granary. A trail guide available at the start tells about the Anasazi and the local plants.

Cave Spring Trail

- Distance: 0.6 miles round-trip
- Duration: 45 minutes
- Elevation change: 50 feet
- Effort: easy
- Trailhead: Cave Spring
- Directions: Turn left 0.7 miles past the visitors center and follow signs about 1 mile to the trailhead.

Don't miss the Cave Spring Trail, which introduces the geology and ecology of the park and leads to an old cowboy line camp. Pick up the brochure at the beginning. The loop goes clockwise, crossing some slickrock; two ladders assist hikers on the steep sections. Native Americans first used these rock overhangs for shelter, and faint pictographs still decorate the rock walls. Much later—from the late 1800s until the park was established in 1964—cowboys used these open caves as a line camp. The park service has recreated the line camp, just

POTHOLE ECOSYSTEMS

At Canyonlands it's easy to be in awe of the deep canyons and big desert rivers. But the little details of Canyonlands geology and ecology are pretty wonderful too. Consider the potholes: shallow depressions dusted with wind-blown dirt. These holes, which range from less than an inch to several feet deep, fill after rain-storms and bring entire little ecosystems to life.

Pothole dwellers must be able to survive long periods of dryness, then pack as much living as possible into the short wet periods. Some creatures, like the tadpole shrimp, live only for a couple of weeks. Others, like the spadefoot toad, hatch from drought-resistant eggs when water is present, quickly pass through the critical tadpole stage, then move onto dry land, re-turning to mate and lay eggs in potholes.

Although pothole dwellers are tough enough to survive in a dormant form during the long dry spells, most are very sensitive to sud-den water-chemistry changes, temperature changes, sediment input, being stepped on, and being splashed out onto dry land. Humans should never use pothole water for swimming, bathing, or drinking, as this can drastically change the salinity or pH of a pool. Organisms are unable to adapt to these human-generated changes, which occur suddenly, unlike slow, natural changes. While the desert pothole eco-systems may seem unimportant, they act as an indicator of the health of the larger ecosystems in which they occur.

50 yards in from the trailhead, with period furnishings and equipment. If you're not up for the full hike, or would rather not climb ladders, the cowboy camp and the pictographs are just a five-minute walk from the trailhead.

This trail is a good introduction to hiking on slickrock and using rock cairns to find your way. Signs identify plants along the way.

Pothole Point Nature Trail

- Distance: 0.6 miles round-trip
- Duration: 40 minutes
- Elevation change: 20 feet
- Effort: easy
- Trailhead: parking area on the left side of Big Spring Canyon Overlook Scenic Drive, five miles past the visitors center

Highlights of this hike across the slickrock are the many potholes dissolved in the Cedar Mesa sandstone. A brochure illustrates the fairy shrimp, tadpole shrimp, horsehair worms, snails, and other creatures that spring to life when rain fills the potholes. Desert varnish rims the potholes; it forms when water evaporates,

leaving mineral residues on the surface of the rocks. In addition to the potholes, you'll enjoy fine views of distant buttes from the trail.

Slickrock Trail

- Distance: 2.4 miles round-trip
- Duration: 2 hours
- Elevation change: 150 feet
- Effort: easy-moderate
- Trailhead: parking area on the right side of Big Spring Canyon Overlook Scenic Drive, 6.2 miles past the visitors center

The Slickrock Trail leads north to a series of four viewpoints, including a panoramic view over much of southeastern Utah, and overlooks of Big Spring and Little Spring Canyons. As its name indicates, much of the trail is across slickrock, but there are enough pockets of soil to support a good springtime display of wildflowers. The trailhead is almost at the end of the paved road, where **Big Spring Canyon Overlook,** 6.5 miles past the visitors center, marks the end of the scenic drive but not the scenery.

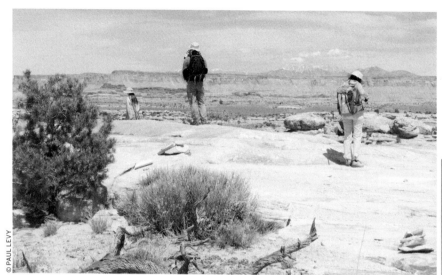

CANYONLANDS

© PAUL LEVY

The Slickrock Trail has several great viewpoints.

Confluence Overlook Trail

- Distance: 5.5 miles one-way
- Duration: 5 hours
- Elevation change: 1,250 feet
- Effort: moderate-strenuous
- Trailhead: Big Spring Canyon Overlook

The Confluence Overlook Trail begins at the end of the paved road and winds west to an overlook of the Green and Colorado Rivers 1,000 feet below; there's no trail down to the rivers. The trail starts with some ups and downs, crossing Big Spring and Elephant Canyons, and follows a jeep road for a short distance. Much of the trail is through open country, so it can get quite hot. Higher points have good views of the Needles to the south. You might see rafts in the water or bighorn sheep on the cliffs. Except for a few short steep sections, this trail is level and fairly easy; it's the length of this 10-mile round-trip to the confluence as well as the hot sun that make it challenging. A very early start is recommended in summer because there's little shade. Carry water even if you don't plan to go all the way. This enchanting country has lured many a hiker beyond his or her original goal.

Peekaboo Trail

- Distance: 5 miles one-way
- Duration: 5-6 hours
- Elevation change: 550 feet
- Effort: strenuous
- Trailhead: Squaw Flat trailhead
- Directions: A road to Squaw Flat Campground and Elephant Hill turns left 2.7 miles past the ranger station. The Squaw Flat trailhead sits a short distance south of the campground and is reached by a separate signed road. You can also begin from a trailhead in the campground itself.

Peekaboo Trail winds southeast over rugged up-and-down terrain, including some steep sections of slickrock (best avoided when wet, icy, or covered with snow) and a couple of ladders.

There's little shade, so carry water. The trail follows Squaw Canyon, climbs over a pass to Lost Canyon, then crosses more slickrock before descending to Peekaboo Campground on Salt Creek Road (accessible by 4WD vehicles). Look for Anasazi ruins on the way and rock art at the campground. A rockslide took out Peekaboo Spring, which is still shown on some maps. Options on this trail include a turnoff south through Squaw or Lost Canyon to make a loop of 8.75 miles or more.

Squaw Canyon Trail

- Distance: 3.75 miles one-way
- Duration: 4 hours
- Elevation change: 700 feet
- Effort: moderate
- Trailhead: parking area on the left of the main road, 5 miles past the visitors center
- Directions: A road to Squaw Flat Campground and Elephant Hill turns left 2.7 miles past the ranger station. The Squaw Flat Trailhead is a short distance south of the campground and is reached by a separate signed road. You can also begin from a trailhead in the campground itself.

Squaw Canyon Trail follows the canyon south. Intermittent water can often be found until late spring. You can take a connecting trail (Peekaboo, Lost Canyon, or Big Spring Canyon) or cross a slickrock pass to Elephant Canyon.

Lost Canyon Trail

- Distance: 3.25 miles one-way
- Duration: 4-5 hours
- Elevation change: 360 feet
- Effort: moderate-strenuous
- Trailhead: parking area on the left of the main road, 5 miles past the visitors center
- Directions: A road to Squaw Flat Campground and Elephant Hill turns left 2.7 miles past the ranger station. The Squaw

Flat trailhead sits a short distance south of the campground and is reached by a separate signed road. You can also begin from a trailhead in the campground itself.

Lost Canyon Trail is reached via Peekaboo or Squaw Canyon Trails and makes a loop with them. Lost Canyon is surprisingly lush, and you may be forced to wade through water. Most of the trail is in the wash bottom, except for a section of slickrock to Squaw Canyon.

Big Spring Canyon Trail

- Distance: 3.75 miles one-way
- Duration: 4 hours
- Elevation change: 370 feet
- Effort: moderate-strenuous
- Trailhead: parking area on the left of the main road, 5 miles past the visitors center
- Directions: A road to Squaw Flat Campground and Elephant Hill turns left 2.7 miles past the ranger station. The Squaw Flat trailhead is a short distance south of the campground and is reached by a separate signed road. You can also begin from a trailhead in the campground itself.

Big Spring Canyon Trail crosses an outcrop of slickrock from the trailhead, then follows the canyon bottom to the head of the canyon. It's a lovely springtime hike with lots of flowers, including the fragrant cliffrose. Except in summer, you can usually find intermittent water along the way. At canyon's end, a steep slickrock climb leads to Squaw Canyon Trail and back to the trailhead for a 7.5-mile loop. Another possibility is to turn southwest to the head of Squaw Canyon, then hike over a saddle to Elephant Canyon, for a 10.5-mile loop.

◖ Chesler Park

- Distance: 3 miles one-way
- Duration: 3-4 hours
- Elevation change: 920 feet

- Effort: moderate
- Trailhead: Elephant Hill parking area or Squaw Flat trailhead (increases the distance slightly)
- Directions: Drive west 3 miles past the Squaw Flat campground turnoff (on passable dirt roads) to the Elephant Hill picnic area and trailhead at the base of Elephant Hill.

The Elephant Hill parking area doesn't always inspire confidence: Sounds of racing engines and burning rubber can often be heard from above as vehicles attempt the difficult 4WD road that begins just past the picnic area. However, the noise quickly fades as you hit the trail. Chesler Park is a favorite hiking destination. A lovely desert meadow contrasts with the red and white spires that give the Needles District its name. An old cowboy line camp is on the west side of the rock island in the center of the park. The trail winds through sand and slickrock before ascending a small pass through the Needles to Chesler Park. Once inside, you can take the Chesler Park Loop Trail (5 miles) completely around the park. The loop includes the unusual 0.5-mile Joint Trail, which follows the bottom of a very narrow crack. Camping in Chesler Park is restricted to certain areas; check with a ranger.

Druid Arch

- Distance: 5.5 miles one-way
- Duration: 5-7 hours
- Elevation change: 1,000 feet
- Effort: strenuous
- Trailhead: Elephant Hill parking area or Squaw Flat trailhead (increases the round-trip distance by 2 miles)
- Directions: Drive west 3 miles past the Squaw Flat campground turnoff (on passable dirt roads) to the Elephant Hill picnic area and trailhead at the base of Elephant Hill.

Druid Arch reminds many people of the massive slabs at Stonehenge in England, which are popularly associated with the druids. Follow the Chesler Park Trail two miles to Elephant Canyon, turn up the canyon for 3.5 miles, and then make a steep 0.25-mile climb, which includes a ladder and some scrambling, to the arch. Upper Elephant Canyon has seasonal water but is closed to camping.

Lower Red Lake Canyon Trail

- Distance: 9.5 miles one-way
- Duration: 2 days
- Elevation change: 1,000 feet
- Effort: strenuous
- Trailhead: Elephant Hill parking area or Squaw Flat trailhead (increases the distance by 2 miles)
- Directions: Drive west 3 miles past the Squaw Flat campground turnoff (on passable dirt roads) to the Elephant Hill picnic area and trailhead at the base of Elephant Hill.

Lower Red Lake Canyon Trail provides access to the Colorado River's Cataract Canyon. This long, strenuous trip is best suited for experienced hikers and is ideally completed in two days. Distance from the Elephant Hill trailhead is 19 miles round-trip; you'll be walking on 4WD roads and trails. If you can drive Elephant Hill 4WD Road to the trail junction in Cyclone Canyon, the hike is only eight miles round-trip. The most difficult trail section is a steep talus slope that drops 700 feet in 0.5 miles into the lower canyon. The canyon has little shade and lacks any water source above the river. Summer heat can make the trip grueling; temperatures tend to be 5-10°F hotter than on other Needles trails. The river level drops between midsummer and autumn, allowing hikers to go along the shore both downstream to see the rapids and upstream to the confluence. Undertows and strong currents make the river dangerous to cross.

Upper Salt Creek Trail

- Distance: 12 miles one-way
- Duration: 2 days

- Elevation change: 1,650 feet
- Effort: strenuous
- Trailhead: end of Salt Creek Road
- Directions: Drive to the end of the rugged 13.5-mile 4WD road up Salt Creek to start this hike.

Several impressive arches and many inviting side canyons attract adventurous hikers to the extreme southeast corner of the Needles District. The trail goes south 12 miles up-canyon to Cottonwood Canyon and Beef Basin Road near Cathedral Butte, just outside the park boundary. The trail is nearly level except for a steep climb at the end. Water can usually be found. Some wading and bushwhacking may be necessary. The famous "All-American Man" pictograph, shown on some topographic maps (or ask a ranger), is in a cave a short way off to the east at about the midpoint of the trail; follow your map and unsigned paths to the cave, but don't climb in—it's dangerous to you, the ruins, and the pictograph inside. Many more archaeological sites are near the trail, but they're all fragile, and great care should be taken when visiting them.

MOUNTAIN BIKING AND 4WD EXPLORATION

Visitors with bicycles or 4WD vehicles can explore the many backcountry roads that lead to the outback. More than 50 miles of challenging roads link primitive campsites, remote trailheads, and sites with ancient cultural remnants. Some roads in the Needles District are rugged and require previous experience in handling 4WD vehicles on steep inclines and in deep sand. Be aware that towing charges from this area commonly run over $1,000.

The best route for mountain bikers is the seven-mile-long Colorado Overlook Road, which starts near the visitors center. Although very steep for the first stretch and busy with 4WD vehicles spinning their wheels on the hill, Elephant Hill Road is another good bet,

with just a few sandy parts. Start here and do a combination ride and hike to the Confluence Overlook. It's about eight miles from the Elephant Hill parking area to the confluence; the final 0.5 miles is on a trail, so you'll have to lock up your bike and walk this last bit. Horse Canyon and Lavender Canyon are too sandy for pleasant biking.

All motor vehicles and bicycles must purchase a $10 day-use permit and remain on designated roads. Overnight backcountry trips with bicycles or motor vehicles require a permit ($30 per group).

Salt Creek Canyon 4WD Road

This rugged route begins near Cave Spring Trail, crosses sage flats for the next 2.5 miles, and then terminates at Peekaboo campground. Hikers can continue south into a spectacular canyon on Upper Salt Creek Trail.

Horse Canyon 4WD Road turns off to the left shortly before the mouth of Salt Canyon. The round-trip distance, including a side trip to Tower Ruin, is about 13 miles; other attractions include Paul Bunyan's Potty, Castle Arch, Fortress Arch, and side canyon hiking. Salt and Horse Canyons can easily be driven in 4WD vehicles. Salt Canyon is usually closed in summer because of quicksand after flash floods and in winter due to shelf ice.

Davis and Lavender Canyons

Both canyons are accessed via Davis Canyon Road off Highway 211; contain great scenery, arches, and Native American historic sites; and are easily visited with high-clearance vehicles. Davis is about 20 miles round-trip, while sandy Lavender Canyon is about 26 miles round-trip. Try to allow plenty of time in either canyon, because there is much to see and many inviting side canyons to hike. You can camp on BLM land just outside the park boundaries, but not in the park itself.

Colorado Overlook 4WD Road

This popular route begins beside the visitors

CANYONLANDS

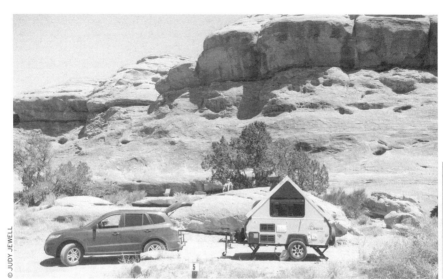

© JUDY JEWELL

camping in style at Needles Outpost

center and follows Salt Creek to Lower Jump Overlook. It then bounces across slickrock to a view of the Colorado River, upstream from the confluence. Driving, for the most part, is easy-moderate, although it's very rough for the last 1.5 miles. Round-trip distance is 14 miles. This is also a good mountain bike ride.

Elephant Hill 4WD Loop Road

This rugged backcountry road begins three miles past the Squaw Flat Campground turn-off. Only experienced drivers with stout vehicles should attempt the extremely rough and steep climb up Elephant Hill (coming up the back side of Elephant Hill is even worse). The loop is about 10 miles round-trip. Connecting roads go to the Confluence Overlook trailhead (the viewpoint is one mile round-trip on foot), the Joint trailhead (Chesler Park is two miles round-trip on foot), and several canyons. Some road sections on the loop are one-way. The parallel canyons in this area are grabens caused by faulting, where a layer of salt has shifted deep underground. In addition to Elephant Hill, a few other difficult spots must be negotiated.

This area can also be reached by a long route south of the park using Cottonwood Canyon and Beef Basin Road from Highway 211, about 60 miles one-way. You'll enjoy spectacular vistas from the Abajo Highlands. Two very steep descents from Pappys Pasture into Bobbys Hole effectively make this section one-way; travel from Elephant Hill up Bobbys Hole is possible but much more difficult than going the other way, and it may require hours of road-building. The Bobbys Hole route may be impassable at times; ask about conditions at the BLM office in Monticello or at the Needles visitors center.

CAMPGROUNDS

The **Squaw Flat Campground** (year-round, no reservations, $15) about six miles from the visitors center, has 26 sites, many snuggled under the slickrock, and has water. RVs must be less than 28 feet long. Rangers present evening programs at the campfire circle on Loop A spring through autumn.

If you can't find a space at Squaw Flat, a common occurrence in spring and fall, the private campground at **Needles Outpost** (435/979-4007, www.canyonlandsneedlesoutpost.com, mid-Mar.-late Oct., $20 tents or RVs, no hookups, showers $3), just outside the park entrance, is a good alternative.

Nearby BLM land also offers a number of places to camp. A string of campsites along **Lockhart Basin Road** are convenient and inexpensive. Lockhart Basin Road heads north from Highway 211 about five miles east of the entrance to the Needles District. **Hamburger Rock Campground** (no water, $6) is about one mile up the road. North of Hamburger Rock, camping is dispersed, with many small (no water, free) campsites at turnoffs from the road.

Not surprisingly, the road gets rougher the farther north you travel; beyond Indian Creek Falls, it's best to have 4WD. These campsites are very popular with climbers who are here to scale the walls at Indian Creek.

There are two first-come, first-served campgrounds ($12) in the Canyon Rims Special Recreation Management Area (www.blm.gov). **Windwhistle Campground,** backed by cliffs to the south, has fine views to the north and a nature trail; follow the main road from U.S. 191 for six miles and turn left. At **Hatch Point Campground,** in a piñon-juniper woodland, you can enjoy views to the north. Go 24 miles in on the paved and gravel roads toward Anticline Overlook, then turn right and continue for one mile. Both campgrounds have water mid-April-mid-October, tables, grills, and outhouses.

The Maze District

Only adventurous and experienced travelers will want to visit this rugged land west of the Green and Colorado Rivers. Vehicle access wasn't even possible until 1957, when mineral-exploration roads first entered what later became Canyonlands National Park. Today, you'll need a high-clearance 4WD vehicle, a horse, or your own two feet to get around, and most visitors spend at least three days in the district. The National Park Service plans to keep this district in its remote and primitive condition. An airplane flight, which is recommended if you can't come overland, provides the only easy way to see the scenic features.

The names of erosional forms describe the landscape—Orange Cliffs, Golden Stairs, the Fins, Land of Standing Rocks, Lizard Rock, the Doll House, Chocolate Drops, the Maze, and Jasper Canyon. The many-fingered canyons of the Maze gave the district its name; although it is not a true maze, the canyons give that impression.

It is extremely important to have a good map before entering this part of Canyonlands. National Geographic/Trails Illustrated makes a good one, called *Canyonlands National Park Maze District, NE Glen Canyon NRA.*

Getting to the Maze District

Dirt roads to the **Hans Flat Ranger Station** (435/259-2652, 8am-4:30pm daily) and Maze District branch off from Highway 24 (across from the Goblin Valley State Park turnoff) and Highway 95 (take the usually unmarked Hite-Orange Cliffs Road between the Dirty Devil and Hite Bridges at Lake Powell). The easiest way in is the graded 46-mile road from Highway 24; it's fast, although sometimes badly corrugated. The 4WD Hite Road (also called Orange Cliffs Rd.) is longer, bumpier, and, for some drivers, tedious; it's 54 miles from the turnoff at Highway 95 to the Hans Flat Ranger Station via the Flint Trail. All roads to the Maze District cross Glen Canyon

National Recreation Area. From Highway 24, two-wheel-drive vehicles with good clearance can travel to Hans Flat Ranger Station and other areas near, but not actually in, the Maze District. From the ranger station it takes at least three hours of skillful four-wheeling to drive into the canyons of the Maze.

One other way of getting to the Maze District is by river. **Tex's Riverways** (435/259-5101 or 877/662-2839, www.texsriverways.com, about $110 pp) can arrange a jet-boat shuttle on the Colorado River from Moab to the Spanish Bottom. After the two-hour boat ride, it's 1,260 vertical feet uphill in a little over one mile to the Doll House via the Spanish Bottom Trail.

Planning an Expedition

Maze District explorers need a backcountry permit ($30) for overnight trips. Note that a backcountry permit in this district is not a reservation. You may have to share a site, especially in the popular spring months. As in the rest of the park, only designated sites can be used for vehicle camping. You don't need a permit to camp in the adjacent Glen Canyon National Recreation Area (NRA) or on BLM land.

There are no developed sources of water in the Maze District. Hikers can obtain water from springs in some canyons (check with a ranger to find out which are flowing) or from the rivers; purify all water before drinking. The Maze District has nine camping areas (two at Maze Overlook, seven at Land of Standing Rocks), each with a 15-person, three-vehicle limit.

The National Geographic/Trails Illustrated topographic map of the Maze District describes and shows the few roads and trails here; some routes and springs are marked on it too. Agile hikers experienced in desert and canyon travel may want to take off on cross-country routes, which are either unmarked or lightly cairned.

Extra care and preparation must be undertaken for travel in both Glen Canyon NRA and the Maze. Always ask rangers beforehand for current conditions. Be sure to leave an itinerary with someone reliable who can contact the rangers if you're overdue returning. Unless the rangers know where to look for you in case of breakdown or accident, a rescue could take weeks.

◖ LAND OF STANDING ROCKS

Here in the heart of the Maze District, strangely shaped rock spires stand guard over myriad canyons. Six camping areas offer scenic places to stay (permit required). Hikers have a choice of many ridge and canyon routes from the 4WD road, a trail to a confluence overlook, and a trail that descends to the Colorado River near Cataract Canyon.

Getting to the Land of Standing Rocks takes some careful driving, especially on a three-mile stretch above Teapot Canyon. The many washes and small canyon crossings here make for slow going. Short-wheelbase vehicles have the easiest time, of course. The turnoff for Land of Standing Rocks Road is 6.6 miles from the junction at the bottom of the Flint Trail via a wash shortcut (add about three miles if driving via the four-way intersection). The lower end of the Golden Stairs foot trail is 7.8 miles in; the western end of the Ernies Country route trailhead is 8.6 miles in; the Wall is 12.7 miles in; Chimney Rock is 15.7 miles in; and the Doll House is 19 miles in, at the end of the road. If you drive from the south on Hite-Orange Cliffs Road, stop at the self-registration stand at the four-way intersection, about 31 miles in from Highway 95; you can write your own permit for overnights in the park.

Tall, rounded rock spires near the end of the road reminded early visitors of dolls, hence the name Doll House. The Doll House is a great place to explore, or you can head out on nearby routes and trails.

NORTH POINT

Hans Flat Ranger Station and this peninsula, which reaches out to the east and north, are at an elevation of about 6,400 feet. Panoramas from North Point take in the vastness of Canyonlands, including the Maze, Needles, and Island in the Sky Districts. From **Millard Canyon Overlook,** just 0.9 miles past the ranger station, you can see arches, Cleopatra's Chair, and features as distant as the La Sal Mountains and Book Cliffs. For the best views, drive out to Panorama Point, about 10.5 miles one-way from the ranger station. A spur road to the left goes two miles to Cleopatra's Chair, a massive sandstone monolith and area landmark.

HIKING
North Canyon Trail

- Distance: 7 miles one-way
- Duration: overnight
- Elevation change: 1,000 feet
- Effort: strenuous
- Trailhead: on North Point Road
- Directions: From Hans Flat Ranger Station, drive 2.5 miles east, turn left onto North Point Road, and continue about 1 mile to the trailhead.

This is just about the only trailhead in the Maze District that two-wheel-drive vehicles can usually reach. The trail leads down through the Orange Cliffs. At the eastern end of the trail, ambitious hikers can follow 4WD roads an additional six miles to the Maze Overlook Trail, then one more mile into a canyon of the Maze. Because North Point belongs to the Glen Canyon NRA, you can camp here without a permit.

Maze Overlook Trail

- Distance: 3 miles one-way (to Harvest Scene)
- Duration: 3-4 hours
- Elevation change: 550 feet
- Effort: strenuous
- Trailhead: at the end of the road in the Maze District

Here, at the edge of the sinuous canyons of the Maze, the Maze Overlook Trail drops one mile into the South Fork of Horse Canyon; bring a 25-foot-long rope to help lower backpacks through one difficult section. Once in the canyon, you can walk around to the Harvest Scene, a group of prehistoric pictographs, or do a variety of day hikes or backpacking trips. These canyons have water in some places; check with the ranger when you get your permit. At least four routes connect with the 4WD road in Land of Standing Rocks, shown on the Trails Illustrated map. Hikers can also climb Petes Mesa from the canyons or head downstream to explore Horse Canyon, but a dry fall blocks access to the Green River. You can stay at primitive camping areas (backcountry permit required) and enjoy the views.

The Golden Stairs

- Distance: 2 miles one-way
- Duration: 3 hours
- Elevation change: 800 feet
- Effort: moderate
- Trailhead: bottom of Flint Trail, at Golden Stairs camping area
- Directions: Drive the challenging Flint Trail, a 4WD route, to its bottom. The top of the Golden Stairs is 2 miles east of the road junction at the bottom of the Flint Trail.

Hikers can descend this steep foot trail to the Land of Standing Rocks Road in a fraction of the time it takes for drivers to follow the roads. The trail offers good views of Ernies Country, the vast southern area of the Maze District, but it lacks shade or water. The eponymous stairs are not actual steps carved into the rock, but a series of natural ledges.

Chocolate Drops Trail

- Distance: 4.5 miles one-way
- Duration: 5 hours
- Elevation change: 550 feet

- Effort: strenuous
- Trailhead: Chocolate Drops
- Directions: The Land of Standing Rocks turnoff is 6.6 miles from the junction at the bottom of the Flint Trail. The trailhead is just east of the Wall camping area.

The well-named Chocolate Drops can be reached by a trail from the Wall near the beginning of the Land of Standing Rocks. A good day hike makes a loop from Chimney Rock to the Harvest Scene pictographs; take the ridge route (toward Petes Mesa) in one direction and the canyon fork northwest of Chimney Rock in the other. Follow your topographic map through the canyons and the cairns between the canyons and ridge. Other routes from Chimney Rock lead to lower Jasper Canyon (no river access) or into Shot and Water Canyons and on to the Green River.

Spanish Bottom Trail

- Distance: 1.2 miles one-way
- Duration: 3 hours
- Elevation change: 1,260 feet
- Effort: strenuous
- Trailhead: Doll House, near Camp 1, just before the end of the Land of Standing Rocks Road

This trail drops steeply to Spanish Bottom beside the Colorado River; a thin trail leads downstream into Cataract Canyon and the first of a long series of rapids. **Surprise Valley Overlook Trail** branches to the right off the Spanish Bottom Trail after about 300 feet and winds south past some dolls to a T junction (turn right for views of Surprise Valley, Cataract Canyon, and beyond); the trail ends at some well-preserved granaries, after 1.5 miles one-way. From the same trailhead, the **Colorado-Green River Overlook Trail** heads north five miles one-way from the Doll House to a viewpoint of the confluence. See the area's Trails Illustrated map for routes, trails, and roads.

4WD EXPLORATION
Flint Trail 4WD Road

This narrow, rough 4WD road connects the Hans Flat area with the Maze Overlook, Doll House, and other areas below. The road, driver, and vehicle should all be in good condition before attempting this route. Winter snow and mud close the road late December-March, as can rainstorms anytime. Check on conditions with a ranger before you go. If you're starting from the top, stop at the signed overlook just before the descent to scout for vehicles headed up (the Flint Trail has very few places to pass). The top of the Flint Trail is 14 miles south of Hans Flat Ranger Station; at the bottom, 2.8 nervous miles later, you can turn left and go two miles to the Golden Stairs Trailhead or 12.7 miles to the Maze Overlook; keep straight 28 miles to the Doll House or 39 miles to Highway 95.

Horseshoe Canyon Unit

This canyon contains exceptional prehistoric rock art in a separate section of Canyonlands National Park. Ghostly life-size pictographs in the Great Gallery provide an intriguing look into the past. Archaeologists think that the images had religious importance, although the meaning of the figures remains unknown. The Barrier Canyon Style of these drawings has been credited to an archaic culture beginning at least 8,000 years ago and lasting until about AD 450. Horseshoe Canyon also contains rock art left by the subsequent Fremont and Anasazi people. The relationship between the earlier and later prehistoric groups hasn't been determined.

Call the **Hans Flat Ranger Station** (435/259-2652) to inquire about ranger-led

CANYONLANDS

© TERRY WOOD/FLICKR.COM

some of the figures in the Great Gallery, the largest panel of pictographs and petroglyphs in the Horseshoe Canyon Unit

hikes to the Great Gallery (Sat.-Sun. spring); when staff are available, additional walks may be scheduled. In-shape hikers will have no trouble making the hike on their own, however.

HIKING
C Great Gallery Trail

- Distance: 3.25 miles one-way
- Duration: 4-6 hours
- Elevation change: 800 feet
- Effort: moderate-strenuous
- Trailhead: parking area on the canyon's west rim
- Directions: From Highway 24, turn east across from the Goblin Valley State Park turnoff, then continue east 30 miles on a dirt road; keep left at the Hans Flat Ranger Station and Horseshoe Canyon turnoff 25 miles in.

Horseshoe Canyon is northwest of the Maze District. The easiest and most common way to reach Horseshoe Canyon is from the west and Highway 24. In dry weather, cars with good

clearance can reach a trailhead on the canyon's west rim. From the rim and parking area, the trail descends 800 feet in one mile on an old jeep road, which is now closed to vehicles. At the canyon bottom, turn right and go two miles upstream to the Great Gallery. The sandy canyon floor is mostly level; trees provide shade in some areas.

Look for other rock art along the canyon walls on the way to the Great Gallery. Take care not to touch any of the drawings, because they're fragile and irreplaceable. The oil from your hands will remove the paints. Horseshoe Canyon also offers pleasant scenery and spring wildflowers. Carry plenty of water. Neither camping nor pets are allowed in the canyon, although horses are OK, but you can camp on the rim. Contact the Hans Flat Ranger Station or the Moab office for road and trail conditions.

Horseshoe Canyon can also be reached via primitive roads from the east. A 4WD road runs north 21 miles from Hans Flat Ranger Station and drops steeply into the canyon from the east side. The descent on this road is so rough that most people prefer to park on the rim and hike the last mile of road. A vehicle barricade prevents driving right up to the rock-art panel, but the 1.5-mile walk is easy. A branch off the jeep road goes to the start of **Deadman's Trail** (1.5 miles one-way), which is less used and more difficult.

The River District

The River District is the name of the administrative unit of the park that oversees conservation and recreation for the Green and Colorado Rivers.

Generally speaking, there are two boating experiences on offer in the park's River District. First are the relatively gentle paddling and rafting experiences on the Colorado and Green Rivers above their confluence. After these rivers meet, deep in the park, the resulting Colorado River then tumbles into Cataract Canyon, a white-water destination par excellence with abundant Class III-V rapids.

While rafting and canoeing enthusiasts can plan their own trips to any section of these rivers, by far the vast majority of people sign on with outfitters, often located in Moab, and let them do the planning and work. Do-it-yourselfers must start with the knowledge that permits are required for most trips but are not always easily procured; because these rivers flow through rugged and remote canyons, most trips require multiple days and can be challenging to plan.

No matter how you execute a trip through the River District, there are several issues to think about beforehand. There are no designated campsites along the rivers in Canyonlands. During periods of high water, camps can be difficult to find, especially for large groups. During late summer and fall, sandbars are usually plentiful and make ideal

CANYONLANDS

© BILL MCRAE

Rafters set out on the Colorado River.

camps. There is no access to potable water along the river, so river runners either need to bring along their own water or be prepared to purify river water.

While it's possible to fish in the Green and Colorado Rivers, these desert rivers don't offer much in the way of species that most people consider edible. You'll need to bring along all your foodstuffs.

The park requires all river runners to pack out their solid human waste. Specially designed portable toilets that fit into rafts and canoes can be rented from most outfitters in Moab.

RIVER-RUNNING ABOVE THE CONFLUENCE

The Green and Colorado Rivers flow smoothly through their canyons above the confluence of the two rivers. Almost any shallow-draft boat can navigate these waters: Canoes, kayaks, rafts, and powerboats are commonly used. Any travel requires advance planning because of the remoteness of the canyons and the scarcity of river access points. No campgrounds, supplies, or other facilities exist past Moab on the Colorado River or the town of Green River on the Green River. All river runners must follow park regulations, which include carrying life jackets, using a fire pan for fires, and packing out all garbage and solid human waste. The river flow on both the Colorado and the Green Rivers averages a gentle 2-4 mph (7-10 mph at high water). Boaters typically do 20 miles per day in canoes and 15 miles per day on rafts.

The Colorado has one modest rapid, called the Slide (1.5 miles above the confluence), where rocks constrict the river to one-third of its normal width; the rapid is roughest during high water levels in May-June. This is the only difficulty on the 64 river miles from Moab. Inexperienced canoeists and rafters may wish to portage around it. The most popular launch points on the Colorado are the Moab Dock

(just upstream from the U.S. 191 bridge near town) and the Potash Dock (17 miles downriver on Potash Rd./Hwy. 279).

On the Green River, boaters at low water need to watch for rocky areas at the mouth of Millard Canyon (33.5 miles above the confluence, where a rock bar extends across the river) and at the mouth of Horse Canyon (14.5 miles above the confluence, where a rock and gravel bar on the right leaves only a narrow channel on the left side). The trip from the town of Green River through Labyrinth and Stillwater Canyons is 120 miles. Launch points include Green River State Park (in the town of Green River) and Mineral Canyon (52 miles above the confluence and reached on a fairweather road from Hwy. 313). Boaters who launch at Green River State Park pass through Labyrinth Canyon; a free interagency permit is required for travel along this stretch of the river. Permits are available from the BLM office (82 Dogwood Ave., Moab, 435/259-2100, 7:45am-noon Mon.-Fri.), the Canyonlands National Park Headquarters (2282 SW Resource Blvd., Moab, 435/719-2313, 8am-4pm Mon.-Fri.), Green River State Park in Green River, or the John Wesley Powell River History Museum (1765 E. Main St., Green River, 435/564-3427, 8am-7pm daily). A permit can also be downloaded from the BLM website (www.blm.gov).

No roads go to the confluence. The easiest return to civilization for nonmotorized craft is a pickup by jet boat from Moab by **Tex's Riverways** (435/259-5101, www.texsriverways. com) or **Tag-A-Long Tours** (800/453-3292, www.tagalong.com). A far more difficult way out is hiking either of two trails just above the Cataract Canyon Rapids to 4WD roads on the rim. Don't plan to attempt this unless you're a very strong hiker and have a packable watercraft.

National park rangers require that boaters above the confluence obtain a backcountry permit ($30) either in person from the Moab National Park Service office (2282 SW

ENDANGERED FISH OF THE COLORADO RIVER BASIN

Colorado pikeminnow (*Ptychocheilus lucius*): Native only to the Colorado and its tributaries, this species is the largest minnow in North America. It has been reported to weigh up to 100 pounds and measure six feet long. Loss of habitat caused by dam construction has greatly curtailed its size and range. Fishers often confuse the smaller, more common roundtail chub (*Gila robusta*) with the Colorado pikeminnow; the chub is distinguished by a smaller mouth extending back only to the front of the eye.

Humpback chub (*Gila cypha*): Scientists first described this fish only in 1946 and know little about its life. This small fish usually weighs less than two pounds and measures less than 13 inches. Today the humpback chub hangs on the verge of extinction; it has retreated to a few small areas of the Colorado River where the water still runs warm, muddy, and swift. The bonytail chub (*Gila elegans*) has a similar size and shape, but without a hump; its numbers are also rapidly declining.

Humpback or razorback sucker (*Xyrauchen texanus*): This large sucker grows to weights of 10-16 pounds and lengths of about three feet. Its numbers have been slowly decreasing, especially above the Grand Canyon. It requires warm, fast-flowing water to reproduce. Mating is a bizarre ritual in the spring: When the female has selected a suitable spawning site, two male fish press against the sides of her body. The female begins to shake her body until the eggs and spermatozoa are expelled simultaneously. One female can spawn three times, but she uses a different pair of males each time.

CANYONLANDS

Resource Blvd., Moab, 435/719-2313, 8am-4pm Mon.-Fri.) or by mail (National Park Service Reservation Office, 2282 SW Resource Blvd., Moab, UT 84532-3298) or fax (435/259-4285) at least two weeks in advance.

Notes on boating the Green and Colorado Rivers are available on request from the National Park Service's Moab office (435/259-3911). Bill and Buzz Belknap's *Canyonlands River Guide* has river logs and maps pointing out items of interest on the Green River below the town of Green River and all of the Colorado River from the upper end of Westwater Canyon to Lake Powell.

◖ RIVER-RUNNING THROUGH CATARACT CANYON

The Colorado River enters Cataract Canyon at the confluence and picks up speed. The rapids begin four miles downstream and extend for the next 14 miles to Lake Powell. Especially in spring, the 26 or more rapids give a wild ride equal to the best in the Grand Canyon. The current zips along at up to 16 mph and forms waves more than seven feet high. When the excitement dies down, boaters have a 34-mile trip across Lake Powell to Hite Marina; most people either carry a motor or arrange for a powerboat to pick them up. Depending on water levels, which can vary wildly from year to year, the dynamics of this trip and the optimal take-out point can change. Depending on how much motoring is done, the trip through Cataract Canyon takes 2-5 days.

Because of the real hazards of running the rapids, the National Park Service requires boaters to have proper equipment and a permit ($30). Many people go on commercial trips with Moab outfitters on which everything has been taken care of. Private groups must contact the Canyonlands River Unit of the National Park Service far in advance for permit details (435/259-3911, www.nps.gov/cany).

MOAB

By far the largest town in southeastern Utah, Moab (population 5,150, elevation 4,025 feet) makes an excellent base for exploring Arches and Canyonlands National Parks and the surrounding canyon country. Moab is near the Colorado River in a green valley enclosed by high red sandstone cliffs. The biblical Moab was a kingdom at the edge of Zion, and early settlers must have felt themselves at the edge of their world too, being so isolated from Salt Lake City—the Mormon version of Zion. Moab's existence on the fringe of Mormon culture and the sizable young non-Mormon population give the town a unique character.

Moab's first boom came during the 1950s, when vast deposits of uranium, important fuel for the atomic age, were discovered. By the 1970s the uranium mines were largely abandoned, but all the rough roads that had been built to access the mines set the stage for exploration with jeeps, ATVs, and mountain bikes. Another legacy of the uranium boom can be seen along the highway at the north end of town, where the area around the Colorado River bridge is the site of a massive environmental cleanup, slated to take years to complete.

In recent years Moab has become nearly synonymous with mountain biking. The slickrock canyon country seems made for exploration by bike, and people come from all over the world to pedal the backcountry. River trips on the Colorado River are nearly as popular, and a

© JUDY JEWELL

HIGHLIGHTS

LOOK FOR 《 TO FIND RECOMMENDED SIGHTS, ACTIVITIES, DINING, AND LODGING.

《 **Dead Horse Point State Park:** Thirty minutes northwest of Moab, this peninsula of land perched 2,000 feet above the Colorado River has spectacular viewpoints, great camping, and mountain bike trails suitable for the whole family (page 74).

《 **Corona Arch and Bowtie Arch Trail:** This hike doesn't require a lot of exertion, but there's plenty of payback. Three arches are visible from the short trail, including 140-foot-wide Corona Arch, larger than many in Arches National Park (page 82).

《 **Fisher Towers:** These thin rock columns reach nearly 1,000 feet into the desert sky just south of Highway 128, northeast of Moab. Hiking trails loop through the unworldly landscape, ringing the mast-like formations and leading to overlooks of rugged Onion Creek Canyon (page 84).

《 **Gemini Bridges Trail:** Skip the pros and posers at the Slickrock Trail and have some real fun on the mostly downhill ride from the trailhead near Dead Horse Point State Park to U.S. 191. Most cyclists do this 14-mile one-way ride with a shuttle vehicle (page 86).

《 **Air Tours:** It's hard to grasp the scale of Moab's canyon country without getting up above it. Local aviators offer flightseeing trips, providing the chance to see this amazing landscape from the viewpoint of an eagle (page 92).

host of other outdoor recreational diversions—from horseback riding to 4WD jeep exploring to hot-air ballooning—combine to make Moab one of the most popular destinations in Utah.

As Moab's popularity has grown, so have concerns that the town and the surrounding countryside are simply getting loved to death. On a busy day, hundreds of mountain bikers form queues to negotiate the trickier sections of the famed Slickrock Trail, and more than 20,000 people crowd into town on busy weekends to bike, hike, float, and party. As noted in an article in *Details* magazine, "Moab is pretty much the Fort Lauderdale of the intermountain West." Whether this old Mormon town and the delicate desert environment can endure such an onslaught of popularity is a question of increasing concern.

PLANNING YOUR TIME

While many people come to Moab because of what it's near, there's certainly enough to do in the town to justify adding an extra day to a park-focused itinerary just for exploring Moab and environs. It's easy to spend a few hours lounging by the hotel pool or shopping for books, crafts, and gifts, and the quality of

MOAB AND VICINITY

the food and locally brewed beer has its own appeal, particularly after several days of hiking or driving the Utah outback.

Moab is also central for expeditions into the less regulated red-rock canyon country not included in the national parks. Take a break from exploring the parks themselves and devote a day to nonpark adventures, such as jet-boat tours on the Colorado River, horseback rides in Castle Valley, ATV tours into the backcountry, hikes with your dog, or even tasting local vintages.

Moab is the most hospitable town in this part of Utah, so don't blow right through. Take time to stop and enjoy its quirky charms. However, be forewarned that the adrenaline (or is it testosterone?) level reaches a fever pitch here during spring break, so don't plan a quiet weekend in Moab anytime around Easter.

Sights

It's fair to say that Moab doesn't tempt travelers with a lot of traditional tourism establishments, but all you have to do is raise your eyes to the horizon. The locale is so striking that you'll want to get outdoors and explore, and the astonishing sights of Canyonlands and Arches National Parks are just minutes from town. But there's nothing wrong with just enjoying the enthusiastic vibe of the town.

MUSEUM OF MOAB

The regional Museum of Moab (118 E. Center St., 435/259-7985, www.moabmuseum.org, 10am-5pm Mon.-Fri., noon-5pm Sat. Mar.-Oct., noon-5pm Mon.-Sat. Nov.-Feb., $5 over age 17, $10 families) tells the story of Moab's and Grand County's past, from prehistoric and Ute artifacts to the explorations of Spanish missionaries. Photos and tools show pioneer Moab life, much of which centered on ranching or mining. You'll also find displays of rocks and minerals as well as the bones of huge dinosaurs, including the backbone of a sauropod found by a rancher just outside town.

HOLE 'N THE ROCK

Fifteen miles south of Moab, Albert Christensen worked 12 years to excavate his dream home within a sandstone monolith south of town. When he died in 1957, his wife, Gladys, worked another eight years to complete the 5,000-square-foot house, called Hole 'n the Rock (11037 S. U.S. 191, 435/686-2250, www.theholeintherock.com, 9am-5pm daily, $5 adults, $3.50 ages 5-10). It's now a full-on roadside attraction. The interior has notable touches like a 65-foot chimney drilled through the rock ceiling, paintings, taxidermy exhibits, and a lapidary room. The 14-room home is open for 12-minute-long guided tours and offers a gift shop, petting zoo, picnic area, and snack bar.

MILL CANYON DINOSAUR TRAIL

The 0.5-mile Mill Canyon Dinosaur Trail, with numbered stops, identifies the bones of dinosaurs that lived in the wet climate that existed here 150 million years ago. You'll see fossilized wood and dinosaur footprints too. Pick up the brochure from the Moab Information Center (25 E. Center St., at Main St., 435/259-8825 or 800/635-6622, www.discovermoab.com) or at the trailhead.

To reach the dinosaur site, drive 15 miles north of Moab on U.S. 191, then turn left (west) at an intersection just north of milepost 141. Cross the railroad tracks and continue two miles on a rough dirt road (impassable when wet) to the trailhead.

You'll find many other points of interest nearby. A copper mill and tailings dating from the late 1800s are across the canyon. The ruins of Halfway Stage Station, where travelers once stopped on the Thompson-Moab run, are a short distance down the other road fork. Jeepers and mountain bikers can do a 13-14-mile loop to Monitor and Merrimac Buttes; a sign just off U.S. 191 has a map and details.

COPPER RIDGE SAUROPOD TRACKS

Apatosaurus, a.k.a. brontosaurus, and theropod tracks crisscross an ancient riverbed at the Copper Ridge Sauropod Tracks site. It's easy to make out the two-foot-wide hind footprints of the brontosaurus, but its small front feet didn't leave much of a dent in the sand. Three-toed tracks of the carnivorous theropods, possibly allosaurus, are 8-15 inches long, and some show an irregular gait—perhaps indicating a limp.

The Copper Ridge tracks are 23 miles north of Moab on U.S. 191; turn right (east) 0.75 miles north of milepost 148. Cross the railroad tracks and turn south, following signs two miles to the tracks.

MOAB

MOAB

To **DEAD HORSE POINT STATE PARK,**
Colorado River, Arches
National Park, and I-70

**SLICKROCK CAMPGROUND/
WESTERN RIVER EXPEDITIONS**

**BUCK'S
GRILL
HOUSE**

191

Colorado River

Scott M. Matheson
Wetlands Preserve

Mill
Creek

**MOAB
REGIONAL
HOSPITAL**

0   0.5 mi

0   0.5 km

ADOBE ABODE

KANE CREEK BLVD.

Moab Rim Trail

W 400 N

N 500 W

**JEFFREY'S
STEAKHOUSE**

W 200 N

E 200 N

**BOWEN
MOTEL**

N MAIN ST

N 100 E

**LOVE
MUFFIN**

**RIM
CYCLERY**

**JAILHOUSE
CAFÉ**

E 100 N

**RED ROCK
LODGE
MOTEL**

N 100 W

**POST
OFFICE**

**MIGUEL'S
BAJA GRILL**

**SLICKROCK
CAFÉ**

E CENTER ST

**MUSEUM OF
MOAB**

**BEST WESTERN
CANYONLANDS
INN**

RIO

S 100 W

**MOAB
INFORMATION
CENTER**

S MAIN ST

S 100 E

**PUBLIC
LIBRARY**

**RED ROCK
BAKERY**

**DESERT
BISTRO**

ZAX

**EDDIE
MCSTIFF'S**

**KOKOPELLI
LODGE**

W 100 S

E 100 S

**BEST WESTERN
GREENWELL MOTEL**

© AVALON TRAVEL

MOAB

Slickrock Bike Trail

Mt View Cave

Swiss Cheese Ridge

SUNSET GRILL

ECHO POINT

ABYSS VIEW POINT

Practice Loop

MCGILL

POISON SPIDER BICYCLES

TAG-A-LONG EXPEDITIONS

CLIFFVIEW

City Park

N 100 W

EKLECTICAFE

Slickrock Bike Trail

Start One-Way Loop

SWIMMING POOL

PARK DR

SLICKROCK

SEE DETAIL

E 200 N

SUNFLOWER HILL LUXURY INN

WALNUT LN

N MAIN ST

N 100 E

E 100 N

S 300 E

Swiss Cheese Ridge

WILLIAMS WAY

3 DOGS & A MOOSE

E CENTER ST

S 200 E

SAND FLATS RD

CITY DUMP

E 100 S

E 100 S

GONZO INN

MOAB DINER & ICE CREAM SHOPPE

TUSHER ST

E 200 S

WOODY'S TAVERN

VIRGINIAN MOTEL

E 300 S

S MAIN ST

MOAB CYCLERY

UP THE CREEK

BIG HORN LODGE

MILT'S STOP & EAT

MILL CREEK DR

RED STONE INN

BAR M CHUCKWAGON'S LIVE WESTERN SHOW AND COWBOY SUPPER

MULBERRY LN

MOUNTAINVIEW AVE

SLICKROCK CINEMAS

CANYONLANDS CAMPGROUND

S 400 E

Mill Creek

BLM DISTRICT OFFICE

POWERHOUSE LN

Moab Rim

MOAB BREWERY

Pack Creek

MILL CREEK DR

191

To Hole 'n the Rock and Monticello

LAZY LIZARD HOSTEL

HOLYOAK LN

MOAB

THE ELK MOUNTAIN MISSION

The Old Spanish Trail, which opened in 1829 between New Mexico and California, ran north from Santa Fe into Utah, crossing the Colorado River near present-day Moab. The Mormons under Brigham Young reached Utah in 1847, and by the 1850s they were establishing settlements across Utah. Young determined that a Mormon outpost was needed at the Colorado River crossing to control settlement and to proselytize the local Ute people.

In 1855, a group of 41 missionaries left the Wasatch Front to explore and build settlements in the Spanish Valley, home to present-day Moab. In those days, travel in roadless Utah was challenging—entering Moab Canyon required that wagons be taken apart and lowered by rope down a precipice near today's entry gate to Arches National Park.

By July 15, 1855, the missionaries and 75 head of cattle had arrived in Spanish Valley, and construction began on a 4,100-square-foot stone fort called the Elk Mountain Mission. The fort's walls were north of today's downtown Moab, near the edge of the current Motel 6 parking lot. They also built a corral, planted various crops, and tried to establish friendships with the Ute people, who controlled a large part of southern Utah. The Spanish Valley area had traditionally been used as a shared common ground for

gathering and trading among the Native Americans, particularly the Utes and the Navajo.

Initially the Mormon missionaries found success, tending their abundant gardens and baptizing more than a dozen Utes. Some of the Utes became concerned about the motives of the new settlers, however, and tensions between them and the missionaries grew. By early fall, it had become increasingly difficult to keep the peace.

After the Utes started helping themselves to the Mormons' garden produce, such as melons and squash, events quickly escalated. On September 23, 1855, one of the Mormon missionaries was shot by a Ute and a fierce gun battle ensued at the fort. At least two Utes were killed and many more wounded during the hostilities. Two other Mormons, who were returning from a hunting trip, were ambushed and killed. The hay and cornfields surrounding the fort were set ablaze by the Utes.

The next morning, the remaining missionaries abandoned the fort, packing what they could and leaving behind five horses and 25 head of cattle. The three dead missionaries were buried within the walls of the fort.

The Elk Mountain Mission marked one of the rare failures of a Mormon settlement during the church's colonization of the West under Brigham Young. For more than two decades afterward, no permanent settlers lived in the Moab area.

◖ DEAD HORSE POINT STATE PARK

Just east of Canyonlands National Park's Island in the Sky District and a short drive northwest of Moab is one of Utah's most spectacular state parks. At Dead Horse Point (435/259-2614, www.stateparks.utah.gov, day-use $10 per vehicle), the land drops away in sheer cliffs, and 2,000 feet below the Colorado River twists through a gooseneck on its long journey to the sea. The river and its tributaries have carved canyons that reveal a geologic layer cake of colorful rock formations. Even in a region with impressive views around nearly every corner, Dead

Horse Point stands out for its exceptionally breathtaking panorama. You'll also see below you, along the Colorado River, the result of powerful underground forces: Salt, under pressure, has pushed up overlying rock layers into an anticline. This formation, the Shafer Dome, contains potash that is being processed by the Moab Salt Plant. You can see the mine buildings, processing plant, and evaporation ponds, which are tinted blue to hasten evaporation.

A narrow neck of land only 30 yards wide connects the point with the rest of the plateau. Cowboys once herded wild horses onto the point, then placed a fence across the neck to make a

MOAB

Dead Horse Point State Park, just northwest of Moab, is full of outstanding views.

40-acre corral. They chose the desirable animals from the herd and let the rest go. According to one tale, a group of horses left behind after such a roundup became confused by the geography of the point. They couldn't find their way off and circled repeatedly until they died of thirst within sight of the river below. You may also hear other stories of how the point got its name.

Besides the awe-inspiring views, the park also has a **visitors center** (8am-6pm daily mid-Mar.-mid-Oct., 9am-5pm daily mid-Oct.-mid-Mar.), a very popular campground, a picnic area, a group area, a nature trail, hiking trails, and great mountain biking on the **Intrepid Trail System.** Spectacularly scenic hiking trails run along the east and west rims of the peninsula-like park; hikers are also allowed to use the Intrepid trails. Rangers lead hikes during the busy spring season and on some evenings during the summer, including monthly full-moon hikes. Whether you're visiting for the day or camping at Dead Horse Point, it's best to bring plenty of water. Although water is available here, it is trucked in.

Dead Horse Point is easily reached by paved road, either as a destination itself or as a side trip on the way to the Island in the Sky District of Canyonlands National Park. From Moab, head northwest 10 miles on U.S. 191, then turn left and travel 22 miles on Highway 313. The drive along Highway 313 climbs through a scenic canyon and tops out on a ridge with panoramas of distant mesas, buttes, mountains, and canyons. There are several rest areas along the road.

SCENIC DRIVES

Each of the following routes is at least partly accessible to standard low-clearance highway vehicles. If you have a 4WD vehicle, you have the option of additional off-road exploring.

You'll find detailed travel information on these and other places in Charles Wells's *Guide to Moab, UT Backroads & 4-Wheel Drive Trails,* which, along with a good selection of maps, is

MOAB'S MINING BOOM AND BUST

Moab is within the Paradox Salt Basin, a geologic formation responsible for the area's famous arch formations and accumulations of valuable minerals relatively near the surface. In addition to significant mineral wealth, mining and oil exploration has provided the region with some of its liveliest history and most colorful characters. French scientist Marie Curie, who discovered the element radium in uranium ore in 1898, visited the Moab area in 1899 to inspect a uranium-processing operation near the Dolores River.

Oil exploration in the 1920s caused some excitement in Moab, but nothing like that of the uranium boom that began in 1952. A down-on-his-luck geologist from Texas named Charles Steen struck it rich at his Mi Vida claim southeast of Moab. Steen's timing was exquisite: Uranium was highly sought-after by the federal government, primarily for use in Cold War-era atomic weapons and in nuclear power plants. An instant multimillionaire, Steen built a large mansion overlooking Moab and hosted lavish parties attended by Hollywood celebrities (his home is now the Sunset Grill restaurant). The Mi

Vida mine alone would ultimately be worth more than $100 million, and it put Moab on the map.

By the end of 1956, Moab was dubbed "The Richest Town in the USA" and "The Uranium Capital of the World." In the wake of Steen's discovery, thousands of prospectors, miners, laborers, and others descended on the area, hoping to cash in on the mother lode. Moab's population tripled in just three years as eager prospectors swarmed into the canyons.

By the mid-1960s, the boom had died out. As the uranium played out, however, mining operations began in 1965 in one of the largest potash deposits in the world, on the Colorado River between Moab and Dead Horse Point, and work continues there today. Other valuable materials mined in the Moab area over the years include vanadium (used in steel processing), lead, gold, copper, and silver, along with helium, natural gas, and oil.

Cleanup of 16 million tons of uranium tailings is now underway near the U.S. 191 Colorado River crossing. The toxic tailings are being hauled 30 miles north to a disposal site near I-70. It's expected that this project will be completed no sooner than 2019.

available at the **Moab Information Center** (25 E. Center St., at Main St., 435/259-8825 or 800/635-6622, www.discovermoab.com). Staff at the info center usually know current road and trail conditions.

Utah Scenic Byway 279

Highway 279 goes downstream along the west side of the Colorado River Canyon on the other side of the river from Moab. Pavement extends 16 miles past fine views, prehistoric rock art, arches, and hiking trails. A potash plant marks the end of the highway; a rough dirt road continues to Canyonlands National Park. From Moab, head north 3.5 miles on U.S. 191, then turn left on Highway 279. The highway enters the canyon at the "portal," 2.7 miles from the turnoff. Towering sandstone cliffs rise on the

right, and the Colorado River drifts along just below on the left.

Stop at a signed pullout on the left, 0.6 miles past the canyon entrance, to see **Indian Ruins Viewpoint,** a small prehistoric Native American ruin tucked under a ledge across the river. The stone structure was probably used for food storage.

Groups of **petroglyphs** cover cliffs along the highway 5.2 miles from U.S. 191, which is 0.7 miles beyond milepost 11. Look across the river to see the Fickle Finger of Fate among the sandstone fins of Behind the Rocks. A petroglyph of a bear is 0.2 miles farther down the highway. Archaeologists think that the Fremont people and the later Utes did most of the artwork in this area.

A signed pullout on the right, 6.2 miles from U.S. 191, points out **dinosaur tracks** and petroglyphs visible on rocks above. Sighting tubes help locate the features. It's possible to hike up the steep hillside for a closer look.

Ten miles west of the highway turnoff is the trailhead for the **Corona Arch Trail** (3 miles round-trip).

The aptly named **Jug Handle Arch,** with an opening 46 feet high and 3 feet wide, is close to the road on the right, 13.6 miles from U.S. 191. Ahead the canyon opens up where underground pressure from salt and potash has folded the rock layers into an anticline.

At the **Moab Salt Plant,** mining operations inject water underground to dissolve potash and other chemicals, then pump the solution to evaporation ponds. The ponds are dyed blue to hasten evaporation, which takes about a year. You can see these colorful ponds from Dead Horse Point and Anticline Overlook on the canyon rims.

High-clearance vehicles can continue on the unpaved road beyond the plant. The road passes through varied canyon country, with views overlooking the Colorado River. At a road junction in Canyonlands National Park's Island in the Sky District, you have a choice of turning left for the 100-mile White Rim Trail (4WD vehicles only past Musselman Arch), continuing up the steep switchbacks of the Shafer Trail Road (4WD recommended) to the paved park road, or returning the way you came.

Utah Scenic Byway 128

Highway 128 turns northeast from U.S. 191 just south of the Colorado River Bridge, two miles north of Moab. This exceptionally scenic canyon route follows the Colorado for 30 miles upstream before crossing at Dewey Bridge and turning north to I-70. The entire highway is paved. The Lions Park picnic area at the turnoff from U.S. 191 is a pleasant stopping place. Big Bend Recreation Site is another good spot 7.5 miles up Highway 128.

The rugged scenery along this stretch of the Colorado River has been featured in many films—mostly Westerns, but also *Thelma and*

Louise—and commercials. If you're intrigued, stop by the free **Film Museum** at Red Cliffs Ranch, a resort near mile marker 14.

The paved and scenic **La Sal Mountains Loop Road,** with viewpoints overlooking Castle Valley, Arches and Canyonlands National Parks, Moab Rim, and other scenic features, has its northern terminus at Castle Valley, climbs high into the La Sals, and then loops back to Moab. Vegetation along the drive runs the whole range from the cottonwoods, sage, and rabbitbrush of the desert to forests of aspen, fir, and spruce. The 62-mile loop road can easily take a full day with stops for scenic overlooks, a picnic, and a bit of hiking or fishing. Because of the high elevations, the loop's season usually lasts May-October. Before venturing off the Loop Road, it's a good idea to check current back-road conditions with the Moab Information Center (25 E. Center St., at Main St., 435/259-8825 or 800/635-6622, www.discovermoab.com). You can also ask for a road log of sights and side roads. The turnoff from Highway 128 is 15.5 miles up from U.S. 191.

A graded county road, **Onion Creek Road** turns southeast off Highway 128 about 20 miles from U.S. 191 and heads up Onion Creek, crossing it many times. Avoid this route if storms threaten. The unpleasant-smelling creek contains poisonous arsenic and selenium. Colorful rock formations of dark red sandstone line the creek. After about eight miles, the road climbs steeply out of Onion Creek to upper Fisher Valley and a junction with Kokopelli's Trail, which follows a jeep road over this part of its route.

One of the area's most striking sights are the gothic spires of **Fisher Towers,** which soar as high as 900 feet above Professor Valley. Supposedly, the name Fisher is not that of a pioneer but a corruption of the geologic term *fissure* (a narrow crack). In 1962, three climbers from Colorado made the first ascent of Titan Tower, the tallest of the three towers. The almost vertical rock faces, overhanging bulges,

MOAB

ROCK ART AROUND MOAB

The fertile valley around Moab has been home to humans for thousands of years. Prehistoric Fremont and Anasazi people once lived and farmed in the bottoms of the canyons around Moab. Their rock art, granaries, and dwellings can still be seen here. Nomadic Utes had replaced the earlier groups by the time the first white settlers arrived. They left fewer signs of settlement but added their artistry to the area's rock-art panels. You don't need to travel far to see excellent examples of native pictographs and petroglyphs.

Sego Canyon: If you approach Moab along I-70, consider a side trip to one of the premier rock-art galleries in Utah. Sego Canyon is about five miles north of I-70; take exit 185, the Thompson Springs exit. Drive through the slumbering little town and continue up the canyon behind it (BLM signs also point the way). A side road leads to a parking area where the canyon walls close in. Sego Canyon is a showcase of prehistoric rock art–it preserves rock drawings and images that are thousands of years old. The Barrier Canyon Style drawings may be 8,000 years old; the more recent Fremont Style images were created in the last 1,000 years. Compared to these ancient pictures, the Ute etchings are relatively recent: Experts speculate that they may have been drawn in the 1800s, when Ute villages still lined Sego Canyon. The newer petroglyphs and pictographs are more representational than the older ones. The ancient Barrier Canyon figures are typically horned ghostlike beings that look like aliens from early Hollywood sci-fi thrillers. The Fremont Style images depict stylized human figures made from geometric shapes; the crudest figures are the most recent. The Ute images are of bison and hunters on horseback.

Potash Road (Hwy. 279): From U.S. 191 just north of the Colorado River bridge, take Highway 279 west along the river 5.2 miles to these easily accessed petroglyphs. There's even a sign ("Indian Writing") to guide you to them.

Golf Course Rock Art: Take U.S. 191 south to the Moab Golf Course, which is about four miles from the corner of Main and Center Streets in downtown Moab. Turn left and proceed to Spanish Trail Road. Approximately one mile past the fire station, turn right onto Westwater Drive. Proceed 0.5 miles to a small pullout on the left side of the road. An area approximately 30 by 90 feet is covered with human and animal figures, including "Moab Man" and what is popularly referred to as the "reindeer and sled."

Kane Creek Boulevard: Kane Creek Boulevard (south of downtown Moab; watch for the McDonald's) follows the Colorado River and leads to a number of excellent rock-art sites. From the junction with U.S. 191, turn west and proceed 0.8 miles to the intersection of Kane Creek Drive and 500 West. Keep left and continue along Kane Creek Drive approximately 2.3 miles to the mouth of Moon Flower Canyon. Along the rock cliff just beyond the canyon, you will see a rock-art panel behind a chain-link fence (vandalism has been a problem). Continue another 1.2 miles to another rock-art panel, where a huge rock surface streaked with desert varnish is covered with images of bighorn sheep, snakes, and human forms. For a unique rock-art image, continue on Kane Creek Boulevard past the cattle guard, where the road turns from pavement to graded gravel road. After traveling 1.7 miles from the previous site, a total of 5.3 miles from the intersection of Kane Creek Drive and 500 West, watch for two pullouts. Down the slope from the road is a large boulder with rock art on all four sides. The most amazing image is of a woman giving birth.

Courthouse Wash: Although this site is located within Arches National Park, it is accessed from a parking lot off U.S. 191 just north of the Colorado River bridge, one mile north of Moab. A 0.5-mile hike leads to the panel, which is almost 19 feet high and 52 feet long. It has both pictographs and petroglyphs, with figures resembling ghostly humans, bighorn sheep, scorpions, and a large beaked bird.

A *Rock Art Auto Tour* brochure is available at the Moab Information Center (25 E. Center St., at Main St., Moab, 435/259-8825 or 800/635-6622, www.discovermoab.com, 8am-8pm Mon.-Sat. and 9am-7pm Apr.-Sept., reduced hours Mon.-Sat. Oct.-Mar.).

The Fisher Towers are nearly 1,000 feet tall.

and sections of rotten rock made for an exhausting 3.5 days of climbing; the party descended to the base for two of the nights. Their final descent from the summit took only six hours. In 2008 a slackliner walked a rope strung between the two tallest towers, and visitors to the towers can frequently see climbers and occasionally slackline walkers. The Bureau of Land Management (BLM) has a small campground and picnic area nearby, and a hiking trail skirts the base of the three main towers. An unpaved road turns southeast off Highway 128 near milepost 21, which is 21 miles from U.S. 191, and continues two miles to the picnic area.

The existing **Dewey Bridge,** 30 miles up the highway, replaced a picturesque wood-and-steel suspension bridge built in 1916, which burned in 2008. Here, the BLM has built the Dewey Bridge Recreation Site, with a picnic area, a trailhead, a boat launch, and a small campground.

Upstream from Dewey Bridge are the wild rapids of **Westwater Canyon.** The Colorado River cut this narrow gorge into dark metamorphic rock. You can raft or kayak down the river in one day or a more leisurely two days; many local outfitters offer trips. Camping is limited to a single night. Unlike most desert rivers, this section of the Colorado River also offers good river-running at low water levels in late summer and autumn. Westwater Canyon's inner gorge, where boaters face their greatest challenge, is only about 3.5 miles long; however, you can enjoy scenic sandstone canyons both upstream and downstream.

The rough 4WD **Top-of-the-World Road** climbs to an overlook with outstanding views of Fisher Towers, Fisher Valley, Onion Creek, and beyond. Pick up a map at the Moab Information Center (25 E. Center St., at Main St., 435/259-8825 or 800/635-6622, www.discovermoab.com) to guide you to the rim. The elevation here is 6,800 feet, nearly 3,000 feet higher than the Colorado River.

Kane Creek Scenic Drive

Kane Creek Road heads downstream along the

MOAB

Colorado River on the same side as Moab. The four miles through the Colorado River Canyon are paved, followed by six miles of good dirt road through Kane Springs Canyon. This route also leads to several hiking trails and campgrounds. People with high-clearance vehicles or mountain bikes can continue across Kane Springs Creek to Hurrah Pass and an extensive network of 4WD trails. From Moab, drive south on Main Street (U.S. 191) for one mile, then turn right onto Kane Creek Boulevard, which becomes Kane Creek Road.

Recreation

Moab is at the center of some of the most picturesque landscapes in North America. Even the least outdoorsy visitor will want to explore the river canyons, natural arches, and mesas. Mountain biking and river tours are the recreational activities that get the most attention in the Moab area, although hikers, climbers, and horseback riders also find plenty to do. If you're less physically adventurous, you can explore the landscape on scenic flights or follow old mining roads in a jeep to remote backcountry destinations.

It's easy to find outfitters and sporting goods rental operations in Moab; it's the largest business segment in town. And there's a remarkable cohesion to the town's operations: It seems that everyone markets everyone else's excursions and services, so just ask the closest outfitter for whatever service you need, and chances are excellent you'll get hooked up with what you want.

Make the **Moab Information Center** (25 E. Center St., at Main St., 435/259-8825 or 800/635-6622, www.discovermoab.com) your first stop in town. It's an excellent source for information about the area's recreational options. The center is staffed by representatives of the National Park Service, the BLM, the U.S. Forest Service, and the Canyonlands Field Institute; they can direct you to the adventure of your liking. The center also has literature, books, and maps for sale. BLM officials can point you to the developed and undeveloped designated campsites near the Moab Slickrock Bike Trail, Kane Creek, and along the Colorado River; you must use the designated sites in these areas.

To reach most of Moab's prime hiking trails requires a short drive to trailheads. For more options, head to nearby Arches and Canyonlands National Parks. **Canyonlands Field Institute** (435/259-7750 or 800/860-5262, www.canyonlandsfieldinst.org) leads day hikes from (Sat.-Sun. mid-Apr.-mid-Oct., $40-45, includes transportation and park admission) at various locations near Moab; join one to really learn about the area's natural history.

HIKING KANE CREEK SCENIC DRIVE AND U.S. 191 SOUTH

The high cliffs just southwest of town provide fine views of the Moab Valley, the highlands of Arches National Park, and the La Sal Mountains.

Moab Rim Trail

- Distance: 6 miles round-trip
- Duration: 4 hours
- Elevation change: 940 feet
- Effort: moderate
- Trailhead: Kane Creek Boulevard, 2.6 miles northwest of its intersection with U.S. 191 in Moab

If you're hiking, expect to share this route with mountain bikers and 4WD enthusiasts. The trail climbs northeast 1.5 miles along tilted rock strata of the Kayenta Formation to the top of the plateau west of Moab, with the first of several great views over town and the Spanish

ODD FORMATIONS BEHIND THE ROCKS

A look at a topographic map will show that something strange is going on in the area called **Behind the Rocks.** Massive fins of Navajo sandstone, 100-500 feet high, 50-200 feet thick, and up to 0.5 miles long cover a large area. Narrow vertical cracks, sometimes only a few feet wide, separate the fins. The concentration of arches in the area is similar to that in Arches National Park, with more than 20 major named arches. Where canyon drainages penetrate the sandstone, pour-offs form into 400-1,000-foot-deep sheer-walled canyons, often exposing perennial springs at the bottom. Behind the Rocks was inhabited extensively by the Anasazi and Fremont peoples, the two cultures apparently overlapping here. Petroglyph panels, habitation caves, stone ruins, and middens abound throughout the area.

No maintained trails exist, and some routes require technical climbing skills. The maze offers endless routes for exploration. If you get lost, which is very easy to do, remember that the fins are oriented east-west; the rim of the Colorado River Canyon is reached by going west, and Spanish Valley is reached by going east. Bring plenty of water, a topographic map (Moab 7.5-minute), and a compass. Access routes are Moab Rim and Hidden Valley Trails (from the north and east) and Pritchett Canyon (from the west and south). Although it is only a couple of miles from Moab, Behind the Rocks seems a world away.

Valley. Once on top, hikers can follow jeep roads southeast to Hidden Valley Trail, which descends to U.S. 191 south of Moab—a 5.5-mile trip one-way. Experienced hikers can also head south from the rim to Behind the Rocks, a fantastic maze of sandstone fins.

Hidden Valley Trail

• Distance: 2.3 miles round-trip to Behind the Rocks overlook

• Duration: 3 hours

• Elevation change: 680 feet

• Effort: moderate

• Trailhead: 3 miles south of Moab on U.S. 191 and right onto Angel Rock Road. After two blocks, turn right onto Rimrock Road and drive to the parking area.

You'll see not only a hidden valley from this trail, but also panoramas of the Moab area and the Behind the Rocks area. The trail ascends a series of switchbacks to a broad shelf below the Moab Rim, then follows the shelf (hidden valley) to the northwest. It then crosses a low pass and follows a second shelf in the same direction. Near the end of the second shelf, the trail turns

left to a divide, where you can see a portion of the remarkable fins of Behind the Rocks. The trail continues 0.3 miles from the divide down to the end of the Moab Rim Trail, with the possibility of hiking on loop trails. Instead of turning left to the divide, you can make a short side trip (no trail) to the right for views of Moab.

Hunters Canyon

• Distance: 4 miles round-trip

• Duration: 4 hours

• Elevation change: 240 feet

• Effort: moderate

• Trailhead: on Kane Creek Scenic Drive, 7.5 miles west of its intersection with U.S. 191. Hunters Canyon is on the left, 1 mile beyond the switchbacks.

• Directions: To reach the trailhead from Moab, drive eight miles on Kane Creek Boulevard along the Colorado River and up Kane Creek Canyon. The road is asphalted where it fords Hunters Creek, but the asphalt is usually covered with dirt washed over it by the creek.

A rock arch and other rock formations in the canyon walls and the lush vegetation along the creek are highlights of a Hunters Canyon hike. Off-road vehicles have made tracks a short way up; you'll be walking, mostly along the creek bed. Short sections of trail lead around thickets of tamarisk and other water-loving plants. Look for Hunters Arch on the right, about 0.5 miles up. Most of the water in Hunters Canyon comes from a deep pool surrounded by hanging gardens of maidenhair ferns. A dry fall and a small natural bridge are above the pool. This pretty spot marks the hike's three-mile point and an elevation gain of 240 feet. At this point, the hike becomes very brushy.

You can make a longer hike by going up Hunters Canyon and descending on Pritchett Canyon Road. The road crosses the normally dry creek bed just upstream from the deep pool. To bypass the dry fall above the pool, backtrack 300 feet down the canyon and rock-scramble up a short steep slope on the right heading upstream. At a junction just east of here, a jeep road along the north rim of Hunters Canyon meets Pritchett Canyon Road. Walk northeast

Bowtie Arch was formed when a pothole in the cliffs above met a cave below.

0.5 miles on Pritchett Canyon Road to a spur trail (on the left) leading to Pritchett Arch. Then continue 4.5 miles on Pritchett Canyon Road to Kane Creek Boulevard. This country is more open and desertlike than Hunters Canyon. A 3.2-mile car shuttle or hike is required for the return to Hunters Canyon trailhead.

HIKING HIGHWAY 279
Portal Overlook Trail

- Distance: 4 miles round-trip
- Duration: 3 hours
- Elevation change: 980 feet
- Effort: moderate
- Trailhead: JayCee Park Recreation Site, Highway 279, 4.2 miles west of the Highway 279-U.S. 191 junction

The Portal Overlook Trail switchbacks up a slope, then follows a sloping sandstone ledge of the Kayenta Formation for two miles to an overlook. A panorama (the "portal") takes in the Colorado River, Moab Valley, Arches National Park, and the La Sal Mountains. This trail is a twin of the Moab Rim Trail across the river. Expect to share it with mountain bikers.

◖ Corona Arch and Bowtie Arch Trail

- Distance: 3 miles round-trip
- Duration: 2 hours
- Elevation change: 200 feet
- Effort: moderate
- Trailhead: Highway 279, 10 miles west of the Highway 279-U.S. 191 junction

If you have time for only one hike in the Moab area, this one is especially recommended. The trail leads across slickrock country to two impressive arches. You can't see them from the road, although a third arch—Pinto—is visible. The trail climbs 1.5 miles up from the parking area, crosses railroad tracks, and follows a jeep road and a small wash to an ancient gravel bar. Pinto Arch, also called Gold Bar Arch, stands to the left, but there's no trail to it. Follow rock cairns to Corona and Bowtie Arches. Handrails and a ladder help in the few steep spots.

Despite being only a few hundred yards apart, each arch has a completely different character and history. Bowtie formed when a pothole in the cliffs above met a cave underneath. It used to be called Paul Bunyan's Potty before that name was appropriated for an arch in Canyonlands National Park. The hole is about 30 feet in diameter. Corona Arch, reminiscent of the larger Rainbow Bridge, eroded out of a sandstone fin. The graceful span is 140 feet long and 105 feet high. Both arches are composed of Navajo sandstone.

HIKING HIGHWAY 128
Negro Bill Canyon

- Distance: 4 miles round-trip
- Duration: 3-4 hours
- Elevation change: 330 feet
- Effort: easy-moderate
- Trailhead: Highway 128, 3 miles east of the Highway 128-U.S. 191 junction

One of the most popular hiking destinations in the Moab area, the Negro Bill Canyon trail follows a lively stream dammed by beavers and surrounded by abundant greenery and sheer cliffs. The high point of the hike is Morning Glory Natural Bridge, the sixth-longest natural rock span in the country at 243 feet.

William Granstaff was the first non-Native American to live in the area, about 1877-1881; modern sensibilities have changed his nickname to "Negro Bill." The trailhead and a large parking area are on the right just after crossing a concrete bridge three miles from U.S. 191. The Granstaff campground, run by the BLM, is on the banks of the Colorado River just across the road from the trailhead.

The trail follows the creek up the canyon, with numerous stream crossings. Although the crossings are not difficult, hikers must be comfortable with stepping from rock to rock.

To see Morning Glory Natural Bridge, head two miles up the main canyon to the second side canyon on the right, then follow a good but fairly steep side trail for 0.5 miles up to the long slender bridge. The spring and small pool underneath

MOAB

© PAUL LEVY

The trail up Negro Bill Canyon is cooler and shadier than many trails around Moab.

keep the air cool even in summer; ferns, columbines, and abundant poison ivy grow here.

Experienced hikers can continue up the main canyon about eight miles and rock-scramble (there's no trail) up the right side, then drop into Rill Creek, which leads to the North Fork of Mill Creek and into Moab. The total distance is about 16 miles one-way; you'll have to find your own way between canyons. The upper Negro Bill and Rill Canyons can also be reached from Sand Flats Road. The Moab and Castle Valley 15-minute and Moab 1:100,000 topographic maps cover the route. This makes a good overnight trip, although fast hikers have done it in a day. Expect to do some wading and rock scrambling. Water from the creeks and springs is available in both canyon systems, but be sure to purify it first.

A car shuttle is necessary between the Negro Bill and Mill Creek trailheads. You can reach Mill Creek from the end of Powerhouse Lane on the east edge of Moab, but don't park here: Vehicle break-ins are a serious problem. Have someone meet you or drop you off here or park closer to town near houses. A hike up the North Fork offers very pretty scenery. A deep pool and waterfall are 0.75 miles upstream; follow Mill Creek upstream and take the left (north) fork. Negro Bill and Mill Creek Canyons are BLM wilderness study areas.

◖ Fisher Towers

- Distance: 4.4 miles round-trip
- Duration: 4 hours
- Elevation change: 670 feet
- Effort: moderate
- Trailhead: off Highway 128; 21 miles east of the Highway 128-U.S. 191 junction, turn right and go 2.2 miles on an improved dirt road to a parking lot

These spires of dark-red sandstone rise 900 feet above Professor Valley. You can hike around the base of these needle rocks on a trail accessed by a short flight of stairs from the BLM picnic area. The trail follows a small slickrock-covered ridge leading away from the main cliffs; when the ridge narrows, go left into the ravine through a small cut in the ridge. From the bottom of the ravine, the trail heads steeply up and then begins to wind directly beneath the Fisher Towers. After skirting around the largest tower, the Titan, the trail ascends and ends after 2.2 miles on a ridge with a panoramic view. The Fisher Towers attract many very good rock climbers, and hikers may find that they linger along the trail to watch some spectacular climbing exploits. Carry water, as much of the trail is exposed and is frequently quite hot.

BIKING

The first mountain bikes came to Moab in 1982, when they were used to herd cattle. That didn't work out so well, but within a decade or so, Moab had become the West's most noted mountain bike destination. In addition to riding the famed and challenging slickrock trails (slickrock is the exposed sandstone that composes much of the land's surface here, and despite its name, bike tires grab it quite nicely) that wind through astonishing desert landscapes, cyclists can pedal through alpine meadows in the La Sal Mountains or take nearly abandoned 4WD tracks into the surrounding backcountry. Beware: The most famous trails—like the Slickrock Bike Trail—are not for beginners. Other trails are better matched to the skills of novices.

It's a good idea to read up on Moab-area trails before planning a trip; heaps of books and pamphlets are available. You can also hire an outfitter to teach you about the special skills needed to mountain-bike in slickrock country, or join a guided tour. The Moab Information Center's website (www.discovermoab.com) also has good information about bike trails.

Most people come to Moab to mountain bike mid-March-late May, and then again in

MOUNTAIN BIKE ETIQUETTE

When mountain biking in the Moab area, don't expect an instant wilderness experience. Because of the popularity of the routes, the fragile desert environment is under quite a bit of stress, and you'll need to be considerate of the thousands of other people who share the trails. By keeping these rules in mind, you'll help keep Moab from being loved to death.

· **Ride only on open roads and trails.** Much of the desert consists of extremely fragile plant and animal ecosystems, and riding recklessly through cryptobiotic soils can destroy desert life and lead to erosion. If you pioneer a trail, chances are someone else will follow the tracks, leading to ever more destruction.

· **Protect and conserve scarce water sources.** Don't wash, swim, walk, or bike through potholes, and camp well away from isolated streams and water holes. The addition of your insect repellent, body oils, suntan lotion, or bike lubrication can destroy the thriving life of a pothole. Camping right next to a remote stream can deprive shy desert wildlife of life-giving water access.

· **Leave all Native American sites and artifacts as you find them.** First, it's against the law to disturb antiquities; second, it's stupid. Enjoy looking at rock art, but don't touch the images—body oils hasten their deterioration. Don't even think about taking potsherds, arrowheads, or artifacts from where you find them. Leave them for others to enjoy or for archaeologists to interpret.

· **Dispose of solid human waste thoughtfully.** The desert can't easily absorb human fecal matter. Desert soils have few microorganisms to break down organic material, and, simply put, mummified turds can last for years. Be sure to bury solid waste at least 6-12 inches deep in sand and at least 200 feet away from streams and water sources. Pack out toilet paper in plastic bags.

MOAB

the fall mid-September-end of October. Unless you are an early riser, summer is simply too hot for extended bike touring in these desert canyons. Be prepared for crowds, especially in mid-March during spring break. The Slickrock Trail alone has been known to attract more than 150,000 riders per year.

If you've never biked on slickrock or in the desert, here are a few basic guidelines. Take care if venturing off a trail—it's a long way down some of the sheer cliff faces. A trail's steep slopes and sharp turns can be tricky, so a helmet is a must. Knee pads and riding gloves also protect from scrapes and bruises. Fat bald tires work best on the rock; partially deflated knobby tires do almost as well. Carry plenty of water—one gallon in summer, half a gallon in cooler months. Tiny plant associations, which live in fragile cryptobiotic soil, don't want you tearing through their homes; stay on the rock and avoid sandy areas.

Dozens of trails thread through the Moab area;

one good place for beginners to start is on the **Intrepid trail system** at Dead Horse Point State Park. Descriptions of several local trails follow.

MOAB Brand Trails

The interconnected loops and spur trails here form a trail system with several options that are especially good for beginners or riders who are new to slickrock.

The seven-mile **Bar-M** loop is easy and makes a good family ride, although you might share the packed-dirt trail with motor vehicles; try **Circle O** (no motor vehicles) for a good three-mile initiation to slickrock riding.

More experienced slickrock cyclists can find some challenges on the **Deadman's Ridge, Long Branch,** and **Killer-B** routes at the southern end of the trail system.

To reach the trailhead for all these rides, head about eight miles north of town on U.S.

191 to the Bar M Chuckwagon, and park at the south end of their private lot.

Slickrock Bike Trail

Undulating slickrock in the Sand Flats Recreation Area just east of Moab challenges even the best mountain bike riders; this is not an area in which to learn riding skills. Originally, motorcyclists laid out this route, although now most riders rely on leg and lung power. The 1.7-mile practice loop near the trail's beginning allows first-time visitors a chance to get a feel for the slickrock. The "trail" consists only of painted white lines. Riders following it have less chance of getting lost or finding themselves in hazardous areas. Plan on about five hours to do the 10.5-mile main loop, and expect to do some walking.

Side trails lead to viewpoints overlooking Moab, the Colorado River, and arms of Negro Bill Canyon. Panoramas of the surrounding canyon country and the La Sal Mountains add to the pleasure of biking.

To reach the trailhead from Main Street in Moab, turn east and go 0.4 miles on 300 South, turn right and go 0.1 miles on 400 East, turn left (east) and go 0.5 miles on Mill Creek Drive, then turn left and go 2.5 miles on Sand Flats Road. The Sand Flats Recreation Area, where the trail is located, charges $5 for an automobile day pass, $2 for a bicycle or motorcycle. Camping ($10) is available, but there is no water.

Farther up Sand Flats Road, the quite challenging, often rock-strewn **Porcupine Rim Trail** draws motorcyclists, jeeps, and mountain bikers; after about 11 miles, the trail becomes single-track, and four-wheelers drop out. The whole trail is about 15 miles long.

◖ Gemini Bridges Trail

This 14-mile one-way trail passes tremendous twin rock arches (the bridges) and the slickrock fins of the Wingate Formation, making this one of the most scenic of the trails in the Moab area; it's also one of the more moderate trails in terms of necessary skill and fitness. The trail begins 12.5 miles up Highway 313, just before the turnoff to Dead Horse Point State Park. It's a stiff 21-mile uphill ride from Moab to reach the trailhead, so you may want to consider a shuttle. Several companies, including **Coyote Shuttle** (435/260-2097, $20), provide this service, enabling cyclist to concentrate on the fun, mostly downhill ride back toward Moab. The Gemini Bridges Trail, which is shared with motorcycles and 4WD vehicles, ends on U.S. 191 just north of town.

Intrepid Trail System

Mountain bikers, including novices, should bring their rides to Dead Horse Point, where the Intrepid Trail System offers about 15 miles of slickrock and sand single-track trails in three loops that range from a one-mile beginner's loop to a more challenging nine-mile loop. All routes start at the visitors center and have great views into the canyon country. To reach Dead Horse Point State Park (435/259-2614, $10) from Moab, take U.S. 191 nine miles north, then turn west on Highway 313 and follow it 23 miles to the park entrance.

Monitor and Merrimac Trail

A good introduction to the varied terrains of the Moab area, the 13.2-mile Monitor and Merrimac Trail also includes a trip to a dinosaur fossil bed. The trail climbs through open desert and up Usher Canyon, then explores red sandstone towers and buttes across slickrock before dropping down Mill Canyon. At the base of the canyon, you can leave your bike and hike the Mill Canyon Dinosaur Trail before completing the loop to the parking area. Reach the trailhead by traveling 15 miles north of Moab on U.S. 191 and turning west (left) onto Mill Canyon Road, just past mile marker 141.

Sovereign Single Track

Not every bike trail here is over slickrock; the

challenging single-track Sovereign trail is good to ride in hot weather. The trail, which contains rocky technical sections, a bit of slickrock, and more flowing single track, is shared with motorcycles. Several trailheads access this trail; a popular one is from Willow Springs Road. From Moab, travel 11 miles north on U.S. 191 and turn right onto Willow Springs Road, following this sandy road 2.5 miles to the trailhead. To best see the options, pick up a map at a local bike store.

Kokopelli's Trail

Mountain bikers have linked a 142-mile series of back roads, paved roads, and bike trails through the magical canyons of eastern Utah and western Colorado. The trail is usually ridden from east to west, starting in Loma, Colorado, and passing Rabbit Valley, Cisco Boat Landing, Dewey Bridge, Fisher Valley, and Castle Valley before landing on Sand Flats Road in Moab. Lots of optional routes, access points, and campsites allow for many possibilities. This multiday trip requires a significant amount of advance planning; **Bikerpelli Sports** (www.bikerpelli.com) is a good place to start this process.

Moab Canyon Pathway (Road Biking)

Although the Moab area is great for biking, riding along busy U.S. 191 is no fun. The recently completed Moab Canyon Pathway starts at the Colorado River bridge at the north end of town and closely parallels the highway north to Arches National Park. From the entrance to the park, the path, which is separated from the road, continues north, climbing to the junction of Highways 191 and 313, the road to Dead Horse Point State Park and Canyonlands' Island in the Sky district. From this intersection, the bike path is on a relatively wide shoulder; it's a 35-mile ride to Canyonlands' Grand View Point, or a mere 24-mile uphill chug to Dead Horse Point.

The paved route provides easy cycling access to the MOAB Brand mountain bike trails just off U.S. 191 and a more challenging ride to the Intrepid trails in Dead Horse Point State Park and the Gemini Bridges trail, which starts just outside the park.

Bike Tours

Most of the bicycle rental shops in Moab offer day-long mountain bike excursions, while outfitters offer multiday tours that vary in price depending on the difficulty of the trail and the degree of comfort involved. The charge for these trips is usually around $200-250 per day, including food and shuttles. Be sure to inquire whether rates include bike rental.

Rim Tours (1233 S. U.S. 191, 435/259-5223 or 800/626-7335, www.rimtours.com) is a well-established local company offering several half-day (around $85 pp for 2-3 cyclists), full-day (around $120 pp for 2-3 cyclists), and multiday trips. **Magpie Cycling** (800/546-4245, magpieadventures.com) is a small local business that runs day trips that include instruction on mountain biking techniques and overnight rides, mostly in Canyonlands, including a four-day tour of the White Rim Trail ($875).

Western Spirit Cycling (478 Mill Creek Dr., 435/259-8732 or 800/845-2453, www.western-spirit.com) offers mountain and road bike tours in the western United States, with about one-third of them in Utah. Moab-area trips include the White Rim, the Maze, and the Kokopelli Trail (5 days, $1,200). Another Moab-based company with tours all over the West is **Escape Adventures** (Moab Cyclery, 391 S. Main St., 435/259-7423 or 800/596-2953, www.escapeadventures.com), which leads multiday mountain bike trips, including one into the remote Maze section of Canyonlands National Park (5 days, $1,270); some of the tours combine cycling with rafting, climbing, and hiking.

Rentals and Repairs

Rim Cyclery (94 W. 100 N., 435/259-5333

or 888/304-8219, www.rimcyclery.com, 9am-6pm daily) is Moab's oldest bike and outdoor gear store, offering both road and mountain bike sales, rentals, and service. Mountain bike rentals are also available at **Poison Spider Bicycles** (497 N. Main St., 435/259-7882 or 800/635-1792, www.poisonspiderbicycles.com, 8am-7pm daily spring and fall, 9am-6pm daily winter and summer) and **Chile Pepper** (702 S. Main St., 435/259-4688 or 888/677-4688, www.chilebikes.com, 8am-6pm daily Mar.-Nov., 9am-5pm daily Dec.-Feb.). **Moab Cyclery** (391 S. Main St., 435/259-7423 or 800/559-1978, www.moabcyclery.com, 8am-6pm daily) offers rentals, tours, shuttles, and gear. Expect to pay about $45-70 per day to rent a mountain bike, a little less for a road bike.

Shuttle Services

Several of the Moab area's best mountain bike trails are essentially one-way, and unless you want to cycle back the way you came, you'll need to arrange a shuttle service to pick you up and bring you back to Moab or your vehicle. Also, if you don't have a vehicle or a bike

© BILL MCRAE

Colorado River Canyon, just outside Moab

rack, you will need to use a shuttle service to get to more distant trailheads. **Coyote Shuttle** (435/260-2097, www.coyoteshuttle.com) and **Roadrunner Shuttle** (435/260-2724, www.roadrunnershuttle.com) both operate shuttle services; depending on distance, the usual fare is $15-25 pp. Both companies also shuttle hikers to trailheads and pick up rafters.

RAFTING AND BOATING

Even a visitor with a tight schedule can get out and enjoy the canyon country on rafts and other watercraft. Outfitters offer both laid-back and exhilarating day trips, which usually require little advance planning. Longer multiday trips include gentle canoe paddles along the placid Green River and thrilling expeditions down the Colorado River.

You'll need to reserve well in advance for most of the longer trips because the BLM and the National Park Service limit trips through the backcountry, and space, especially in high season, is at a premium. Experienced rafters can also plan their own unguided trips, although you'll need a permit for all areas except for the day-long Fisher Towers float upstream from Moab.

The rafting season runs April-September, and jet-boat tours run February-November. Most do-it-yourself river-runners obtain their permits by applying in January-February for a March drawing; the Moab Information Center's BLM ranger can advise on this process and provide the latest information about available cancellations.

Rafting and Kayaking Trips

For most of the following trips, full-day rates include lunch and beverages, while part-day trips include just lemonade and soft drinks. On overnight trips you'll sleep in tents in backcountry campgrounds.

The **Colorado River** offers several exciting options. The most popular day run near Moab starts upstream near Fisher Towers and bounces through several moderate rapids on the way back to town. Full-day raft trips (about $65 pp adults) run from Fisher Towers to near Moab. Half-day trips ($45-50 pp adults) run over much the same stretch of river but don't include lunch.

For a more adventurous rafting trip, the Colorado's rugged **Westwater Canyon** offers lots of white water and several class III-IV rapids near the Utah-Colorado border. These long day trips are more expensive, typically around $160-170 per day. The Westwater Canyon is also often offered as part of multiday adventure packages. The **Dolores River** joins the Colorado about two miles upstream from Dewey Bridge, near the Colorado border. The Dolores River offers exciting white water in a narrow canyon during the spring runoff; the season is short, though, and the river is too low to run by mid-June. With plenty of class III-IV rapids, this 32-mile trip usually takes 2-5 days and costs around $325-975 pp.

The **Cataract Canyon** section of the Colorado River, which begins south of the river's confluence with the Green River and extends to the backwater of Lake Powell, usually requires four days of rafting to complete. However, if you're in a hurry, some outfitters offer time-saving trips that motor rather than float through placid water and slow down only to shoot rapids, enabling these trips to conclude in as little as two days. This is the wildest white water in the Moab area, with big boiling class III-IV rapids. Costs range $600-1,200, depending on what kind of craft, the number of days, and whether you fly, hike, or drive out at the end of the trip.

The **Green River** also offers class II-III rafting and canoeing opportunities, although they are milder than those on the Colorado. Trips on the Green make good family outings. Most trips require five days, leaving from the town of Green River and taking out at Mineral Bottom, just before Canyonlands National Park. Highlights of the Green River include Labyrinth Canyon and Bowknot Bend. Costs range $650-900 for a five-day rafting trip.

Rafting or Kayaking on Your Own

The class II-III **Fisher Towers** section of the Colorado River is gentle enough for amateur rafters to negotiate on their own. A popular one-day raft trip with mild rapids begins from the Hittle Bottom Recreation Site (Hwy. 128, 23.5 miles north of Moab, near Fisher Towers) and ends 14 river miles downstream at Take-out Beach (Hwy. 128, 10.3 miles north of U.S. 191). You can rent rafts and the mandatory life jackets in Moab, but you won't need a permit on this section of river.

Experienced white-water rafters can obtain permits from the BLM's Westwater Ranger Station (82 E. Dogwood Ave., 435/259-7012, www.blm.gov, 8am-noon Mon.-Fri.) up to two months prior to launch date. Don't show up at the office expecting to get a same-day or next-day permit; it's important to plan well in advance. The usual put-in is at the Westwater ranger station nine miles south of I-70's exit 227; another option is the Loma boat launch in Colorado. A start at Loma adds a day or two to the trip along with the sights of Horsethief and Ruby Canyons. Normal takeout is at Cisco, although it's possible to continue 16 miles on slow-moving water through open country to Dewey Bridge.

Canyon Voyages (211 N. Main St., 435/259-6007 or 800/733-6007, www.canyonvoyages.com) and **Navtec Expeditions** (321 N. Main St., 435/259-7983 or 800/833-1278, www.navtec.com) are two local rafting companies that rent rafts (from $60 per day) and kayaks (about $35 per day) for those who would rather organize their own river adventures.

Rafting Outfitters

Moab is full of river-trip companies, and most offer a variety of day and multiday trips; in addition, many will combine raft trips with biking, horseback riding, hiking, or 4WD

MOAB

excursions. Check out the many websites at www.discovermoab.com/tour.htm. The following list includes major outfitters offering a variety of rafting options. Most lead trips to the main river destinations on the Colorado and Green Rivers as well as other rivers in Utah and the West. Red River Adventures runs trips in smaller self-paddled rafts and inflatable kayaks. Inquire about natural history or petroglyph tours if these specialty trips interest you.

- **Adrift Adventures** (378 N. Main St., 435/259-8594 or 800/874-4483, www.adrift.net)
- **Canyon Voyages** (211 N. Main St., 435/259-6007 or 800/733-6007, www.canyonvoyages.com)
- **Navtec Expeditions** (321 N. Main St., 435/259-7983 or 800/833-1278, www.navtec.com)
- **Red River Adventures** (1140 S. Main St., 435/259-4046 or 877/259-4046, www.redriveradventures.com)
- **Sheri Griffith Expeditions** (503/259-8229 or 800/332-2439, www.griffithexp.com)
- **Tag-A-Long Expeditions** (452 N. Main St., 435/259-8946 or 800/453-3292, www.tagalong.com)
- **Western River Expeditions** (225 S. Main St., 435/259-7019 or 866/904-1163, www.westernriver.com)

Canoeing

Canoeists can also sample the calm waters of the Green River on multiday excursions with **Moab Rafting and Canoe Company** (805 N. Main St., 435/259-7722, www.moab-rafting.com), which runs scheduled guided trips (about $150 pp per day) to four sections of the Green and to calmer stretches of the Colorado River. They also rent canoes (around $35 per day), including the necessary equipment.

Another good source for DIY canoe and kayak trips on the Green is **Tex's Riverways** (435/259-5101 or 877/662-2839, www.texsriverways.com), which specializes in rentals, shuttles, and support for self-guided trips.

Jet Boats and Motorboats

Guided jet-boat excursions through Canyonlands National Park start at around $75 for a half-day trip. **Tag-A-Long Expeditions** (452 N. Main St., 435/259-8946 or 800/453-3292, www.tagalong.com) and **Adrift Adventures** (378 N. Main St., 435/259-8594 or 800/874-4483, www.adrift.net) both offer half-day trips and full-day combination jet boat-jeep excursions.

Canyonlands by Night & Day (435/259-5261 or 800/394-9978, www.canyonlandsbynight.com, Apr.-mid-Oct., $65 adults, $55 ages 4-12) tours leave at sunset in an open motorboat and go several miles upstream on the Colorado River; a guide points out canyon features. The sound and light show begins on the way back; music and historic narration accompany the play of lights on the canyon walls. Package tours with chuckwagon dinners are available. Reservations are a good idea because the boat fills up fast. Daytime jet-boat tours ($80 adults, $70 children) are longer—about four hours—and go a little farther. Trips depart from the Spanish mission-style office just north of Moab, across the Colorado River.

4WD EXPLORATION

Road tours offer visitors a special opportunity to view unique canyon-country arches and spires, indigenous rock art, and wildlife. An interpretive brochure at the Moab Information Center (25 E. Center St., at Main St., 435/259-8825 or 800/635-6622, www.discovermoab.com) outlines the Moab Area Rock Art Auto Tour, which routes motorists to petroglyphs tucked away behind golf courses and ranches. You might also pick up a map of Moab-area 4WD trails: four rugged 15-54-mile loop routes through the desert that take 2.5-4 hours to drive. Those who left their trusty four-by-fours and off-road-driving skills at home can take an off-road jeep tour with a private operator. Most Moab outfitters offer jeep or Hummer tours,

© JUDY JEWELL

Four-wheeling and outlandish art both find homes in Moab.

often in combination with rafting or hiking options. The **Moab Adventure Center** (452 N. Main St., 435/259-7019 or 888/622-4097, www.moabadventurecenter.com) runs two-hour ($81 adults, $49 youths) and half-day ($169 adults, $122 youths) guided Hummer safaris. The Adventure Center, which can book you on any number of trips, can also arrange jeep rentals (from $180 per day).

Jeep and other 4WD-vehicle rentals are available at a multitude of Moab outfits, including **Farabee Jeep Rentals** (35 Grand Ave., 435/259-74944 or 877/970-5337, www.moabjeeprentals.com), **Canyonlands Jeep Adventures** (225 S. Main St., 435/259-4412, www.canyonlandsjeep.com), and **Cliffhanger Jeep Rentals** (40 W. Center St., 435/259-0889, www.cliffhangerjee-prental.com). Expect to pay from $180 per day.

ATVS AND DIRT BIKES

As an alternative to four-by-four touring in the backcountry, there's all-terrain vehicle (ATV)

and motorcycle "dirt biking," typically but not exclusively geared toward youngsters and families. Although youths ages 8-15 may operate an ATV, provided they possess an Education Certificate issued by Utah State Parks and Recreation or an equivalent certificate from their home state, parents should research ATV safety before agreeing to such an outing. Much of the public land surrounding Moab is open to ATV exploration, with many miles of unpaved roads and existing trails on which ATVs can travel. However, ATV and dirt bike riding is not allowed within either Arches or Canyonlands National Park.

One particularly popular area for ATVs is **White Wash Sand Dunes,** with many miles of dirt roads in a strikingly scenic location. It is 48 miles northwest of Moab, reached by driving 13 miles south from I-70's exit 175, just east of Green River. The dunes are interspersed with large cottonwood trees and bordered by red sandstone cliffs. In addition to the dunes,

White Wash is a popular route around three sides of the dunes.

ATVs and dirt bikes are available from a number of Moab-area outfitters, including **High Point Hummer** (281 N. Main St., 435/259-2972 or 877/486-6833, www.highpointhummer.com) and **Moab Tour Company** (543 N. Main St., 435/259-4080 or 877/725-7317, www.moabtourcompany.us). A half-day dirt bike or ATV rental starts at around $150.

◖ AIR TOURS

You'll have a bird's-eye view of southeastern Utah's incredible landscape from Moab's Canyonlands Field with **Redtail Aviation** (435/259-7421 or 800/842-9251, www.redtailaviation.com). Flights (minimum 2 people, $165 pp) include Canyonlands National Park's Needles, Island in the Sky, and Maze Districts. Longer tours are also available, and flights operate year-round. A 3.5-hour tour (minimum 4 people, $435 pp) over Canyonlands, Natural Bridges, Lake Powell, and the Capitol Reef area includes a stop for lunch (extra cost) at the Marble Canyon Lodge.

SKYDIVING

If you think the Arches and Canyonlands area looks dramatic from an airplane, imagine the excitement of parachuting into the desert landscape. **Skydive Moab** (Canyonlands Fields Airport, U.S. 191, 16 miles north of Moab, 435/259-5867, www.skydivemoab.com) offers jumps for both first-time and experienced skydivers. First-timers receive 30 minutes of ground schooling, followed by a half-hour flight before a tandem parachute jump with an instructor from 10,000 feet. A tandem skydive, including instruction and equipment, starts at $215. For experienced skydivers with their own equipment, jumps start at $18; equipment and parachutes are available for rent.

CLIMBING

Just outside town, the cliffs along Highway 279 and Fisher Towers attract rock climbers.

For world-class crack climbing, head south to Indian Creek, near the Needles District of Canyonlands National Park.

Moab has a couple of stores with rock climbing gear and informative staff: **Gearheads** (471 S. Main St., 435/259-4327) and **Pagan Mountaineering** (59 S. Main St., 435/259-1117, www.paganclimber.com). The friendly folks at Pagan also offer a climbing guide service to the local rock. **Moab Desert Adventures** (415 N. Main St., 435/260-2404 or 877/765-6622, www.moabdesertadventures.com) offers rock climbing and canyoneering lessons, both for beginners and experienced climbers; families are welcome. A half day of climbing instruction is $165 pp; rates are lower for groups of 2-3 students.

HORSEBACK RIDING

Head up the Colorado River to **Red Cliffs Lodge** (milepost 14, Hwy. 128, 435/259-2002 or 866/812-2002, www.redcliffslodge.com) for guided trail rides amid the dramatic scenery of Castle Valley. Half-day rides are $80 pp; children must be at least eight years old, and an adult must accompany children. Riders must weigh less than 220 pounds. Several tour operators, including **Adrift Adventures** (378 N. Main St., 435/259-8594 or 800/874-4483, www.adrift.net) and the **Moab Adventure Center** (225 S. Main St., 435/259-7019 or 866/904-1163, www.moabadventurecenter.com), offer horseback rides in conjunction with rafting, hiking, and jeep exploration.

GOLF

The **Moab Golf Club** (2705 SE Bench Rd., 435/259-6488, www.moabcountryclub.com/golf, $47) is an 18-hole par-72 public course in a well-watered oasis amid stunning red-rock formations. To get here from Moab, go south five miles on U.S. 191, turn left on Spanish Trail Road, follow it two miles; then go right on Murphy Lane, and follow it to Bench Road and the golf course.

LOCAL PARKS

The **city park** (181 W. 400 N.) has shaded picnic tables and a playground. It's also home to the **Moab Recreation and Aquatic Center** (374 Park Ave., 435/259-8226), a new community center with indoor and outdoor swimming pools, a weight room, and group exercise classes.

Two miles north of town, **Lions Park** (U.S. 191 and Hwy. 128) offers picnicking along the Colorado River, although ongoing bridge construction makes it less than peaceful. **Rotary Park** (Mill Creek Dr.) is family-oriented and has lots of activities for kids.

Entertainment and Events

For a town of its size, Moab puts on a pretty good nightlife show, with lots of young hikers, bikers, and rafters reliving their daily conquests in bars and brewpubs. There are also notable seasonal music events, ranging from folk to classical.

NIGHTLIFE

A lot of Moab's nightlife focuses on the rowdy and well-loved **Eddie McStiff's** (57 S. Main St., 435/259-2337, www.eddiemcstiffs.com, 11:30am-close daily), right downtown, with 12 handcrafted beers on draft, two outdoor seating areas, and live music several times a week. Although the **Moab Brewery** (686 S. Main St., 435/259-6333, www.themoabbrewery.com) brews on the premises and is a pleasant place to sample good beer, it is more a restaurant than a bar.

Woody's Tavern (221 S. Main St., 435/259-9323) has live bands on the weekend—you might hear bluegrass, roots rock, reggae, or jam bands.

Come for some barbecue and stay for the blues (or vice versa; both are good) at **Blu Pig** (811 S. Main St., 435/259-3333). Another restaurant with a lively bar scene is **Buck's Grill House** (1393 U.S. 191, 435/259-5201); they bring in bands a couple of times a week.

For a more family-friendly evening out, consider the **Bar M Chuckwagon's Live Western Show and Cowboy Supper** (7000 N. U.S. 191, 435/259-2276, http://barmchuckwagon.com, hours vary), a kind of Western-themed dinner theater that includes mock gunfights, live

country music, and other Old West entertainment in addition to a chuckwagon buffet dinner.

Another longtime tradition for evening entertainment is **Canyonlands by Night** (435/259-5261, www.canyonlandsbynight.com), a cruise on the Colorado River that ends with a sound-and-light presentation along the sandstone cliffs. Dinner packages are available; children under age four are not permitted, per Coast Guard regulations.

For a selection of movies, head for **Slickrock Cinemas** (580 Kane Creek Blvd., 435/259-4441).

EVENTS

To find out about local happenings, contact the Moab Information Center (25 E. Center St., at Main St., 435/259-8825 or 800/635-6622, www.discovermoab.com) or browse *Moab Happenings,* available free around town or online (www.moabhappenings.com). Unsurprisingly, Moab offers quite a few annual biking events. The **Moab Skinny Tire Festival,** held the first week of March, and the **Moab Century Tour,** held in September, are both supported road bike events that benefit the Lance Armstrong Foundation. For information on both, visit www.skinnytirefestival.com or call 435/259-3193. The mountain bike endurance race event **24 Hours of Moab** (www.grannygear.com/Races/Moab), held in early October, pits four-person relay teams against the rugged terrain of the Behind the Rocks area. This is one of North America's major events

MOAB

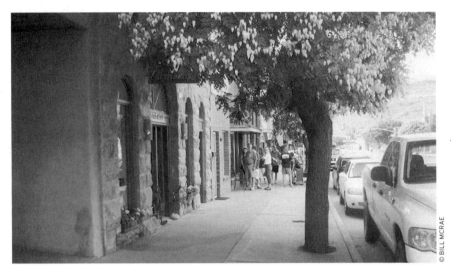

Moab's old downtown

for mountain bikers, bringing more than 500 teams and 5,000 spectators to Moab.

Other major annual athletic events include the **Canyonlands Half Marathon and Five Mile Run** (www.moabhalfmarathon.org), held the third Saturday in March. A women's half marathon, the **Thelma and Louise Half Marathon,** run in May, is organized by the same group.

Moab's most popular annual event, more popular than anything celebrating two wheels, is the **Easter Jeep Safari** (www.rr4w.com), which is the Sturgis or Daytona Beach of recreational four-wheeling. Upward of 2,000 4WD vehicles (it's not exclusively for jeeps, although ATVs are not allowed) converge on Moab for a week's worth of organized backcountry trail rides. "Big Saturday" (the day before Easter) is the climax of the event, when all participating vehicles parade through Moab. Plan well ahead for lodging if you are planning to visit Moab during this event, as hotel rooms are often booked a year in advance.

Memorial Day weekend brings artists, musicians, and art cars to the city park for the **Moab Arts Festival** (435/259-2742, www.moabarts-festival.org).

The dust is kicked up at the Spanish Trail Arena (3641 S. U.S. 191, just south of Moab) with the professional **Canyonlands PRCA Rodeo,** held the first weekend in June, with a rodeo, a parade, a dance, horse racing, and a 4-H gymkhana.

The **Moab Music Festival** (435/259-7003, www.moabmusicfest.org) is first and foremost a classical chamber music festival, but every year a few jazz, bluegrass, or folk artists are included in the lineup. More than 30 artists are currently involved in the festival, held the first two weeks of September. Many of the concerts are held in dramatic outdoor settings. The **Moab Folk Festival** (www.moabfolkfestival.com) is the town's other big annual musical event, attracting top-notch acoustic performers to Moab the first weekend of November.

SHOPPING

Main Street, between 200 North and 200 South, has nearly a dozen galleries and gift shops with T-shirts, outdoor apparel, Native American art, and other gifts. **Back of Beyond Books** (83 N. Main St., 435/259-5154) features an excellent selection of regional books and maps. Pick up those missing camping items at **Gearheads** (471 S. Main St., 435/259-4327, 8am-10pm daily spring-fall, shorter hours winter), an amazingly well-stocked outdoor store. If you're heading out to camp or hike in the desert, Gearheads is a good place to fill your water jugs with free filtered water.

Moab's largest grocery store, **City Market** (425 S. Main St., 435/259-5181, 6am-11pm daily), is a good place to pick up supplies; it has a pharmacy and a gas station.

Stop by the **Moonflower Market** (39 E. 100 N., 435/259-5712, 9am-8pm daily) for natural-food groceries; it's a well-stocked store.

Accommodations

Moab has been a tourism destination for generations and offers a wide variety of lodging choices, ranging from older motels to new upscale resorts. U.S. 191 is lined with all the usual chain motels, but we tend to go for the smaller local operations, and that's mostly what you'll find listed here.

Moab/Canyonlands Central Reservations (435/259-5125 or 800/505-5343, www.moabutahlodging.com) can make bookings at area vacation homes, which include some relatively inexpensive apartments. Another handy tool is www.moab-utah.com, which has a complete listing of lodging websites for the Moab area.

The only time Moab isn't busy is in the dead of winter, November-February. At all other times, be sure to make reservations well in advance. Summer room rates are listed here; in winter rates typically drop 40 percent.

UNDER $50

The **Lazy Lizard Hostel** (1213 S. U.S. 191, 435/259-6057, www.lazylizardhostel.com) costs just $10 for simple dorm-style accommodations. To stay at this casual classic Moab lodging, you won't need a hostel membership, and all guests share access to a hot tub, a kitchen, a barbecue, a coin-operated laundry, and a common room with cable TV. Showers for nonguests ($3) and private guest rooms ($26) are also offered. Log cabins can sleep two ($34) to six ($48) people. The Lazy Lizard is one mile south of town,

behind A-1 Storage; the turnoff is about 200 yards south of Moab Lanes.

$50-100

There's nothing fancy about the **Red Rock Lodge Motel** (51 N. 100 W., 435/259-5431 or 877/253-5431, www.red-rocklodge.com, from $60), but it has a great location, pet-friendly guest rooms with fridges and coffeemakers, a hot tub, and a locked bicycle storage facility.

A simple but quite adequate place is the **Bowen Motel** (169 N. Main St., 435/259-7132 or 800/874-5439, www.bowenmotel.com, from $74), a homey motel with an outdoor pool and included continental breakfast. The Bowen offers a variety of room types, including three-bedroom family suites and an 1,800-square-foot three-bedroom house with full kitchen. A couple of older but well-cared-for motels just north of downtown have guest rooms starting at about $75: the **Adventure Inn** (512 N. Main St., 435/662-2466 or 866/662-2466, www.adventureinnmoab.com) and the **Inca Inn** (570 N. Main St., 435/259-7261 or 866/462-2466, www.incainn.com).

A reasonably priced motel that's simple, friendly, and noncorporate is the **C Kokopelli Lodge** (72 S. 100 E., 435/259-7615 or 888/530-3134, www.kokopellilodge.com, from $76), offering small but colorful pet-friendly guest rooms and a convenient location one block off the main drag. Kokopelli also offers a number of condos on its website if you're looking for a

MOAB

© JUDY JEWELL

Moab has a few modest but well-kept motels such as the Kokopelli Lodge.

relatively inexpensive option with multiple beds and full kitchens.

A few blocks south of downtown, the **Red Stone Inn** (535 S. Main St., 435/259-3500 or 800/772-1972, www.moabredstone.com, from $90) is a one-story, knotty pine-sided motel; all guest rooms have efficiency kitchens. Other amenities include a bicycle maintenance area, a covered patio with a gas barbecue grill, a hot tub, and guest laundry. Motel guests have free access to the hotel pool next door. Pets are permitted only in smoking rooms.

$100-150

The Red Stone's sister property, the sprawling **Big Horn Lodge** (550 S. Main St., 435/259-6171 or 800/325-6171, www.moabbighorn.com, from $99) has similar knotty-pine guest rooms equipped with microwaves and fridges as well as a pool and a steak restaurant. Package deals for a guest room plus jeep tours, raft trips, and other activities are offered.

At the heart of downtown Moab, **Best Western Greenwell Motel** (105 S. Main St., 435/259-6151 or 800/528-1234, www.bestwesternmoab.com, from $139) has a pool, fitness facilities, an on-premises restaurant, and some kitchenettes.

At the **Virginian Motel** (70 E. 200 S., 435/259-5951 or 800/261-2063, www.moab-utah.com/virginian, $109), more than half of the guest rooms have kitchenettes, and pets are permitted. During the winter, room rates are less than half the high-season rates.

Eight very long blocks from downtown, on a quiet property that backs on the Mill Creek and Nature Conservancy holdings, is **Adobe Abode** (778 Kane Creek Blvd., 435/259-7716, www.adobeabodemoab.com, from $139), a B&B-style inn with large guest rooms done up in handsome Southwestern style. The inn also offers a pool table and evening refreshments, a large and tasty breakfast, and a hot tub.

If you want seclusion in a quiet community

18 miles east of Moab, stay at the **Castle Valley Inn B&B** (424 Amber Lane, Castle Valley, 435/259-6012, www.castlevalleyinn.com, $105-220). The inn adjoins a wildlife refuge in a stunning landscape of red-rock mesas and needle-pointed buttes. You can stay in one of the main house's five guest rooms or in one of the three bungalows with kitchens. Facilities include a hot tub. To reach Castle Valley Inn, follow Highway 128 east from Moab for 16 miles, turn south, and continue 2.3 miles toward Castle Valley.

OVER $150

The **Best Western Canyonlands Inn** (16 S. Main St., 435/259-2300 or 800/649-5191, www.canyonlandsinn.com, from $170) is at the heart of Moab, with suites, a pool, a fitness room and spa, a restaurant, and a bike storage area.

One of the most interesting accommodations options in Moab is the ◖ **Gonzo Inn**

© BILL MCRAE

Saddle horses await their riders at Sorrel River Ranch.

(100 W. 200 S., 435/259-2515 or 800/791-4044, www.gonzoinn.com, from $169). With a look somewhere between an adobe inn and a postmodern warehouse, the Gonzo doesn't try to appear anything but hip. Expect large guest rooms with vibrant colors and modern decor, a pool, and a friendly welcome.

Located in a lovely and quiet residential area, the ◖ **Sunflower Hill Luxury Inn** (185 N. 300 E., 435/259-2974 or 800/662-2786, www.sunflowerhill.com, from $165) offers high-quality accommodations. Choose from a guest room in one of Moab's original farmhouses, a historic ranch house, or a garden cottage. All 12 guest rooms have private baths, air-conditioning, and queen beds; there are also two suites. Guests share access to an outdoor swimming pool and a hot tub, bike storage, patios, and large gardens. Children over age seven are welcome, and the place is open year-round.

Families or groups might want to rent a condo at **Moab Springs Ranch** (1266 N. U.S. 191, 435/259-7891 or 888/259-5759, www.moabspringsranch.com, from $274), located on the north end of town on the site of Moab's oldest ranch. The townhomes have a parklike setting with a swimming pool and a hot tub, and they sleep up to 10.

A cluster of four charming and pet-friendly cottages dubbed **3 Dogs & a Moose** (171 and 173 W. Center St., 435/260-1692, www.3dogsandamoosecottages.com) is just off the main drag. The two smaller cottages ($125-175) are perfect for couples, and the larger cottages ($275-285) sleep up to six.

GUEST RANCHES

A short drive from Moab along the Colorado River's red-rock canyon is the region's premium luxury guest ranch, the ◖ **Sorrel River Ranch** (Hwy. 128, 17 miles northeast of Moab, 435/259-4642 or 877/317-8244, www.sorrelriver.com, from $399). The ranch sits on 240 acres in one of the most dramatic landscapes

MOAB

in the Moab area—just across the river from Arches National Park and beneath the soaring mesas of Castle Valley. Accommodations are in a series of beautifully furnished wooden lodges, all tastefully fitted with Old West-style furniture. All units have kitchenettes and a patio with a porch swing or back deck overlooking the river; some guest rooms have both. Horseback rides are offered into the arroyos behind the ranch, and kayaks and bicycles are available for rent. The ranch's restaurant, the River Grill (435/259-4642, 7am-2pm and 6pm-9pm daily Apr.-Oct., 7am-10am and 6pm-9pm daily Nov.-Mar., $28-36), has some of the best views in Utah and an adventurous menu offering everything from blue corn-dusted halibut to grilled elk chops.

Sharing a similar view of the Colorado River and Castle Valley but three miles closer to Moab is the sprawling **Red Cliffs Lodge** (milepost 14, Hwy. 128, 435/259-2002 or 866/812-2002, www.redcliffslodge.com, from $239), which houses guests in "mini suites" in the main lodge building and in a number of riverside cabins that can sleep up to six ($339). The lodge offers the Cowboy Grill bar and restaurant, horseback rides, and mountain bike rentals and will arrange river raft trips. The lodge is also the headquarters for Castle Creek Winery and the site of the free Moab Museum of Film & Western Heritage, which displays a collection of movie memorabilia from westerns filmed in the area.

CAMPGROUNDS
Moab Campgrounds

It's really easy and comfy to camp at ◖ **Up the Creek** (210 E. 300 S., 435/260-1888, www.moabupthecreek.com, mid-Mar.-early Nov., $25 for 1 person, $30 for 2, $35 for 3, $5 dogs), a walk-in, tents-only campground tucked into a residential neighborhood near downtown

Shade trees, an in-town location, and a nice bathhouse make Up the Creek campground a pleasant place to stay.

Moab. The shady campground, with a bathhouse and showers, picnic tables, and a few propane grills (campfires are prohibited), is right alongside a bike path.

RV parks cluster at the north and south ends of town. **Moab Valley RV Resort** (1773 N. U.S. 191, at Hwy. 128, 2 miles north of Moab, 435/259-4469, www.moabvalleyrv.com, $25 tents, from $40 RVs) is open year-round; it has showers, a pool, a playground, and free wireless Internet access. There's also a selection of cabins (bedding provided, $57-80) available—some are simple sleeping rooms, others have baths and fridges. Pets are allowed only in RVs. Although this place is convenient, it is pretty close to a large ongoing environmental cleanup project involving removal of radioactive mine tailings. **Moab KOA** (3225 S. U.S. 191, 435/259-6682 or 800/562-0372, http://moabkoa.com, Mar.-Nov., $25 tents, from $65 RVs with hookups, $65-170 cabins), just off the highway four miles south of town, has showers, a laundry room, a store, miniature golf, and a pool.

More convenient to downtown, **Canyonlands Campground** (555 S. Main St., 435/259-6848 or 800/522-6848, www.canyonlandsrv.com, $26-33 tents, $40-46 RVs, $60-65 cabins) is open year-round; it has showers, a laundry room, a store, a pool, and two-person air-conditioned cabins—bring your own bedding. One mile north of Moab, **Slickrock Campground** (1301½ N. U.S. 191, 435/259-7660 or 800/448-8873, http://slickrockcampground.com, $25 tents or RVs without hookups, $32-39 with hookups, $52 cabins with air-conditioning and heat but no bath or kitchen) remains open year-round; it has nice sites with some shade as well as showers, a store, an outdoor café, and a pool.

You'll also find campgrounds farther out at Arches and Canyonlands National Parks, Dead Horse Point State Park, Canyon Rims Recreation Area, and east of town in the cool La Sal Mountains.

BLM Campgrounds

There are 26 BLM campgrounds (most $8-12) in the Moab area. Although these spots can't be reserved, sites are abundant enough that campers are rarely unable to find a spot. The campgrounds are concentrated on the banks of the Colorado River—along Highway 128 toward Castle Valley, along Highway 279 toward the potash factory, and along Kane Creek Road—and at the Sand Flats Recreation Area near the Slickrock Trail. Only a few of these campgrounds can handle large RVs, none have hookups, and few have piped water. For a full list of BLM campground and facilities, visit www.discovermoab.com/campgrounds_blm.htm.

Dead Horse Point State Park Campground

Soak in Dead Horse Point's spectacular scenery at the park's **Kayenta Campground** (reservations 800/322-3770, www.reserveamerica.com, $20 camping, $9 reservations fee), just past the visitors center, which offers sites with water and electric hookups but no showers. The campground nearly always fills up during the main season, so it's almost essential to reserve well in advance. Winter visitors may camp on the point; no hookups are available, but the restrooms have water.

If you aren't able to secure a spot inside the park, try the BLM's **Horsethief Campground** (no drinking water, $12) on Highway 313 a few miles east of the state park entrance. It has nearly 60 sites, all first-come, first-served, so it's usually possible to find a site.

MOAB

Food

Moab has the largest concentration of good restaurants in southern Utah; no matter what else the recreational craze has produced, it has certainly improved the food. Several Moab-area restaurants are closed for vacation in February, so call ahead if you're visiting in winter.

BREAKFAST AND LIGHT MEALS

Food isn't limited to muffins at **C Love Muffin** (139 N. Main St., 435/259-6833, www.lovemuffincafe.com, 7am-1pm daily, $6-8), but if you decide to skip the breakfast burritos or insanely tasty red quinoa, the Burple Nurple muffin may be just what you need. While you're eating breakfast, order a Muffaletta or barbecued tofu sandwich to pack along for lunch.

Another good option for a tasty but healthy breakfast or lunch is **C EklectiCafe** (352 N. Main St., 435/259-6896, 7am-2:30pm Mon.-Sat., 7am-1pm Sun., $6-9), a charming and busy little café serving delicious organic and vegetarian dishes. For a more traditional breakfast, try the **Jailhouse Café** (101 N. Main St., 435/259-3900, 7am-noon daily, $7-11), a Moab classic.

Dense, chewy bagels and good sandwiches make the **Red Rock Bakery** (74 S. Main St., 435/259-5941, 7am-2pm daily) worth a visit.

Two Moab diners have an old-fashioned ambience and really good food. At the **Moab Diner & Ice Cream Shoppe** (189 S. Main St., 435/259-4006, http://moabdiner.com, 6am-9pm Mon.-Sat., $5-12), the breakfasts are large, with a Southwestern green chili edge to much of the food. The ice cream is delicious. Another spot with great burgers and shakes is **C Milt's Stop & Eat** (356 Millcreek Dr., 435/259-7424, www.miltsstopandeat.com, 11am-8pm, $3.50-7)—it's a local classic, and just the place to stop after a day of biking or hiking.

CASUAL DINING

Unless otherwise noted, each of the following establishments has a full liquor license.

Zax (96 S. Main St., 435/259-6555, www.zaxmoab.com, 6:30am-close daily, $7-13) is a high-volume all-things-to-all-people restaurant in the heart of downtown. If you're with kids, this might be the ticket for sandwiches, steaks, pasta, pizza, or salad.

The **Slickrock Café** (5 N. Main St., 435/259-8004, www.slickrockcafe.com, 11am-close daily, $10-27) is another versatile restaurant in a historic building downtown. The Slickrock is a casual place serving a wide range of American standards; large salads ($4-14) are a decent bet.

Check out **Miguel's Baja Grill** (51 N. Main St., 435/259-6546, www.miguelsbajagrill.com, 5pm-9pm daily, $10-20) for well-prepared Baja-style seafood, including good fish tacos. It's a busy place, so make a reservation or be prepared to wait.

Get away from high-volume assembly-line restaurants at **Sabaku Sushi** (90 E. Center St., 435/259-4455, 5pm-10pm daily, rolls $4-15), which offers surprisingly good sushi in a friendly atmosphere. Arrive at 5pm for the sushi happy hour.

For a Western night out, consider **Bar M Chuckwagon Supper** (541 S. Mulberry Lane, 435/259-2276, www.barmchuckwagon.com, show starts at 6:30pm Apr.-Oct., days vary by season, beer only, $28 over age 12, $14 ages 4-12, free under age 4), located on the banks of Mill Creek just southeast of town. Tasty cowboy-style cooking is served up from chuckwagons, followed by a variety of live Western entertainment including mock gunfights and live music.

BREWPUBS

After a hot day out on the trail, who can blame you for thinking about a cold brew and a hearty meal? Luckily, Moab has two excellent pubs to

MOAB-AREA WINERIES

Southern Utah is not exactly the first place you think of when you envision fine wine, but for a handful of wine pioneers, the Moab area is the *terroir* of choice. Actually, conditions around Moab are similar to parts of Spain and the eastern Mediterranean, where wine grapes have flourished for millennia. The area's first wine grapes were planted in the 1970s through the efforts of the University of Arizona and the Four Corners Regional Economic Development Commission. The results were positive, as the hot days, cool nights, and deep sandy soil produced grapes of exceptional quality and flavor. A fruit-growing cooperative was formed in Moab to grow wine grapes, and by the 1980s the co-op was producing wine under the Arches Winery label. As teetotal Utah's first winery, Arches Winery was more than a novelty—its wines were good enough to accumulate nearly 40 prizes at national wine exhibitions.

Arches Winery was a true pioneer, and now two wineries produce wine in the Moab area, both open for wine tasting. In addition, many of Moab's fine restaurants offer wine from these local wineries.

Castle Creek Winery (Red Cliffs Lodge, Hwy. 128, 14 miles east of Moab, 435/259-3332, http://redcliffslodge.com/winery, noon-5:30pm Mon.-Sat.), formerly Arches Winery, produces pinot noir, merlot, cabernet sauvignon, chenin blanc, chardonnay, and late-harvest gewürztraminer.

Spanish Valley Vineyards and Winery (4710 Zimmerman Lane, 6 miles south of Moab, 435/259-8134, www.moab-utah.com/spanishvalleywinery, noon-7pm Mon.-Sat. Mar.-Oct., noon-5pm Mon.-Sat. Feb. and Nov.) produces riesling, gewürztraminer, cabernet sauvignon, and syrah.

fill the bill. **Eddie McStiff's** (57 S. Main St., 435/259-2337, www.eddiemcstiffs.com, 11:30am-close daily, $9-19) is an extremely popular place to sip a cool beer or a mojito, eat standard pub food (the pizza is a good bet), and meet other travelers; in good weather there's seating in a nice courtyard. You'd have to try hard not to have fun here.

There's more good beer and perhaps better food at the **Moab Brewery** (686 S. Main St., 435/259-6333, www.themoabbrewery.com, 11:30am-10pm Sun.-Thurs., 11:30am-11pm Fri.-Sat., $8-21), although it doesn't attract the kind of scene you'll find at Eddie McStiff's. The atmosphere is light and airy, and the food is good—steaks, sandwiches, burgers, and a wide selection of salads. Try the spinach salad with smoked salmon ($9) or prime rib ($19). There's deck seating when weather permits.

FINE DINING

The **Desert Bistro** (36 S. 100 W., 435/259-0756, www.desertbistro.com, reservations recommended, dinner from 5:30pm Tues.-Sun.

Mar.-Nov., $22-50), a longtime favorite for regional fine dining, has moved to a new location in downtown Moab. Its seasonal, sophisticated Southwest-meets-continental cuisine features local meats and game plus fresh fish and seafood. The patio dining is some of the nicest in Moab, and the indoor dining rooms are pretty and peaceful.

Buck's Grill House (1393 N. U.S. 191, 435/259-5201, www.bucksgrillhouse.com, 5pm-close daily, $9-33) is a steak house with an easygoing Western atmosphere and imaginative refinements on standard steak house fare. Dishes like duck tamales, elk stew with root vegetables, and a vegetarian meatless loaf are excellent.

Jeffrey's Steakhouse (218 N. 100 W., 435/259-3588, www.jeffreyssteakhouse.com, 5pm-close daily, $22-40), tucked off the main drag in an elegantly renovated small house with an upstairs bar, is about as classy and upscale as you'll find in Moab, with a small menu of steaks, chicken, lamb, and salmon.

The **River Grill** (Sorrel River Ranch, Hwy. 128, 17 miles northeast of Moab,

MOAB

435/259-4642, www.sorrelriver.com, 7am-2pm and 6pm-9pm daily Apr.-Oct., 7am-10am and 6pm-9pm daily Nov.-Mar., $28-36) has a lovely dining room that overlooks spires of red rock and the dramatic cliffs of the Colorado River. The scenery is hard to top, and the food is good, with a focus on prime beef and continental specialties. Dinner reservations are strongly recommended.

The **Sunset Grill** (900 N. U.S. 191, 435/259-7146, www.moab-utah.com/sunsetgrill, 5pm-close Mon.-Sat., $14-24) is located in uranium king Charlie Steen's mansion, situated high above Moab, with million-dollar sweeping views of the valley. Choose from steaks, fresh seafood, and a selection of pasta dishes—what you'll remember is the road up here and the view.

Information and Services

Moab is a small town, and people are generally friendly. Between the excellent Moab Information Center (25 E. Center St., at Main St., 435/259-8825 or 800/635-6622, www.discovermoab.com) and the county library—and the friendly advice of people in the street—you'll find it easy to assemble all the information you need to have a fine stay.

INFORMATION

The **Moab Information Center** (25 E. Center St., at Main St., 435/259-8825 or 800/635-6622, www.discovermoab.com, 8am-8pm Mon.-Sat. and 9am-7pm Apr.-Sept., reduced hours Mon.-Sat. Oct.-Mar.) is the place to start for nearly all local and area information. The National Park Service, the BLM, the U.S. Forest Service, the Grand County Travel Council, and the Canyonlands Natural History Association are all represented here. Visitors who need help from any of these agencies should start at the information center rather than at the agency offices. Free literature is available, the selection of books and maps for sale is large, and the staff is knowledgeable. The center's website is also well organized and packed with information.

The **BLM district office** (82 E. Dogwood Ave., 435/259-2100, 7:45am-4:30pm Mon.-Fri.) is on the south side of town behind Comfort Suites. Some land-use maps are sold here, and this is the place to pick up river-running permits.

SERVICES

The **Grand County Public Library** (257 E. Center St., 435/259-1111, 9am-8pm Mon.-Fri., 9am-5pm Sat.) is a good place for local history and general reading.

The **post office** (50 E. 100 N., 435/259-7427) is downtown. **Moab Regional Hospital** (450 W. Williams Way, 435/719-3500) provides medical care. For ambulance, sheriff, police, or fire emergencies, dial 911.

GETTING THERE

Great Lakes Airlines (800/554-5111, www.greatlakesav.com) provides daily scheduled air service between Canyonlands Field (CNY, U.S. 191, 16 miles north of Moab, 435/259-4849) and Denver. Grand Junction, Colorado, is 120 miles east of Moab via I-70 and has better air service; Salt Lake City is 240 miles northwest of Moab.

Moab Luxury Coach (435/940-4212, www.moabluxurycoach.com) runs SUVs and buses between Moab and Salt Lake City ($149 one-way); advance reservations are required. **Red Rock Express** (435/260-0595, www.redrockexpress.com) has SUV shuttles between Moab and the Grand Junction, Colorado, airport ($100).

Enterprise (711 S. Main St., 435/259-8505, www.enterprise.com) rents cars at the airport.

THE SOUTHEASTERN CORNER

Although Arches and Canyonlands capture more attention, Utah's southeastern corner contains an incredible wealth of scenic and culturally significant sites. Consider rounding out your trip to this part of Utah with a tour of Anasazi ruins, remote desert washes, soaring natural bridges, snowy mountain peaks, and a vast reservoir.

Highway 191 runs south from Moab between Canyonlands National Park and the surprisingly tall Abajo Mountains to the west and the La Sal Mountains to the east. In the heat of the summer, these mountains are cool refuges. Also east of the highway, nearly to the Colorado border is Hovenweep National Monument, an Anasazi site with an astounding collection of masonry buildings. Here the

Anasazi lived in more or less of a city until they suddenly departed about 900 years ago.

The San Juan River runs across the southern tier of the region, with Cedar Mesa to the north and Monument Valley and Navajo tribal land to the south. Bluff, a charming town that's now the put-in for most river trips on the San Juan, was settled in 1880 by Mormon pioneers who made the incredible wagon train trip from Escalante through steep canyons, including Hole-in-the-Rock.

Cedar Mesa is a place to explore on foot; canyons here often shelter Anasazi ruins. To the west of the mesa, Natural Bridges National Monument is often overlooked, probably because it's rather remote. But its soaring stone

HIGHLIGHTS

© AVALON TRAVEL

LOOK FOR [TO FIND RECOMMENDED SIGHTS, ACTIVITIES, DINING, AND LODGING.

[**Edge of the Cedars State Park:** Indoor and outdoor archeological exhibits make this Blanding museum a good introduction to the area and its Anasazi, Ute, Navajo, and Anglo history (page 107).

[**Floating the San Juan River:** Take a few days away from the rest of the world and paddle from Bluff to Lake Powell. You'll go through deep canyons, past rock art and ruins, and down a few Class III rapids (page 108).

[**Hovenweep National Monument:** It's worth taking the detour to this impressive collection of masonry dwellings. Six villages with varying architectural styles are among the ruins here (page 111).

[**Natural Bridges National Monument:** Hike an 8.6-mile loop to visit three spectacular natural bridges. If you're short on time or energy, a nine-mile drive with short hikes to each bridge will also do the trick (page 118).

[**Goblin Valley State Park:** Big mushroom-shaped rock formations, some with eroded "eyes," cluster around the valley floor of this state park. Tromp down into the valley and wander among these sandstone oddities (page 126).

bridges (carved by streams and spanning a streambed) are beautiful, even elegant, and a night in the campground will allow you to see stars in one of the nation's darkest places.

At Lake Powell the Colorado River is backed up by the Glen Canyon Dam. Lake Powell draws boaters—including visitors who rent houseboats to motor to the huge reservoir's remote inlets and canyons—but for a quick look, the car ferry across the lake is far less expensive. The surrounding Glen Canyon Recreation Area encompasses the rugged canyons that drop down toward Lake Powell; before the dam was built, Glen Canyon was considered the equal of the Grand Canyon for drama and beauty, and

in low-water years, a few peeks into the past are possible. A popular side trip—usually visited via tour boats from one of the lake's marinas—is to Rainbow Bridge National Monument, where the enormous stone bridge spans an arm of the lake.

On the western edge of the region, about 25 miles south of I-70, Goblin Valley State Park has rock formations that would be worthy of national park status if they weren't so close to Arches. Here you can hike among hoodoos, spires, and balancing rocks, many with wind-carved "eyes" that explain the area's supernatural moniker.

Remember that this is remote country and fill your gas tank when you have the opportunity. Hanksville and Blanding are good places

SOUTHEASTERN CORNER

THE
**SOUTHEASTERN
CORNER**

Cedar Mountain
Recreation Area

Green River

Green River

Crescent
Junction

Cisco

COLORADO
UTAH

Arches

National

Park

Moab

Mt Waas
12,331ft

Manns Pk
12,273ft

Mt Tomasaki
12,230ft

GOBLIN VALLEY
STATE PARK

Horseshoe
Canyon

Dead Horse
Point State
Park

Mt Peale
12,721ft

Hanksville

Canyonlands

Glen Canyon

National

La Sal

Capitol
Reef
National
Park

Mt Ellen
11,522ft

Recreation

National

Park

Area

Cataract Canyon

BLM NEWSPAPER ROCK
HISTORICAL MONUMENT

Mt Pennell
11,320ft

Mt Hillers
10,723ft

River

Dark Canyon

Monticello

Ticaboo

HITE

Abajo Peak
11,362ft

NATURAL BRIDGES
NATIONAL MONUMENT

EDGE OF THE CEDARS
STATE PARK

Waterpocket Fold

Colorado

Fry Canyon

The Bears Ears
9,058ft

BUTLER
WASH
RUINS

Blanding

BURR TRAIL

Circle Cliffs

BULLFROG

HALLS CROSSING

MULE
CANYON
RUIN

Montezuma Canyon

Glen
Canyon
NRA

Cedar

Mesa

Comb Ridge

FLOATING THE
SAN JUAN RIVER

HOVENWEEP
NATIONAL MONUMENT

HOLE-IN-THE-ROCK RD

Hole-in-the-Rock

San Juan River

Bluff

Montezuma
Creek

Aneth

Lake
Powell

DANGLING ROPE
MARINA

Mexican Hat

NAVAJO INDIAN
RESERVATION

FOUR CORNERS
MONUMENT

RAINBOW BRIDGE
NATIONAL MONUMENT

UTAH

Monument
Valley

ARIZONA

© AVALON TRAVEL

To Page, and
Kayenta, AZ

SOUTHEASTERN CORNER

to check your gauge; if it's showing less than half a tank, definitely fill up. Likewise, pack a lunch and plenty of water when exploring remote areas such as Cedar Mesa, Hovenweep, or Glen Canyon.

PLANNING YOUR TIME

Although it's possible to spend many days exploring the backcountry of Cedar Mesa, floating the San Juan River, houseboating to remote reaches of Lake Powell, or really getting to understand the ancient dwellings at Hovenweep National Monument, most travelers will, at least initially, just pass through. Be sure to allow a day to visit Hovenweep and the Edge of the Cedars Museum in Blanding. From there, if you are short on time, head west across Cedar Mesa to Natural Bridges National Monument and north through Hanksville to Goblin Valley State Park.

Although there are motels in all of the towns included in this chapter, you'll have more flexibility if you are camping. There are many campgrounds and even more de facto primitive campsites, where you can make your own camp; however, be certain that you have the necessary permits before camping in the Cedar Mesa area.

South of Moab

U.S. 191 runs south out of Moab, with the La Sal Mountains to the east and Canyonlands National Park to the west. A string of small towns—Monticello, Blanding, and Bluff—offer places to stop for a meal or a motel room as well as opportunities to explore mountains, desert, rivers, and archeological sites.

MONTICELLO

This small Mormon town (population 2,000) is about 50 miles south of Moab and pretty much its polar opposite. Quiet and relatively untouristed, it's the best place to stay if you're visiting the Needles District and don't want to camp. Monticello ("mon-tuh-SELL-o") is at an elevation of 7,069 feet, just east of the Abajo Mountains. It is 46 miles east of the entrance to the Needles District of Canyonlands National Park.

The local golf course, **The Hideout** (549 S. Main St., 435/587-2200, $40 for 18 holes) is popular in the summer because, at over 7,000 feet in elevation, it's not too hot.

Accommodations

Monticello has a number of comfortable and affordable motels. The **Inn at the Canyons** (533 N. Main St., 435/587-2458, www.

monticellocanyonlandsinn.com, from $75) is nicely renovated and has an indoor pool, a pretty basic continental breakfast, and microwaves and fridges in the guest rooms. The **Monticello Inn** (164 E. Central St., 435/587-2274, www.themonticelloinn.org, from $65) is a well-maintained older motel with a pleasant in-town setting and a few guest rooms that allow pets.

Eight miles north of town, the **Runnin' Iron Inn** (milepost 79.5, U.S. 191, 435/587-2351, http://canyonlandsbestkeptsecret.com, from $59) is a small motel with an Old West ambience, fitting for its middle-of-nowhere location, which happens to be pretty convenient to the Needles District. If you don't need a luxurious guest room or a microwave and fridge, this is a fun place to stay. It's part of a faux-Western town called Roughlock, which also houses an RV park ($20) with tent sites ($20), a few camping cabins ($39) that have no bath or cooking facilities, and a steak house.

The local B&B, the **Grist Mill Inn** (64 S. 300 E., 435/587-2597, www.oldgristmillinn.com, from $89) is indeed housed in an old flour mill. But rest assured, you won't be sleeping under an old millstone; the seven guest rooms are all furnished in typical B&B fashion, and all have private baths and TVs.

Camping

Campgrounds in the nearby Manti-La Sal National Forest include Buckboard and Dalton Springs (435/587-2041, $10). **Buckboard,** seven miles west of town on Blue Mountain Road (Forest Rd. 105), is at 8,600 feet in elevation, so it's not your best bet early in the spring. But when the rest of southeastern Utah swelters in the summer, this shady campground is perfect. **Dalton Springs** is along the same road, a couple of miles closer to town, at 8,200 feet. An abandoned ski area nearby is a good place for mountain biking.

Food

Not only can you get a good cup of coffee and freshly made juice at **Peace Tree Juice Cafe** (516 N. Main St., 435/587-5063, 7am-5pm daily, $79), this is also the only place this side of Moab that you're likely to get a vegetarian Thai wrap sandwich (and it tastes really good).

It's just like a backyard cookout at **K&A Chuckwagon** (196 N. Main St., 435/587-3468, 5pm-9pm daily May-Sept., $15). Settle in at one of the long tent-covered picnic tables and wait for your steak or salmon to be cooked on the big kettle grill. Chuckwagon beans and potatoes accompany the meal, and dessert is included. It's all highly informal and friendly, much like all of Monticello.

Up the road at the Roughlock encampment, the **Line Camp** (milepost 79.5, U.S. 191, 435/587-2351, 5pm-8pm daily, $17-26) is another good steak house with sides of potatoes, beans, and salad as well as a big extra helping of Western atmosphere accompanying every meal. Beer is available at this restaurant, and you can bring your own wine (free corkage).

Information and Services

The expansive new **Southeastern Utah Welcome Center** (216 S. Main St., 435/587-

3401, www.southeastutah.com, 9am-6pm Wed.-Mon. Mar.-Oct., 9am-6pm Fri.-Sun. Nov.-Feb.) is a great place to stop for information about southeastern Utah, including Canyonlands National Park.

The **public library** (80 N. Main St., 435/587-2281) is in the city park.

The **San Juan Hospital** (364 W. 100 N., 435/587-2116) is friendly and small, and it's a good place to have any camping-related injuries repaired.

BLANDING

The largest town in San Juan County, Blanding (population 3,290, elevation 6,105 feet) is also a handy stop for travelers, especially for visitors to Hovenweep National Monument. If you're heading east toward Hovenweep or west into the Cedar Mesa area, check your gas gauge; Blanding is a good place to gas up.

Edge of the Cedars State Park

One mile north of present-day Blanding, prehistoric Anasazi people built at least six groups of pueblo structures between 700 and 1220. The **Edge of the Cedars State Park Museum** (660 W. 400 N., 435/678-2238, www.stateparks.utah.gov, 9am-5pm Mon.-Sat., $5 adults, $3 children) features an excellent array of pottery, baskets, sandals, jewelry, and stone tools. The pottery collection on the second floor stands out for its rich variety of styles and decorative designs. The museum also has exhibits and artifacts of the people who followed the Anasazi— the Utes and Navajo and the early Anglo pioneers.

A short trail behind the museum leads past six clusters of ruins, each of which contains both rectangular rooms on the surface and circular depressions of underground kivas and pit houses. Only Complex 4 has been excavated and partly restored to suggest the village's appearance when the Anasazi lived here. You may enter the kiva by descending a ladder through the restored roof; the walls and interior features are original.

The Dinosaur Museum

The Dinosaur Museum (754 S. 200 W.,

435/678-3454, www.dinosaur-museum.org, 9am-5pm Mon.-Sat. Apr. 15-Oct. 15, $3 adults, $2 seniors, $1.50 children) showcases the prehistoric plant and animal life of this corner of Utah. Exhibits include life-size models of dinosaurs as well as fossils and skeletons. Don't miss the models of feathered dinosaurs.

Accommodations

With one exception, Blanding's motels are all pretty generic. That exception is **Stone Lizard Lodging** (88 W. Center St., 435/678-3323, www.stonelizardlodging.com, $59), an older motel with nicely remodeled guest rooms at very reasonable rates. The **Four Corners Inn** (131 E. Center St., 435/678-3257 or 800/574-3150, www.fourcornersinn.com, from $62), which has a restaurant next door and a simple continental breakfast, is a fine enough place to spend a night. Another good option is the **Gateway Inn** (88 E. Center St., 435/678-2278 or 888/921-2279, http://gatewayinnblanding.com, from $66), with an outdoor pool and pet-friendly guest rooms.

CAMPGROUNDS

At the south edge of town, **Blue Mountain RV Park** (1930 S. Main St., 435/678-7840, www.bluemountainrvpark.com, $32 RVs) is also home to a trading post with some high-quality Native American rugs, jewelry, and baskets. Although tent campers are welcome at the RV park, **Devil's Canyon Campground** (reservations 877/444-6777, www.recreation.gov, $10, $9 reservation fee), at an elevation of 7,100 feet in the Manti-La Sal National Forest, is a better bet for tents. It has sites with water early May-late October (no water or fees off-season). A 0.25-mile nature trail begins at the far end of the campground loop. From Blanding, go north eight miles on U.S. 191, then turn west onto a paved road for 1.3 miles; the turnoff from U.S. 191 is between mileposts 60 and 61.

Food

Blanding is a somewhat unlikely spot to find

an outpost of the **Peace Tree Juice Cafe** (164 N. Grayson Pkwy., 435/678-3969, 7am-5pm daily, $3-8), with its vaguely hippie vibe, tasty wraps, and fresh juices. Although **Fattboyz Grillin'** (733 S. Main St., 435/678-3777, 7am-9pm daily, $5-19) is open for all meals, it's best at dinner, when the ribs are well marinated and the locals are shoulder-to-shoulder. In addition to ribs, there are chicken, burgers, and Navajo tacos on the menu. Since Blanding is a dry town, no alcohol is served.

BLUFF

Bluff, a sleepy community of about 300 inhabitants, is nestled in a striking physical location. In the past few years, Bluff has become a rather unlikely mecca for recreationists and escapees from urban congestion. The quality of lodging is better than that of almost any other town of this size in the state, and local outfitters make it easy to get out and enjoy the remarkable scenery hereabouts.

Bluff is the oldest non-Native American community in southeastern Utah; it was settled in 1880 by Mormon pioneers who had traveled the excruciatingly difficult Hole-in-the-Rock Trail from the town of Escalante down into what's now Lake Powell.

Spend an afternoon poking around local washes or examining a large pictograph panel, found along the cliff about 0.3 miles downstream from the Sand Island campground. **Fort Bluff** is being reconstructed; it is located near the north end of town. The visitors center, located in the small museum, is worth a stop; the staff can give you detailed directions for good informal hikes in the nearby washes.

If you want a guided trip into the backcountry of southeastern Utah, **Far Out Expeditions** (425/672-2294, www.faroutexpeditions.com) is a local company with lots of experience leading day trips and overnights in the area.

◖ Floating the San Juan River

From the high San Juan Mountains in southern

© JUDY JEWELL

The San Juan River runs by the town of Bluff.

Colorado, the San Juan River winds its way into New Mexico, enters Utah near Four Corners, and twists through spectacular canyons before ending at Lake Powell. Most boaters put in at Sand Island Campground near Bluff and take out at the town of Mexican Hat, 30 river miles downstream. This trip combines ancient Native American ruins, rock art, and a trip through Monument Upwarp and the Upper Canyon, with fast water for thrills (Class III rapids) and weirdly buckled geology to ponder. Longer trips continue on through the famous Goosenecks, the "entrenched meanders" carved thousands of feet below the desert surface, and through more Class III rapids on the way to Clay Hills Crossing or Paiute Farms (not always accessible) on Lake Powell. Allow at least four days for the full trip, though more time will allow for exploration of side canyons and visits to Anasazi sites. Rafts, kayaks, and canoes can be used. The season usually lasts year-round because of adequate water flow from Navajo Reservoir upstream.

Many commercial river-running companies offer San Juan trips. If you go on your own, you should have river-running experience or be with someone who does. Private groups need to obtain permits ($6-18 pp) from the Bureau of Land Management's San Juan Resource Area office (435/587-1544, www.blm.gov); permits are issued through a preseason lottery, although boaters with flexible schedules can usually get permits close to their time of travel. Permit fees vary depending on how far you're floating.

Some people also like to run the river between Montezuma Creek and Sand Island, a leisurely trip of 20 river miles. The solitude often makes up for the lack of scenery. It's easy to get a river permit for this section because no use limits or fees apply.

If you're looking for a multiday trip on the San Juan River, contact local **Wild Rivers Expeditions** (101 Main St., 435/672-2244 or 800/422-7654, www.riversandruins.com), which offers both day and multiday trips out of Bluff; trips run daily in summer, and only a day's notice is usually needed to join a float. Eight-hour, 26-mile day excursions to Mexican Hat cost $165 adults, $123 under age 13; motors may be used if the water level is low. Some of the larger Moab-based outfitters offer San Juan River trips when interest allows.

Accommodations

Attractive 🄲 **Desert Rose Inn** (701 W. Main St., 735/672-2303 or 888/475-7673, www.desertroseinn.com, from $119) is one of the nicest lodgings in this corner of the state. The large lodge-like log structure has two-story wrap-around porches and guest rooms furnished with pine furniture, quilts, and Southwestern art. At the edge of the property are a number of handsome one-bedroom log cabins. This is definitely a class act.

The other great place to stay is **Recapture Lodge** (220 E. Main St., 435/672-2281, www.recapturelodge.com, $75). For many years the heart and soul of Bluff, the lodge is operated by longtime outfitters and has an easy nonchalance that is immediately welcoming. Besides guest rooms and kitchenettes, Recapture Lodge has trails out the back door, a swimming pool, a hot tub, a coin laundry, tours, and llama pack trips. The Recapture also rents a couple of fully equipped homes in Bluff for families and groups.

Kokopelli Inn Motel (160 E. Main St., 435/672-2322, www.kokoinn.com, from $82), just next door to the Recapture, is a fine place to stay, though it pales in comparison to Bluff's unique lodges.

CAMPGROUNDS

Sand Island Recreation Area (435/587-1500, www.blm.gov, $10) is a Bureau of Land Management (BLM) camping area along the San Juan River, three miles south of town, with piped water. Large cottonwood trees shade this pretty spot, but tenters need to watch for thorns in the grass. River-runners

often put in at the campground, so it can be a busy place. Two RV parks are right in town: **Cadillac Ranch RV Park** (U.S. 191, 435/672-2262, www.cadillacranchrv.com, year-round, $28) is in the center of town and **Cottonwood R.V. Park** (U.S. 191, 435/672-2287, http://cottonwoodrvpark.blogspot.com, Mar. 15-Nov. 15, $30) is at the west end of Bluff.

Food

It's worth spending the night in Bluff just to eat at the 🄲 **San Juan River Kitchen** (435/672-9956, www.sanjuanriverkitchen.com, 5:30-about 9pm Tues.-Sat., $10-18), where as much food as possible comes from the restaurant's organic garden. The food is not just local; it's also delicious. Smoked chicken enchiladas feature homemade green chili, and a steak-and-egg sandwich turns into a real treat when braised chard and grilled mushrooms share the space between slices of *ciabatta*. The kitchen serves good beer and wine, which is not so easy to come by in these parts. Lastly, the space is quite lovely—modern and simple yet warm.

A longtime local hangout and a good place for a meal and a friendly vibe is the **Twin Rocks Cafe** (435/672-2341, www.twinrockscafe.com, 7am-8pm daily, $5-20), next to the trading post just below the impossible-to-miss Twin Rocks. Here you can dine on Navajo tacos (fry bread with chili) or Navajo pizza (fry bread with pizza toppings) as well as more standard fare. Be sure to visit the trading post for high-quality Native American crafts, many of them produced locally by Navajo artisans.

Settle in under the big cottonwood tree for a flame-grilled steak dinner at the **Cottonwood Steakhouse** (Main St. and 4th St. E., 435/672-2282, 5:30pm-9:30pm daily spring-fall, $17-25). Dinners come with salad, beans, and potatoes; for $9, you can split an entrée with someone else and get full servings of side dishes. Indoor dining is also an option.

© PAUL LEVY

Hovenweep was the site of six Anasazi villages.

Stop by the **Comb Ridge Coffee House** (680 S. U.S. 191, 435/672-9931, 7am-5pm Tues.-Sun., sandwiches $5-6.25) for a breakfast muffin or slice of quiche, a cup of coffee, and a dose of friendly community spirit. Premade sandwiches and ice cream round out the menu at this sweet spot.

HOVENWEEP NATIONAL MONUMENT

Delve into the region's cultural history and architecture at remote Hovenweep National Monument (970/562-4283, www.nps.gov/hove, $6 per vehicle, $3 cyclists and pedestrians, $25 annual Local Passport also includes entrance to Canyonlands and Arches National Parks and Natural Bridges National Monument), where the Anasazi built many impressive masonry buildings during the early-mid-1200s, near the end of their 1,300-year stay in the area. A drought that began in 1274 and lasted 25 years probably hastened

their migration from this area. Several centuries of intensive farming, hunting, and wood-cutting had already taken a toll on the land. Archaeologists believe the inhabitants retreated south in the late 1200s to sites in northwestern New Mexico and northeastern Arizona. The Ute word *hovenweep* means "deserted valley," an appropriate name for the lonely high-desert country they left behind. The Anasazi at Hovenweep had much in common with the Mesa Verde culture, although the Dakota sandstone here doesn't form large alcoves suitable for cliff-dweller villages. Ruins at Hovenweep remain essentially unexcavated, awaiting the attention of future archaeologists.

The Anasazi farmers had a keen interest in the seasons because of their need to know the best time for planting crops. Astronomical stations (alignments of walls, doorways, and tiny openings) allowed the sun priests to determine the equinoxes and solstices with an accuracy of 1-2 days. This precision also may have been necessary for a complex ceremonial calendar. Astronomical stations at Hovenweep have been discovered at Hovenweep Castle, House of Square Tower Ruins, and Cajon Ruins.

Planning Your Time

Hovenweep National Monument protects six groups of villages left behind by the Anasazi. The sites are near the Colorado border, southeast of Blanding. **Square Tower Ruins Unit,** where the visitors center is located, has the most ruins and the most varied architecture. In fact, you can find all of the Hovenweep architectural styles here. There are other ruins that are good to visit if you'd like to spend more time in the area; you'll need a map and directions from a ranger to find them because they aren't signed. One group, the Goodman Point, near Cortez, Colorado, offers relatively little to see except unexcavated mounds.

Visitors Center

The visitors center (970/562-4282, 8am-6pm daily May-Sept., 8am-5pm daily Apr. and Oct., 8am-4:30pm daily Nov.-Mar.) has a few exhibits on the Anasazi, photos of local wildlife, and a small bookstore. A ranger can answer your questions, provide brochures and handouts about various aspects of the monument, and give directions for visiting the other groups of ruins. Mesa Verde National Park (970/529-4465, www.nps.gov/meve) administers Hovenweep.

Square Tower Ruins

This extensive group of Anasazi towers and dwellings lines the rim and slopes of Little Ruin Canyon, located a short walk from the visitors center. Obtain a trail-guide booklet from the ranger station. You can take easy walks of less than 0.5 miles on the rim; combine all the trails for a loop of about two miles with only one up-and-down section in the canyon. The booklet has good descriptions of Anasazi life and architecture and of the plants growing along the trail. You'll see towers (D-shaped, square, oval, and round), cliff dwellings, surface dwellings, storehouses, kivas, and rock art. Keep an eye out for the prairie rattlesnake, a subspecies of the Western rattlesnake, which is active at night in summer and during the day in spring and fall. And stay on the trail: Don't climb the fragile walls of the ruins or walk on rubble mounds.

Holly Ruins

Holly Ruins group is noted for its Great House, Holly Tower, and Tilted Tower. Most of Tilted Tower fell away after the boulder on which it sat shifted. Great piles of rubble mark the sites of structures built on loose ground. Look for remnants of farming terraces in the canyon below the Great House. A hiking trail connects the campground at Square Tower Ruins with Holly Ruins; the route follows canyon bottoms and is about eight miles round-trip. Ask a ranger for a map and directions. Hikers can also continue to Horseshoe Ruins (one mile farther) and Hackberry Ruins (just beyond Horseshoe). All of these are just across the Colorado border and about six miles one-way by road from the visitors center.

Horseshoe and Hackberry Ruins

Horseshoe Ruins and Hackberry Ruins are best reached by an easy trail (one mile round-trip) off the road to Holly Ruins. Horseshoe House, built in a horseshoe shape similar to Sun Temple at Mesa Verde, has exceptionally good masonry work. Archaeologists haven't determined the purpose of the structure. An alcove in the canyon below contains a spring and a small shelter. A round tower nearby on the rim has a strategic view. Hackberry House has only one room still intact. Rubble piles and wall remnants abound in the area. The spring under an alcove here still has a good flow and supports lush growths of hackberry and cottonwood trees along with smaller plants.

Cutthroat Castle Ruins

Cutthroat Castle Ruins were remote even in

Anasazi times. The ruins lie along an intermittent stream rather than at the head of a canyon like most other Hovenweep sites. Cutthroat Castle is a large multistory structure with both straight and curved walls. Three round towers stand nearby. Look for wall fragments and the circular depressions of kivas. High-clearance vehicles can get close to the ruins, about 11.5 miles one-way from the visitors center. Visitors with cars can drive to a trailhead and then walk to the ruins, 1.5 miles round-trip on foot.

Cajon Ruins

Cajon Ruins are at the head of a little canyon on Cajon Mesa on the Navajo Reservation in Utah, about nine miles southwest of the visitors center. The site has a commanding view across the San Juan Valley as far as Monument Valley. Buildings include a large multiroom structure, a round tower, and a tall square tower. An alcove just below has a spring and some rooms. Look for pictographs, petroglyphs, and grooves in the rock used for tool grinding. Farming terraces were located on the canyon's south side.

Camping

A small **campground** near the visitors center (no reservations, $10) has 31 sites geared toward tent campers, although a few sites will accommodate RVs up to 36 feet long. Running water is available only during summer, when five gallons are allotted to each camper. Like Hovenweep's ancient inhabitants, campers are often treated to excellent stargazing; the monument is far from light pollution, and the dark night skies are frequently clear.

Getting There

One approach is from U.S. 191 between Blanding and Bluff; head east nine miles on Highway 262, continue straight six miles on a small paved road to Hatch Trading Post, and then follow the signs for 16 miles. A good way in from Bluff is to go east 21 miles on the paved road to Montezuma Creek and Aneth, then follow the signs north for 20 miles. A scenic 58-mile route through Montezuma Canyon begins five miles south of Monticello and follows unpaved roads to Hatch and on to Hovenweep; you can stop at the BLM's Three Turkey Ruin on the way. From Colorado, take a partly paved road west and north 41 miles from U.S. 491 (the turnoff is four miles south of Cortez).

Don't expect your cell phone to work in this remote area.

Cedar Mesa and Vicinity

Head way off the beaten track to explore ancient ruins and stunning geography in the area west of U.S. 191 and east of Glen Canyon and Lake Powell. Experienced hikers can wander deep into this rugged area; those with less experience or fortitude may want to focus on the trails at Natural Bridges National Monument.

CEDAR MESA

Just south of Blanding, Highway 95—here labeled Trail of the Ancients National Scenic Byway—heads west across a high plateau toward the Colorado River, traversing Comb Ridge, Cedar Mesa, and many canyons. This is remote country, so fill up with gas before leaving Blanding; you can't depend on finding gasoline until Hanksville, 122 miles away. Hite and the other Lake Powell marinas do have gas and supplies, but their hours are limited.

Cedar Mesa and its canyons have an exceptionally large number of prehistoric Anasazi sites. Several ruins are just off the highway, and hikers will discover many more. If you would like to explore the Cedar Mesa area, be sure to drop in at the **Kane Gulch Ranger Station** (435/587-1532, www.blm.gov, 8am-noon daily spring and fall), at the west end of Cedar Mesa, four miles south of Highway 95 on Highway 261. BLM staff issue the permits required to explore the Cedar Mesa backcountry for day-use ($2) and for overnight stays ($8 pp) in Grand Gulch, Fish Creek Canyon, and Owl Creek Canyon. The number of people permitted to camp at a given time is limited, so call ahead. BLM staff will also tell you about archaeological sites and their historic value, current hiking conditions, and where to find water. Cedar Mesa is managed for more primitive recreation, so hikers in the area should have good route-finding skills and come prepared with food and water. The ranger station sells maps but has no water.

Butler Wash Ruins

Well-preserved pueblo ruins left by the Anasazi are tucked under an overhang across the wash. Find the trailhead on the north side of Highway 95, 11 miles west of U.S. 191, between mileposts 111 and 112. Follow cairns for 0.5 miles through juniper and piñon pine woodlands and across slickrock to the overlook, where you can see four kivas and several other structures. Parts have been reconstructed, but most of the site is about 900 years old.

Comb Ridge

Geologic forces have squeezed up the earth's crust in a long ridge running 80 miles south from the Abajo Peaks into Arizona. Sheer cliffs plunge 800 feet into Comb Wash on the west side. Engineering the highway down these cliffs took considerable effort. A parking area near the top of the grade offers expansive panoramas across Comb Wash.

Arch Canyon

This tributary canyon of Comb Wash has spectacular scenery and many Native American ruins. Much of the canyon can be seen on a day hike, but 2-3 days are required to explore the upper reaches. The main streambeds usually have water, but purify it before drinking it. To reach the trailhead, turn north onto Comb Wash Road (between mileposts 107 and 108 on Hwy. 95) and go 2.5 miles on the dirt road, past a house and a water tank, then park in a grove of cottonwood trees before a stream. The mouth of pretty Arch Canyon is just to the northwest (it's easy to miss). Look for a Native American ruin just up Arch Canyon on the right. More ruins are tucked under alcoves farther up-canyon.

Arch Canyon Overlook

A road and a short trail to the rim of Arch Canyon provide a beautiful view into the depths. Turn north on Texas Flat Road (County Rd. 263) from Highway 95, between mileposts 102 and 103, continue four miles, park just before the road begins a steep climb, and walk east on an old jeep road to the rim. This is a fine place for a picnic, although there are no facilities or guardrails. Texas Flat Road is dirt but passable when dry for cars with good clearance. Trucks can continue up the steep hill to other viewpoints of Arch and Texas Canyons.

Mule Canyon Ruin

Archaeologists have excavated and stabilized this Anasazi village on the gentle slope of Mule Canyon's South Fork. A stone kiva, circular tower, and 12-room structure are all visible, and all were originally connected by tunnels. Cave Towers, two miles southeast, would have been visible from the top of the tower here. Signs describe the ruins and periods of Anasazi development. Turn north from Highway 95 between mileposts 101 and 102 and continue 0.3 miles on a paved road. Hikers can explore other ruins in the North and South Forks of Mule Canyon; check with the Kane Gulch Ranger Station for advice and directions. You might see pieces of pottery and other artifacts in this area. Federal laws prohibit the removal of artifacts: Please leave every piece in place so that future visitors can enjoy the discovery too. Be sure to have a BLM day hiking permit when exploring this area.

GRAND GULCH PRIMITIVE AREA

Within this twisting canyon system are some of the most captivating scenery and largest concentrations of Anasazi ruins in southeastern Utah. The main canyon begins only about six miles southeast of Natural Bridges National Monument. From an elevation of 6,400 feet, Grand Gulch cuts deeply into Cedar Mesa on a tortuous path southwest to the San Juan River, dropping 2,700 feet in about 53 miles. Sheer cliffs, alcoves, pinnacles, Anasazi cliff dwellings, rock-art sites, arches, and a few natural bridges line Grand Gulch and its many tributaries.

From the Kane Gulch Ranger Station, a trail leads four miles down Kane Gulch to the upper end of Grand Gulch, where a camping area is shaded by cottonwood trees. Junction Ruin, a cave dwelling, is visible from here, and less than one mile farther into Grand Gulch are more ruins and an arch.

© BILL MCRAE

Mexican Hat is about 10 miles south of the Moki Dugway, a series of steep switchbacks.

Kane Gulch and Bullet Canyon provide access to the upper end of Grand Gulch from the east side. A popular loop hike using these canyons is 23 miles long (3-4 days); arrange a 7.5-mile car shuttle or hitch. Ask at the ranger station if a shuttle service is available. Collins Canyon, reached from Collins Spring Trailhead, leads into lower Grand Gulch from the west side. Hiking distance between Kane Gulch and Collins Spring Trailheads is 38 miles one-way (5-7 days). A car shuttle of about 29 miles (including eight miles of dirt road) is required. Be sure to visit the BLM's Kane Gulch Ranger Station or Monticello office for a permit and information. You must have a day-use ($2) or overnight camping permit ($8) to enter the area.

MEXICAN HAT

South of the Kane Gulch Ranger Station, Highway 261 loses its pavement and becomes contorted into a series of steeply banked switchbacks known as the Moki Dugway. Slow down and take this stretch of road (with 1,100 feet of elevation change and 5-10 percent grades) at 5-10 mph. About 10 miles south of the Dugway is the town of Mexican Hat, a modest trade and tourism center.

Spectacular geology surrounds this tiny community perched on the north bank of the San Juan River. Folded layers of red and gray rock stand out dramatically. Alhambra Rock, a jagged remnant of a volcano, marks the southern approach to Mexican Hat. Another rock, which looks just like an upside-down sombrero, gave Mexican Hat its name; you'll see this formation from U.S. 163, two miles north of town. Monument Valley, Valley of the Gods Scenic Drive, Goosenecks State Park, and Grand Gulch Primitive Area are only short drives away. The riverbanks near town can be a busy place in summer as river-runners on the San Juan put in, take out, or just stop for ice and beer.

Goosenecks State Park

The San Juan River winds through a series of

SOUTHEASTERN CORNER

© JUDY JEWELL

The tightly wound San Juan River flows 1,000 feet below this viewpoint at Goosenecks State Park.

incredibly tight bends 1,000 feet below. So closely spaced are the bends that the river takes six miles to cover an air distance of only 1.5 miles. The bends and exposed rock layers form exquisitely graceful curves. Geologists know the site as a classic example of entrenched meanders, caused by gradual uplift of a formerly level plain. Signs at the overlook explain the geologic history and identify the rock formations. Goosenecks State Park (435/678-2238, http://stateparks.utah.gov) is an undeveloped area with a few picnic tables and vault toilets. A **campground** (free) is available but has no water. From the junction of U.S. 163 and Highway 261, four miles north of Mexican Hat, go one mile northwest on Highway 261, then turn left and go three miles on Highway 316 to its end.

Muley Point Overlook

One of the great views in the Southwest is just a short drive from Goosenecks State Park and more than 1,000 feet higher in elevation. Although the view of the Goosenecks below is less dramatic than at the state park, the 6,200-foot elevation provides a magnificent panorama across the Navajo Reservation to Monument Valley and countless canyons and mountains. To get here, travel northwest nine miles on Highway 261 from the Goosenecks turnoff. At the top of the Moki Dugway switchbacks, turn left (southwest) and go 5.3 miles on gravel County Road 241 (the turnoff may not be signed), and follow it toward the point. This road is not suitable for wet-weather travel.

Accommodations and Food

The **San Juan Inn and Trading Post** (435/683-2220 or 800/447-2022, www.sanjuaninn.net, from $84), at a dramatic location above the river, just west of town, offers clean guest rooms without extras, a few yurts, Native American trade goods, and a restaurant, the **Olde Bridge**

Bar and Grill (435/683-2220, 7am-9pm daily, $8-15), serving American, Mexican, and Navajo food. **Hat Rock Inn** (435/683-2221, www.hatrockinn.com, $145) offers the nicest guest rooms in town and a swimming pool. **Mexican Hat Lodge** (435/683-2222, www. mexicanhat.net, from $84) offers guest rooms, a pool, and a fun but somewhat expensive restaurant (lunch and dinner daily) with grilled steaks and burgers.

Valle's Trading Post and RV Park (435/683-2226, year-round, $20), has tent and RV sites with hookups. The camping area is pretty basic, but great scenery surrounds it. The trading post offers crafts, groceries, showers, vehicle storage, and car shuttles. **Goosenecks State Park** has free camping with great views but no amenities.

Valley of the Gods

Great sandstone monoliths, delicate spires, and long rock fins rise from the broad valley. This strange red-rock landscape resembles better-known Monument Valley but on a smaller scale. A 17-mile dirt road winds through the spectacular scenery. Cars can usually travel the road at low speeds if the weather is dry (the road crosses washes). Allow 1-1.5 hours for the drive; it's studded with viewpoints, and you'll want to stop at all of them. The east end of the road connects with U.S. 163 at milepost 29 (7.5 miles northeast of Mexican Hat, 15 miles southwest of Bluff); the west end connects with Highway 261 just below the Moki Dugway switchbacks (four miles north of Mexican Hat on U.S. 163, then 6.6 miles northwest on Hwy. 261).

MONUMENT VALLEY

Towering buttes, jagged pinnacles, and rippled sand dunes make this area along the Utah-Arizona border an otherworldly landscape. Changing colors and shifting shadows during the day add to the enchantment. Most of the natural monuments are remnants of sandstone eroded by wind and water. Agathla Peak and some lesser summits are the roots of ancient volcanoes, whose dark rock contrasts with the pale yellow sandstone of the other formations. The valley is at an elevation of 5,564 feet in the Upper Sonoran Life Zone; annual rainfall averages about 8.5 inches.

In 1863-1864, when Kit Carson was ravaging Canyon de Chelly in Arizona to round up the Navajo, Chief Hoskinini led his people to the safety and freedom of Monument Valley.

Hollywood movies made the splendor of Monument Valley widely known to the outside world. *Stagecoach,* filmed here in 1938 and directed by John Ford, became the first in a series of Westerns that has continued to the present. John Wayne and many other movie greats rode across these sands.

The Navajo have preserved the valley as a park with a scenic drive, visitors center, and campground. From Mexican Hat, drive 22 miles southwest on U.S. 163, and turn left and go 3.5 miles to the visitors center. At the turnoff on U.S. 163 is a village's worth of outdoor market stalls and a modern complex of enclosed shops where you can stop to buy Navajo art and crafts.

Visitors Center

At the entrance to the **Monument Valley Navajo Tribal Park** is a visitors center (435/727-5874, 6am-8pm daily May-Sept., 8am-5pm daily Oct.-Apr., $5 pp age 10 and up, free under age 10) with exhibits and crafts. This is a good place to get a list of Navajo tour guides to lead you on driving or hiking trips into the monument. Lots of folks along the road will also offer these services.

Tours

Take one of several guided tours leaving daily year-round from the visitors center to visit sites such as a hogan, a cliff dwelling, and petroglyphs in areas beyond the self-guided drive. The trips last 1.5-4 hours and cost $45-90 pp.

SOUTHEASTERN CORNER

Guided horseback rides from near the visitors center cost around $75 for two hours; longer day and overnight trips can be arranged too. If you'd like to hike in Monument Valley, you must hire a guide. Hiking tours of two hours to a full day or more can be arranged at the visitors center.

Monument Valley Drive

A 17-mile self-guided scenic drive (6am-8:30pm daily May-Sept., 8am-4:30pm daily Oct.-Apr.) begins at the visitors center and loops through the heart of the valley. Overlooks provide sweeping views from different vantage points. The dirt road is normally OK for cautiously driven cars. Avoid stopping or you may get stuck in the loose sand that sometimes blows across the road. Allow 90 minutes for the drive. No hiking or driving is allowed off the signed route. Water and restrooms are available only at the visitors center.

Accommodations

Don't be surprised to find that lodgings at Monument Valley are expensive; they're also extremely popular, so be sure to book well ahead.

The Navajo-owned **◖ View Hotel** (435/727-5555, www.monumentvalleyview.com, from $199) provides the only lodging in Monument Valley Tribal Park. Views are terrific from this stylish newer hotel; reserve a room well in advance. **◖ Goulding's Lodge and Trading Post** (435/727-3231, www.gouldings.com, from $140) is another great place to stay in the Monument Valley area. Harry Goulding and his wife, Mike, opened this dramatically located trading post in 1924. It's a large complex tucked under the rimrocks two miles west of the U.S. 163 Monument Valley turnoff, just north of the Arizona-Utah border. Modern motel rooms offer incredible views of Monument Valley. Guests can use a small indoor pool; meals are available in the dining room. A gift shop sells a wide range of souvenirs, books, and Native American crafts. The nearby store has groceries and gas pumps, a restaurant is open daily for all meals, and tours and horseback rides are available. The lodge stays open year-round, and rates drop in winter and early spring. Goulding's Museum, in the old trading post building, displays prehistoric and modern artifacts, movie photos, and memorabilia of the Goulding family. The Gouldings **campground** ($25 without hookups, $42 with hookups) is pleasant and well managed.

About 30 minutes south in Kayenta, Arizona, the adobe-style **Hampton Inn** (U.S. 160, 520/697-3170 or 800/426-7866, from $189) is the nicest place in town, and it's only a little more expensive than its Kayenta neighbors.

◖ NATURAL BRIDGES NATIONAL MONUMENT

Streams in White Canyon and its tributaries cut deep canyons, then formed three impressive bridges, now protected as Natural Bridges National Monument (435/692-1234, www.nps.gov/nabr, $6 per vehicle, $3 cyclists and pedestrians, $25 annual Local Passport also includes entrance to Natural Bridges and Hovenweep National Monuments and Arches and Canyonlands National Parks). Silt-laden floodwaters sculpted the bridges by gouging tunnels between closely spaced loops in the meandering canyons. You can distinguish a natural bridge from an arch because the bridge spans a streambed and was initially carved out of the rock by flowing water. In the monument, these bridges illustrate three different stages of development, from the massive, newly formed Kachina Bridge to the middle-aged Sipapu Bridge to the delicate and fragile span of Owachomo. All three natural bridges will continue to widen and eventually collapse under their own weight. A nine-mile scenic drive has overlooks of the picturesque bridges, Anasazi ruins, and twisting canyons. You can

© PAUL LEVY

the fragile and elegant Owachomo Bridge, in Natural Bridges National Monument

follow short trails down from the rim to the base of each bridge or hike through all three bridges on an 8.6-mile loop.

Ruins, artifacts, and rock art indicate a long occupation by Native Americans ranging from archaic groups to the Anasazi. Many fine cliff dwellings built by the Anasazi still stand. In 1883, prospector Cass Hite passed on tales of the huge stone bridges that he had discovered on a trip up White Canyon. Adventurous travelers, including those on a 1904 *National Geographic* magazine expedition, visited this isolated region to marvel at the bridges. The public's desire for protection of the bridges led President Theodore Roosevelt to proclaim the area a national monument in 1908. Federal administrators then changed the original bridge names from Edwin, Augusta, and Caroline to the Hopi names used today. Although the Hopi never lived here, the Anasazi of White Canyon very likely have descendants in the modern Hopi villages in Arizona.

Visitors Center

From the signed junction on Highway 95, it is 4.5 miles on Highway 275 to the visitors center (435/692-1234, 8am-6pm daily May-Sept., 8am-5pm daily Apr. and Oct., 8am-4:30pm daily Nov.-Mar.), at an elevation of 6,505 feet. Monument Valley Overlook, two miles in, offers views south across a vast expanse of piñon pine and juniper to Monument Valley and distant mountains. A slide show in the visitors center illustrates how geologic forces and erosion created the canyons and natural bridges. Exhibits introduce the people who once lived here, as well as the area's geology, wildlife, and plants. Outside, labels identify common plants of the monument.

Rangers can answer your questions about the monument and the surrounding area. If asked, staff will provide details on locations of ruins and rock art sites. You can purchase regional books, topographic and geologic maps, postcards, and slides. Checklists of birds, other wildlife, and plants are available too.

SOUTHEASTERN CORNER

The Bridge View Drive is always open during daylight hours, except after heavy snowstorms. A winter visit can be very enjoyable; ice or mud often close the steep Sipapu and Kachina Trails, but the short trail to Owachomo Bridge usually stays open. Pets aren't allowed on the trails or in the backcountry at any time.

Other than the small but popular campground at the national monument, the nearest accommodations are 40 miles east near Blanding or 50 miles west at Hite.

Bright Sun, Dark Nights

A large **solar electric-power station** is across the road from the visitors center. This demonstration system, the largest in the world when it was constructed in 1980, has 250,000 solar cells spread over nearly an acre and produces up to 100 kilowatts. Batteries, located elsewhere, store a two-day supply of power. The monument is far from the nearest power lines, so the solar cells provide an alternative to continuously running diesel-powered generators.

When the sun sets, Natural Bridges becomes one of the darkest places in the United States. In fact, the International Dark Sky Association has named this the world's first dark-sky park. Come here for some serious stargazing!

Bridge View Drive

This nine-mile drive begins its one-way loop just past the campground. You can stop for lunch at a picnic area. Allow about 1.5 hours for a quick trip around. To make all the stops and do a bit of leisurely hiking takes most of a day. The cross-bedded sandstone of the bridges and canyons is part of the 265-million-year-old Cedar Mesa Formation.

Sipapu Bridge viewpoint is two miles from the visitors center. The Hopi name refers to the gateway from which their ancestors entered this world from another world below. Sipapu Bridge has reached its mature or middle-age stage of development. The bridge is the largest in the monument and has a span of 268 feet and a height of 220 feet. Many people think Sipapu is the most magnificent of the bridges. Another view and a trail to the base of Sipapu are 0.8 miles farther. The viewpoint is about halfway down on an easy trail; allow half an hour. A steeper and rougher trail branches off the viewpoint trail and winds down to the bottom of White Canyon, which is probably the best place to fully appreciate the bridge's size. The total round-trip distance is 1.2 miles, with an elevation change of 600 feet.

Horse Collar Ruin, built by the Anasazi, looks as though it has been abandoned for just a few decades, not 800 years. A short trail leads to an overlook 3.1 miles from the visitors center. The name comes from the shape of the doorway openings in two storage rooms. Hikers walking in the canyon between Sipapu and Kachina Bridges can scramble up a steep rock slope to the site. Like all ancient ruins, these are fragile and must not be touched or entered. Only with such care will future generations of visitors be able to admire the well-preserved structures. Other groups of Anasazi dwellings can also be seen in or near the monument; ask a ranger for directions.

The **Kachina Bridge** viewpoint and trailhead are 5.1 miles from the visitors center. The massive bridge has a span of 204 feet and a height of 210 feet. A trail, 1.5 miles round-trip, leads to the canyon bottom next to the bridge; the elevation change is 650 feet. Look for pictographs near the base of the trail. Some of the figures resemble Hopi kachinas (spirits) and inspired the bridge's name. Armstrong Canyon joins White Canyon just downstream from the bridge; floods in each canyon abraded opposite sides of the rock fin that later became Kachina Bridge.

The **Owachomo Bridge** viewpoint and trailhead are 7.1 miles from the visitors center. An easy walk leads to Owachomo's base—0.5 miles round-trip with an elevation change of 180 feet. Graceful Owachomo spans 180 feet and is 106 feet high. Erosive forces have worn the venerable bridge to a thickness of only nine feet. Unlike the other two bridges, Owachomo spans a smaller tributary stream instead of a major canyon. Two streams played a role in the bridge's formation. Floods coming down the larger Armstrong Canyon surged against a sandstone fin on one side while floods in a small side canyon wore away the rock on the other side. Eventually a hole formed, and waters flowing down the side canyon took the shorter route through the bridge. The word *owachomo* means "flat-rock mound" in the Hopi language; a large rock outcrop nearby inspired the name. Before construction of the present road, a trail winding down the opposite side of Armstrong Canyon provided the only access for monument visitors. The trail, little used now, connects with Highway 95.

Natural Bridges Loop Trail

- Distance: 8.6 miles round-trip
- Duration: 5-6 hours
- Elevation change: 500 feet
- Effort: moderate-strenuous
- Trailhead: Sipapu Bridge

A canyon hike through all three bridges can be the highlight of a visit to the monument. Unmaintained trails make a loop in White and Armstrong Canyons and cross a wooded plateau. The trip is easier if you start from Sipapu and come out on the relatively gentle grades at Owachomo. You can save 2.5 miles by arranging a car shuttle between the Sipapu and Owachomo trailheads. Another option is to go in or out on the Kachina Bridge Trail

midway to cut the hiking distance in half. As you near Owachomo Bridge from below, a small sign points out the trail, which bypasses a deep pool. The canyons remain in their wild state; you'll need some hiking experience, water, proper footwear, a compass, and a map (the handout available at the visitors center is adequate). The USGS 7.5-minute topographic maps also cover this area.

When hiking in the canyons, keep an eye out for natural arches and Native American writing. Try not to step on midget faded rattlesnakes or other living entities (including the fragile cryptobiotic soil). And beware of flash floods, especially if you see big clouds billowing in the sky in an upstream direction. You don't need a hiking permit, although it's a good idea to talk beforehand with a ranger to find out current conditions. Overnight camping within the monument is permitted only in the campground. Backpackers, however, can go up or down the canyons and camp outside the monument boundaries. Note that vehicles can't be parked overnight on the loop drive.

Campgrounds

The **Natural Bridges Campground** (first-come, first-served, year-round, $10) is in a forest of piñon pine and juniper. Obtain water from a faucet in front of the visitors center. Rangers give talks several evenings each week during the summer season. The campground is often full, but there is a rather grim designated overflow area near the intersection of Highways 95 and 261. RVs and trailers longer than 26 feet must use this parking area. To reach the campground, drive 0.3 miles past the visitors center and turn right.

SOUTHEASTERN CORNER

Lake Powell and Glen Canyon

Lake Powell is at the center of the Glen Canyon National Recreation Area (520/608-6404, 7 days $15 per vehicle or $7 cyclists and pedestrians, no charge for passing through Page on U.S. 89), a vast land covering 1.25 million acres in Arizona and Utah. When the Glen Canyon Dam was completed in 1964, conservationists deplored the loss of the remote and beautiful Glen Canyon of the Colorado River beneath the lake's waters. In terms of beauty and sheer drama, Glen Canyon was considered the equal of the Grand Canyon. Today, we have only words, pictures, and memories to remind us of its wonders. On the other hand, the 186-mile-long lake now provides easy access to an area most had not even known existed. Lake Powell is the second-largest artificial lake in the United States. Only Lake Mead,

farther downstream, has a greater water-storage capacity. Lake Powell, however, has three times more shoreline—1,960 miles—and when full, it holds enough water to cover the state of Pennsylvania one foot deep. Just a handful of roads approach the lake, so access is basically limited to boats—bays and coves offer nearly limitless opportunities for exploration by boaters—as well as long-distance hiking trails.

NATURAL BRIDGES TO BULLFROG MARINA BY FERRY

Eight miles west of the entrance to Natural Bridges National Monument, travelers must make a decision: whether to continue on Highway 95 to cross the Colorado by bridge at Hite or to follow Highway 276 to the Halls Crossing Marina and cross the river, at this point tamed by the Glen Canyon Dam and known as Lake Powell, by car ferry.

Obviously, the ferry is the more exotic choice, and both Halls Crossing and Bullfrog Marinas offer lodging and food, a relative scarcity in this remote area. Crossing the Colorado on the ferry also makes it easy to access Bullfrog-Notom Road, which climbs for 60 miles through dramatic landscapes on its way to Capitol Reef National Park's otherwise remote Waterfold Pocket. The road ends at Notom, just four miles from the eastern entrance to Capitol Reef Park on Highway 24. Drivers can also turn west on the Burr Trail and follow back roads to Boulder, near the Escalante River Canyon.

Halls Crossing and Bullfrog Ferry

At the junction of Highways 95 and 276, a large sign lists the departure times for the ferry; note that these may be different than the times listed in the widely circulated flyer or on the website. Confirm the departure times (435/684-3088,

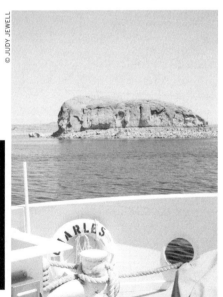

© JUDY JEWELL

SOUTHEASTERN CORNER

A ferry crosses Lake Powell from Halls Crossing to Bullfrog.

www.udot.utah.gov) before making the 42-mile journey to Halls Crossing.

The crossing time for the three-mile trip from Halls Crossing to Bullfrog is 27 minutes. Fares are $25 for cars, which includes the driver and all passengers, $10 bicycles and foot passengers, and $15 motorcycles. Vehicles longer than 20 feet pay $1.50 per foot.

Ferry service runs late April-early October, and there's a trip every other hour daily beginning with the 9am boat from Halls Landing, which then leaves Bullfrog at 10am The final ferry from Halls Crossing departs at 3pm, and the final ferry from Bullfrog departs at 4pm The ferry does not run early October-late April.

If drought or downstream demand lowers the level of Lake Powell beyond a certain point, there may not be enough water for the ferry to operate. If this is the case, there will be notices about the ferry's status at just about every park visitors center in southern Utah.

For reservations and information regarding lodging, camping, tours, boating, and recreation at both Halls Crossing and Bullfrog Marina, contact **Lake Powell Resorts & Marinas** (888/896-3829, www.lakepowell.com).

Arriving at Halls Crossing by road, you'll first reach a small store offering three-bedroom units in trailer houses and an RV park. Continue for 0.5 miles on the main road to the boat ramp and **Halls Crossing Marina** (435/684-2261). The marina has a larger store (groceries and fishing and boating supplies), tours to Rainbow Bridge, a boat-rental office (fishing, waterskiing, and houseboats), a gas dock, slips, and storage. The **ranger station** is nearby, although rangers are usually out on patrol; look for their vehicle in the area if the office is closed.

On the western side of the lake, **Bullfrog Marina** is more like a small town (albeit one run by Aramark), with a **visitors center** (435/684-7420), a clinic, stores, a service station, and a handsome hotel and restaurant. The marina

rents boats ranging from kayaks ($45 per day) to 12-person party boats ($600 per day) to houseboats ($4,320-15,000 per week), but for guided boat tours of Lake Powell, you'll have to go to the Wahweap Marina near Page, Arizona.

Defiance House Lodge (888/896-3829, www.lakepowell.com, from $146) offers comfortable lake-view accommodations and the **Anasazi Restaurant** (breakfast, lunch, and dinner daily summer, $9-32). The front desk at the lodge also handles family units (well-equipped trailers, about $300 per night), an RV park ($46), and houseboat rentals (from $750 per day, 3-day minimum). Showers, a laundry room, a convenience store, and a post office are at **Trailer Village.** Ask the visitors center staff or rangers for directions to primitive camping areas with vehicle access elsewhere along Bullfrog Bay.

Bullfrog Marina can be reached from the north via paved Highway 276. It is 40 miles between Bullfrog and the junction with Highway 95. Ticaboo, 20 miles north of Bullfrog, has another good lodging option. The **Ticaboo Lodge** (435/788-2110 or 800/842-2267, from $122) is a hotel with a swimming pool, a restaurant, and a service-station complex that pretty much constitutes all of Ticaboo.

NATURAL BRIDGES TO LAKE POWELL VIA HIGHWAY 95

If the Lake Powell ferry schedule doesn't match your travel plans, Highway 95 will quickly get you across the Colorado River to the junction with Highway 24 at Hanksville.

Hite

In 1883 Cass Hite came to Glen Canyon in search of gold. He found some at a place later named Hite City, which set off a small gold rush. Cass and a few of his relatives operated a small store and post office, which were the only services for many miles. Travelers who wanted to cross the Colorado River here had the difficult task of swimming their animals across. Arthur Chaffin, a later resident, put through the first road and opened a ferry service in 1946. The Chaffin Ferry served uranium prospectors and adventurous motorists until the lake backed up to the spot in 1964. A steel bridge now spans the Colorado River upstream from Hite Marina. Cass Hite's store and the ferry site are underwater about five miles down the lake from Hite Marina.

Beyond Hite, on the tiny neck of land between the Colorado River bridge and the Dirty Devil bridge, an unmarked dirt road turns north. Called Hite Road, or Orange Cliffs Road, this long and rugged road eventually links up with backcountry routes—including the Flint Trail—in the Maze District of Canyonlands National Park.

The uppermost marina on Lake Powell, Hite is 141 lake miles from Glen Canyon Dam. It is hit hard when water levels drop in Lake Powell, which has been most of the time in recent years. When water is available, boats can continue up the lake to the mouth of Dark Canyon in Cataract Canyon at low water or into Canyonlands National Park at high water. During times of low water, the boat ramp is often high above the lake. Hite tends to be quieter than the other marinas and is favored by some anglers and families. Facilities include a small **store** with gas, three-bedroom housekeeping units in trailer houses (about $300), and a primitive **campground** (free) with no drinking water. Primitive camping is also available nearby, off Highway 95 at Dirty Devil, Farley Canyon, White Canyon, Blue Notch, and other locations. A **ranger station** (435/684-2457) is occasionally open; look for the rangers' vehicle at other times. Contact **Lake Powell Resorts & Marinas** (888/896-3829, www.lakepowell.com) for accommodations reservations.

PAGE, ARIZONA

Although the town of Page is hot, busy, and not particularly appealing, it is the largest community anywhere near Lake Powell, and it offers travelers a number of places to stay and eat. The town overlooks Lake Powell and Glen Canyon Dam; the large Wahweap Resort and Marina is just six miles away.

Accommodations

Nearly all Page motels are on or near Lake Powell Boulevard (U.S. 89L), a 3.25-mile loop that branches off the main highway. Page is a busy place in summer, however, and a call ahead is a good idea if you don't want to chase around town looking for vacancies. Expect to pay top dollar for views of the lake. The summer rates listed here drop in winter (Nov.-Mar.).

In a way, the most appealing lodgings are in the small apartments-turned-motels on and around 8th Avenue, a quiet residential area two blocks off Lake Powell Boulevard. These apartments date back to 1958-1959, when they housed supervisors for the dam construction project. One such place is **Bashful Bob's Motel** (750 S. Navajo Dr., 928/645-3919, www.bashfulbobsmotel.com, from $39), a great little budget place with simple two-bedroom apartments, all with kitchenettes. **Debbie's Hide A Way** (117 8th Ave., 928/645-1224, www.debbieshideaway.com, from $99) is another place with a personal touch and a quiet garden in back; all guest rooms are suites with kitchens. Debbie's also has a two-bedroom apartment ($75) a couple of blocks from the motel. **Lulu's Sleep Ezze** (105 8th Ave., 928/608-0273 or 800/553-6211, www.lulussleepezzemotel.com, from $95, cash discount) is especially sweet.

Courtyard Page (600 Clubhouse Dr., 928/645-5000 or 877/905-4495, www.marriott.com, from $159) is a good chain hotel with a great setting, with views, a restaurant, a pool, a spa, an exercise room, and an adjacent 18-hole golf course.

Food

Dam Bar and Grill (644 N. Navajo Dr., 928/645-2161, 5pm-11pm daily, $8-25), in the

Dam Plaza, serves up steaks, barbecue, seafood, pasta, and sandwiches; it also has a sports bar. **Fiesta Mexicana** (201 S. Lake Powell Blvd., 928/645-3999, 11am-9pm daily, $8-15) is a busy but friendly little Mexican place (and here in Arizona, it's easy to get a margarita).

West of Canyonlands

It's a lonely road that leads north from the Glen Canyon Recreational Area and Lake Powell to I-70, just west of the town of Green River. The crossroads town of Hanksville is a good place to gas up (don't expect any bargains on gas) and grab a burger, and Goblin Valley State Park is worth the detour. Highway 24 north of Hanksville also provides access to Canyonlands National Park's Maze District and the incredible rock art in the park's Horseshoe Canyon Unit.

HANKSVILLE

Even by Utah standards, tiny Hanksville (population just over 200) is pretty remote. Ebenezer Hanks and other Mormon settlers founded this out-of-the-way community in 1882 along the Fremont River, then known as the Dirty Devil River. The isolation attracted polygamists like Hanks and other fugitives from the law. Butch Cassidy and his gang found refuge in the rugged canyon country of "Robbers' Roost," east of town. Several houses and the old stone church on Center Street, one block south of the highway, survive from the 19th century.

Travelers exploring this scenic region find Hanksville a handy if lackluster stopover; Capitol Reef National Park is to the west, Lake Powell and the Henry Mountains are

© JUDY JEWELL

SOUTHEASTERN CORNER

This waterwheel is the most scenic thing in the crossroads town of Hanksville.

to the south, the remote Maze District of Canyonlands National Park is to the east, and Goblin Valley State Park is to the north.

Wolverton Mill

E. T. Wolverton built this ingenious mill during the 1920s at his gold-mining claims in the Henry Mountains. A 20-foot waterwheel, still perfectly balanced, powered ore-crushing machinery and a sawmill. Owners of claims at the mill's original site didn't like a steady stream of tourists coming through to see the mill, so it was moved to the BLM office at Hanksville. Drive south 0.5 miles on 100 West to see the mill and some of its original interior mechanism.

Accommodations

Whispering Sands Motel (68 E. 100 N., 435/542-3238, from $89) has spacious guest rooms with cable TV and phones. In the center of town, the **Red Rock Campground** (435/542-3235 or 800/894-3242, mid-Mar.-Oct., $28 RVs) has showers, laundry, and a restaurant.

Food

Hanksville's restaurants cluster at the south end of town; don't expect anything fancy. The **Red Rock** (26 E. 100 N., 435/542-3235, 8am-8pm or later daily Apr.-Oct., $9-23) is at the campground, with home cooking, beer, and wine. **Blondie's Eatery** (3 N. Hwy. 95, 435/542-3255, 7am-9pm daily, $5-13) is a casual sit-down place with chicken and burgers across from Whispering Sands motel. **Stan's Burger Shack** (140 S. Hwy. 95, 435/542-3441, 7am-10pm daily, $5-8), at the Chevron station, is more a fast-food burger joint that's a step up from the chains.

Information and Services

The **Bureau of Land Management** (435/542-3461) has a field station 0.5 miles south of Highway 24 on 100 West, with information on road conditions, hiking, camping, and the buffalo herd in the Henry Mountains.

◖ GOBLIN VALLEY STATE PARK

Thousands of rock formations, many with goblin-like "faces," inhabit Goblin Valley State Park (435/564-8110, reservations 800/322-3770, www.reserveamerica.com, year-round, $7 per vehicle day-use, $16 camping). All of these so-called goblins have weathered out of the Entrada Formation, here a soft red sandstone and even softer siltstone. **Carmel Canyon Trail** (1.5-mile loop) begins at the northeast side of the parking lot at road's end, then drops down to the desert floor and a strange landscape of goblins, spires, and balanced rocks. Just wander around at your whim; this is a great place for the imagination. A 1.3-mile trail connects the campground and the goblin-studded Carmel Canyon Trail.

Curtis Bench Trail begins on the road between the parking lot and the campground and goes south to a viewpoint of the Henry Mountains; cairns mark the 1.5-mile (one-way) route.

The turnoff from Highway 24 is at milepost 137, which is 21 miles north of Hanksville and 24 miles south of I-70; follow signs west five miles on a paved road, then south seven miles on a gravel road.

Although there are off-road vehicle and motorcycle riding areas just west of the park, bicycling is limited to the park's roads. However, 12 miles north, the **Temple Mountain Bike Trail** traverses old mining roads, ridges, and wash bottoms. Popular hikes near the state park include the Little Wild Horse and Bell Canyons Loop, Chute and Crack Canyons Loop, and Wild Horse Canyon. The park is also a good base for exploring the **San Rafael Swell** area to the northwest.

Camping at Goblin Valley is a real treat; the late-evening and early-morning sun makes the sandstone spires glow. If you're not much of a camper, consider booking one

© PAUL LEVY

Goblin Valley State Park

of the park's two yurts ($60). They're tucked back among the rock formations, and each is equipped with bunk beds and a futon, a swamp cooler, and a propane stove. There are only 26 camping sites, so it's best to reserve well in advance.

GREEN RIVER

Green River (population about 950) is, except for a handful of motels and a lively tavern, pretty run-down, but it's the only real settlement on the stretch of I-70 between Salina and the Colorado border. Travelers can stop for a night or a meal, set off on a trip down the Green River, or use the town as a base for exploring the scenic San Rafael Swell country nearby.

Green River is known for its melons. In summer, stop at roadside stands and partake of wondrous cantaloupes and watermelons. The blazing summer heat and ample irrigation water make such delicacies possible. **Melon Days** celebrates the harvest on the third weekend of September with a parade, a city fair, music, a canoe race, games, and lots of melons.

John Wesley Powell River History Museum

Stop by this fine museum (1765 E. Main St., 435/564-3427, www.johnwesleypowell.com, 8am-7pm daily summer, call for hours fall-spring, $6 adults, $2 ages 3-12) to learn about Powell's daring expeditions down the Green and Colorado Rivers in 1869 and 1871-1872. An excellent multimedia presentation about both rivers uses narratives from Powell's trips. Historic riverboats on display include a replica of Powell's *Emma Dean.*

Labyrinth and Stillwater Canyons

The Green River's Labyrinth and Stillwater Canyons are downstream, between the town of Green River and the river's confluence with the Colorado River in Canyonlands National Park. Primarily a canoeing or kayaking river, the Green River at this point is calm and wide as it passes into increasingly deep, rust-colored

SOUTHEASTERN CORNER

canyons. This isn't a wilderness river; regular powerboats can also follow the river below town to the confluence with the Colorado River and head up the Colorado to Moab, 2-3 days and 186 river miles away.

The most common trip on this portion of the Green River begins just south of town and runs south through the Labyrinth Canyon, ending at Mineral Bottom, a distance of 68 river miles. **Moab Rafting and Canoe Company** (805 N. Main St., Moab, 435/259-7722, http://moab-rafting.com, $625 for a 5-day trip) offers this trip in canoes and has rentals available. **Sherry Griffith Expeditions** (435/259-8229 or 800/332-2439, www.griffithexp.com, $900 for a 5-day trip), also based in Moab, offers the same trip in kayaks. For longer excursions, inquire about special 10-day guided trips that go all the way down the Green to its confluence with the Colorado River. Alternatively, you can plan your own self-guided trip down the Green River. **Tex's Riverways** (435/259-5101, www.texsriverways.com) offers canoe and touring kayak rentals and all the other equipment you need to outfit a multiday trip, plus shuttle services to and from the river. Permits are required to paddle in Labyrinth Canyon; they're free and available to download from the BLM website (www.blm.gov) or can be picked up in town at the John Wesley Powell Museum (1765 E. Main St.) or Green River State Park (150 S. Green River Blvd.).

Crystal Geyser

With some luck, you'll catch the spectacle of this cold-water geyser on the bank of the Green River. The gusher shoots as high as 60 feet, but only 3-4 times daily, so you may have to spend half a day here in order to see it. The eruption, typically lasting seven minutes, is powered by carbon dioxide and other gases. A 2,267-foot-deep petroleum test well drilled in 1935-1936 concentrated the geyser flow, but thick layers of old travertine deposits attest that

mineral-laden springs have long been active at this site. Colorful newer travertine forms delicate terraces around the opening and down to the river. The orange and dark red of the minerals and algae make this a pretty spot, even if the geyser is only quietly gurgling.

Crystal Geyser is 10 miles south of Green River by road; boaters should look for the geyser deposits on the left, about 4.5 river miles downstream from Green River. From downtown, drive east one mile on Main Street, turn left, and go three miles on signed Frontage Road (near milepost 4), then turn right and go six miles on a narrow paved road just after going under a railroad overpass. The road goes under I-70, then is unpaved for the last 4.5 miles; keep right at a fork near some power lines. Some washes have to be crossed, so the drive isn't recommended after rains. When the weather is fair, cars shouldn't have a problem. Buildings and antennas passed on the way belong to the Utah Launch Complex of White Sands Missile Range. From 1963 to 1979 several hundred Pershing and Athena rockets blasted off here for targets at White Sands, New Mexico, 400 miles away.

Accommodations

Green River has a few rather shabby older motels as well as newer chain motels to choose from; unless noted, each of the following has a swimming pool—a major consideration in this often sweltering desert valley.

One of the older places, the **Robber's Roost Motel** (325 W. Main St., 435/564-3452, www.rrmotel.com, from $39) is cheap and basic and right in the center of town; it does not have a pool. Green River's newer motels are on the east end of town. The **Super 8** (1248 E. Main St., 435/564-8888 or 800/888-8888, $75), out by I-70's exit 162, is a good value, with spacious, comfortable guest rooms. The **Holiday Inn Express** (1845 E. Main St., 435/564-4439, $124) is predictably comfortable—not a bad thing if you're coming out of the desert or off the river.

The nicest place to stay in town is 〖 **The River Terrace** (1740 E. Main St., 435/564-3401 or 877/564-3401, www.river-terrace.com, from $106), with somewhat older but large guest rooms, some of which overlook the Green River and some with balconies. Breakfast is included, plus there's a restaurant adjacent to the hotel. The very pleasant outdoor pool area is flanked by patios and shaded tables.

CAMPGROUNDS

Several campgrounds, all with showers, offer sites for tents and RVs year-round. **Green River State Park** (150 S. Green River Blvd., 435/564-3633 or 800/322-3770, www.reserveamerica.com, year-round, $5 day-use, $16 camping) has a great setting near the river; it's shaded by large cottonwoods and has a boat ramp. **Shady Acres RV Park** (350 E. Main St., 435/564-8290 or 800/537-8674, www.shadyacresrv.com, year-round, $20 tents, $27-35 hookups, $42 cabins) is not all that shady and may be a bit too close to the noisy road for tent campers; it has a store, showers, and a laundry. **Green River KOA** (235 S. 1780 E., 435/564-3651, $29 tents,

$46 hookups, from $64 cabins) has campsites and cabins (bring sleeping bags) across from the John Wesley Powell Museum and next to the Tamarisk Restaurant.

Food

Other than motel restaurants and fast food, the one really notable place to eat in Green River is 〖 **Ray's Tavern** (25 S. Broadway, 435/564-3511, 11am-10pm daily, $8-26). Ray's doesn't look like much from the outside, but inside you'll find a friendly welcome, tables made from tree trunks, and some of the best steaks, chops, and burgers in this part of the state. Don't expect haute cuisine, but the food is good, and the atmosphere is truly Western; beer drinkers will be glad for the selection of regional microbrews after a long day navigating the river or driving desert roads.

Directly adjacent to the River Terrace hotel is a decent American-style restaurant, **The Tamarisk** (880 E. Main St., 435/564-8109, 7am-10pm daily, $6-27), with riverfront views.

BACKGROUND

The Colorado Plateau

Southeastern Utah's two national parks and its preserves of public land are all part of the Colorado Plateau, a high, broad physiographic province that includes southern Utah, northern Arizona, southwest Colorado, and northwest New Mexico. This roughly circular plateau, nearly the size of Montana, also contains the Grand Canyon, the Navajo Nation, and the Hopi Reservation.

Created by a slow but tremendous uplift, and carved by magnificent rivers, the plateau is mostly between 3,000 and 6,000 feet elevation, with some peaks reaching nearly 13,000 feet.

Although much of the terrain is gently rolling, the Green and Colorado Rivers have sculpted remarkable canyons, buttes, mesas, arches, and badlands. Think of this area as a layer cake of rock that has been fractured by synclines, anticlines, and folds. Nongeologists can picture the rock layers as blankets on a bed, and then imagine how they look before the bed is made in the morning. This warping, which goes on deep beneath the earth's surface, has affected the overlying rocks, permitting the development of deeply incised canyons.

Isolated uplifts and foldings have formed

© PAUL LEVY

such features as the rock arches in Arches National Park, while the rounded Abajo and La Sal Mountains are examples of intrusive rock—an igneous layer that was formed below the earth's surface and later exposed by erosion.

GEOLOGY

When you visit southeastern Utah, one of the first things you're likely to notice are rocks. Vegetation is sparse, and the soil is thin, so there's not much to hide the geology here. Particularly stunning views are found where rivers have carved deep canyons through the rock layers.

By the standards of the American West, the rocks forming the Colorado Plateau have had it pretty easy. Although faults have cracked and uplifted rocks, and volcanoes have spewed lava across the plateau, it's nothing like the surrounding Rocky Mountains or Basin and Range provinces, both of which are the result of eons of violent geology. Mostly, sediments piled up, younger layers on top of older, then eroded, lifted up, and eroded some more.

Sedimentation

Water made this desert what it is today. Back before the continents broke apart and began drifting to their present-day locations, Utah was near the equator, just east of a warm ocean. Ancient seas washed over the land, depositing sand, silt, and mud. Layer upon layer, the soils piled up and over time were compressed into sandstones, limestones, and shales.

The ancestral Rocky Mountains rose to the east of the ocean, and just to their west, a trough-like basin formed and was intermittently flushed with seawater. Evaporation caused salts and other minerals to collect on the basin floor; when the climate became wetter, more water rushed in.

As the ancestral Rockies eroded, their bulk washed down into the basin. The sea level rose, washing in more mud and sand. When the seas receded, dry winds blew sand across the region, creating enormous dunes.

Over time, the North American continent drifted north, away from the equator, but this region remained near the sea and was regularly washed by tides, leaving more sand and silt. Just inland, freshwater lakes filled, then dried, and the lakebeds consolidated into shales. During wet periods, streams coursed across the area, carrying and then dropping their loads of mud, silt, and sand.

As the ancestral Rockies wore down to mere hills, other mountains rose, then eroded, contributing their sediments. A turn toward dry weather meant more dry winds, kicking up the sand and building it into massive dunes.

Then, about 15 million years ago, the sea-level plateau began to lift, slowly, steadily, and, by geologic standards, incredibly gently. Some areas were hoisted as high as 10,000 feet above sea level.

Erosion

As the Colorado Plateau rose, its big rivers carved deep gorges through the uplifting rocks. Today, the Green, Colorado, and San Juan Rivers are responsible for much of the dramatic scenery in southeastern Utah.

More subtle forms of erosion have also contributed to the plateau's present-day form. Water percolating down through the rock layers is one of the main erosive forces, washing away loose material and dissolving ancient salts, often leaving odd formations such as thin fins of resistant rock.

The many layers of sedimentary rocks forming the Colorado Plateau are all composed of different minerals and have varying densities, so it's not surprising that erosion affects each layer a bit differently. For instance, sandstones and limestones erode more readily than the harder mudstones or shales.

Erosion isn't limited to the force of water against rock. Rocks may be worn down or eaten away by a variety of forces, including wind, freezing and thawing, exfoliation (when sheets of rock peel off), oxidation, hydration and carbonation (chemical weathering), plant roots or

THE COLORADO PLATEAU

WYOMING

Flaming Gorge Reservoir

COLORADO

Rocky Mountains

Salt Lake City

Vernal

UTAH

15

Green River

6
191

Price

24

Green River

70

Grand Junction

70

Moab

La Sal Mtns

89

Aquarius Plateau

Waterpocket Fold

Henry Mtns

Abajo Mtns

Dolores River

Monticello

San Juan Mtns

NEVADA

Cedar City

Escalante

12

Kaiparowits Plateau

Lake Powell

191

Cortez

Durango

St. George

Grand Staircase

Kanab

89

▲ Navajo Mtn

San Juan River

15

Page

89A

Kaibito Plateau

Kayenta

Black Mesa

▲ Ship Rock

Farmington

491

550

Virgin River

160

Chuska Mountains

Colorado River

Grand Canyon

Tuba City

191

Painted Desert

Gallup

Williams

89

Little Colorado River

40

40

Flagstaff

Winslow

Holbrook

ARIZONA

NEW MEXICO

17

CA

N

0   50 mi

0   50 km

191

© AVALON TRAVEL

NATURE'S PALETTE

In Utah, you'll get used to seeing a lot of colorful rock formations. The color gives you clues to the composition and geologic history of the rock. In general:

- **Red rocks** are stained by rusty iron-rich sediments washed down from mountains and are a clue that erosion has occurred.

- **Gray or brown rocks** were deposited by ancient seas.

- **White rocks** are colored by their "glue," the limey remains of dissolved seashells that leach down and harden sandstones.

- **Black rocks** are volcanic in origin, though not all volcanic, or igneous, rocks are black. Igneous rocks are present in the La Sal, Abajo, and Henry Mountains near Canyonlands National Park. These mountains are "laccoliths," formed by molten magma that pushed through the sedimentary layers, leaking deeper into some layers than others and eventually forming broad dome-shaped protuberances, which were eroded into soft peaks, then carved by glaciers into the sharp peaks we see today.

animal burrows, and dissolving of soft rocks. The ever-deepening channel of the Colorado River through Canyonlands National Park, and the slow thinning of pedestals supporting Arches National Park's balanced rocks, are all clues that erosion continues unabated. In fact, the Colorado Plateau is still rising, forcing the various erosional forces to just keep taking bigger bites out of the landscape.

CLIMATE

The main thing for southeastern Utah travelers to remember is that they're in the desert.

The high-desert country of the Colorado Plateau is mostly between 3,000 and 6,000 feet in elevation. Annual precipitation ranges from an extremely dry 3 inches in some areas to about 10 inches in others. Mountainous regions—the Abajos and La Sals—are between 10,000 and 13,000 feet and receive abundant rainfall in summer and heavy snows in winter.

Sunny skies prevail through all four seasons. Spring comes early to the canyon country, with weather that's often windy and rapidly changing. Summer can make its presence known in April, although the real desert heat doesn't set in until late May or early June. Temperatures then soar into the 90s and 100s at midday,

although the dry air makes the heat more bearable. Early morning is the best time for travel in summer. A canyon seep surrounded by hanging gardens or a mountain meadow filled with wildflowers provides a refreshing contrast to the parched desert; other ways to beat the heat include hiking in the mountains and river rafting.

Summer thunderstorm season begins anywhere mid-June–August; huge billowing thunderstorm clouds bring refreshing rains and coolness. During this season, canyon hikers should be alert for flash flooding.

Autumn begins after the rains cease, usually in October, and lasts into November or even December; days are bright and sunny with ideal temperatures, but nights become cold. In both parks, evenings will be cool even in midsummer. Although the day may be baking hot, you'll need a jacket and a warm sleeping bag for the night.

Winter lasts only about two months at the lower elevations. Light snows on the canyon walls add new beauty to the rock layers. Nighttime temperatures commonly dip into the teens, which is too cold for most campers. Otherwise, winter can be a fine time for travel. Heavy snows rarely occur below 8,000 feet.

Flash Floods

Rainwater runs quickly off the rocky desert surfaces and into gullies and canyons. A summer thunderstorm or a rapid late-winter snowmelt can send torrents of mud and boulders rumbling down dry washes and canyons. Backcountry drivers, horseback riders, and hikers need to avoid hazardous locations when storms threaten or unseasonably warm winds blow on the winter snowpack.

Flash floods can sweep away anything in their path, including boulders, cars, and campsites. Do not camp or park in potential flash flood areas. If you come to a section of flooded roadway—a common occurrence on desert roads after storms—wait until the water goes down before crossing (it shouldn't take long). Summer lightning causes forest and brush fires, posing a danger to hikers who are foolish enough to climb mountains when storms threaten.

The bare rock and loose soils so common in the canyon country do little to hold back the flow of rain or meltwater. In fact, slickrock is effective at shedding water as fast as it comes in contact. Logs and other debris wedged high on canyon walls give proof enough of past floods.

FLORA

Within the physiographic province of the Colorado Plateau, several different life zones are represented.

In the low desert, shrubs eke out a meager existence. Climbing higher, you'll pass through grassy steppe, sage, and piñon-juniper woodlands to ponderosa pine. Of all these zones, the piñon-juniper is most common.

But it's not a lockstep progression of plant A at elevation X and plant B at elevation Z. Soils are an important consideration, with sandstones being more hospitable than shales. Plants will grow wherever the conditions will support them, and southeastern Utah's parks and public lands have many microenvironments that can lead to surprising plant discoveries. Look for different plants in these different habitats: slickrock (where cracks can gather enough soil to host a few plants), riparian (moist areas with the greatest diversity of life), and terraces and open space (the area between riverbank and slickrock, where shrubs dominate).

How Plants Survive in the Desert

Most of the plants you'll see in southeastern Utah are well adapted to desert life. Many are succulents, which have their own water storage systems in their fleshy stems or leaves. Cacti are the most obvious succulents; they swell with stored moisture during the spring, then slowly shrink and wrinkle as the stored moisture is used.

Other plants have different strategies for making the most of scarce water. Some, such as yucca, have deep roots, taking advantage of what moisture exists in the soil. The leaves of desert plants are often vertical, exposing less surface area to the sun. Leaves may also have very small pores, slowing transpiration, or stems coated with a resinous substance, which also slows water loss. Hairy or light-colored leaves help reflect sunlight.

Desert wildflowers are annuals; they bloom in the spring, when water is available, then form seeds, which can survive the dry hot summer, and die. A particularly wet spring means a bumper crop of wildflowers.

Even though mosses aren't usually thought of as desert plants, they are found growing in seeps along canyon walls and in cryptobiotic soils. When water is unavailable, mosses dry up; when the water returns, the moss quickly plumps up again.

Junipers have a fairly drastic way of dealing with water shortage. During a prolonged dry spell, a juniper tree can shut off the flow of water to one or more of its branches, sacrificing these branches to keep the tree alive.

Hanging Gardens

Watch for clumps of ferns and mosses lit with

maidenhair ferns, shooting stars, monkey flowers, columbine, orchids, and bluebells along canyon walls. These unexpectedly lush pockets are called "hanging gardens," gemlike islands of plantlife nestled into desert cliffs.

Hanging gardens take advantage of a unique microclimate created by the meeting of two rock layers: Navajo sandstone and Kayenta shale. Water percolates down through porous sandstone and, when it hits the denser shale layer, travels laterally along the top of the harder rock and emerges at cliff's edge. These little springs support lush plantlife.

Tamarisk

One of the Colorado Plateau's most common small trees, the nonnative tamarisk is also one of the peskiest. Imported from the Mediterranean and widely planted along the Colorado River to control erosion, the tamarisk has spread wildly, and its dense stands have crowded out native trees such as cottonwoods. Tamarisks are notoriously thirsty trees, sucking up vast amounts of water, but they give back little in the way of food or habitat for local wildlife. Their thick growth also increases the risk of fire. The National Park Service and the Bureau of Land Management are taking steps to control tamarisk; one big project is at the Sand Flats campground near Bluff.

Cryptobiotic Soil

Over much of the Colorado Plateau, the soil is alive. What looks like a grayish-brown crust is actually a dense network of filament-forming blue-green algae intertwined with soil particles, lichens, moss, green algae, and microfungi. This slightly sticky, crusty mass holds the soil together, slowing erosion. Its sponge-like consistency allows it to soak up water and hold it. Plants growing in cryptobiotic soil have a great advantage over plants rooted in dry, sandy soil.

Crytobiotic soils are extremely fragile. Make every effort to avoid stepping on them—stick to trails, slickrock, or rocks instead.

FAUNA

Although they're not thought of as great "wildlife parks" like Yellowstone or Denali, southeastern Utah's national parks are home to plenty of animals. However, desert animals are often nocturnal and go unseen by park visitors.

Rodents

Rodents include squirrels, packrats, kangaroo rats, chipmunks, and porcupines, most of which spend their days in burrows.

One of the few desert rodents out foraging during the day is the white-tailed antelope squirrel, which looks much like a chipmunk. Its white tail reflects the sunlight, and when it needs to cool down a bit, an antelope squirrel smears its face with saliva (yes, that probably would work for you too, but that's why you have sweat glands). The antelope squirrel lives at lower elevations; higher up you'll see golden-mantled ground squirrels.

Look for rabbits—desert cottontails and jackrabbits—at dawn and dusk. If you're rafting the Green or Colorado River, keep an eye out for beavers.

Kangaroo rats are particularly well adapted to desert life. They spend their days in cool burrows, eat only plants, and never drink water: Instead, a kangaroo rat metabolizes dry food in a way that produces water.

Prairie dogs live together in social groups called colonies or towns, which are laced with burrows, featuring a network of entrances for quick pops in and out of the ground. Prairie dogs are preyed on by badgers, coyotes, hawks, and snakes, so a colony will post lookouts who are constantly searching for danger. When threatened, the lookouts "bark" to warn the colony. Utah prairie dogs hibernate during the winter and emerge from their burrows to mate furiously in early April.

Bats

As night falls in canyon country, bats emerge

© EMILY ROTH

rattlesnake warming against a rock

from the nooks and crannies that protect them from the day's heat and begin to feed on mosquitoes and other insects. The tiny gray western pipistrelle is common. It flies early in the evening, feeding near streams, and can be spotted by its somewhat erratic flight. The pallid creature spends a lot of its time creeping across the ground in search of food, and it is a late-night bat. Another common bat, here and across the United States, is the prosaically named big brown bat.

Large Mammals

Mule deer are common across the region, as are coyotes. Other large mammals include the predators: mountain lions and coyotes. If you're lucky, you'll get a glimpse of a bobcat or a fox.

If you're hiking high-elevation trails early in the morning and see something that looks like a small dog in a tree, it's probably a gray fox. These small (5-10 pounds) foxes live in forested areas and have the catlike ability to climb trees. Kit foxes, which are even tinier than gray

foxes, with prominent ears and a big bushy tail, are common in Arches and Canyonlands. Red foxes also live across the plateau.

Desert bighorn sheep live in Arches and Canyonlands, and in other cliff-dominated terrains; look for them trotting across steep rocky ledges. In Arches, they're frequently sighted along U.S. 191 south of the visitors center. They also roam the talus slopes and side canyons near the Colorado River.

Reptiles

Reptiles are well-suited to desert life. As cold-blooded, or ectothermic, animals, their body temperature depends on the environment rather than on internal metabolism, and it's easy for them to keep warm in the desert heat. When it's cold, reptiles hibernate or drastically slow their metabolism.

The western whiptail lizard is common in Arches. You'll recognize it because its tail is twice as long as its body. Also notable is the western collared lizard, with a bright green body set off by a black collar.

Less flashy but particularly fascinating are the several species of parthenogenetic lizards. All of these lizards are female, and they reproduce by laying eggs that are clones of themselves. Best known is the plateau striped whiptail, but 6 of the 12 species of whiptail present in the area are all-female.

The northern plateau lizard is common at altitudes of about 3,000-6,000 feet. It's not choosy about its habitat—juniper-piñon woodlands, prairies, riparian woodlands, and rocky hillsides are all perfectly acceptable. This is the lizard you'll most often see scurrying across your campsite.

Rattlesnakes are present across the area, but given a chance, they'll get out of your way rather than strike. (Still, they are another good reason to wear sturdy boots.) The midget faded rattlesnake, a small subspecies of the western rattlesnake, lives in burrows and rock crevices and is mostly active at night. Although this

snake has especially toxic venom, full venom injections occur in only one-third of all bites.

Amphibians

Although they're not usually thought of as desert animals, a variety of frogs and toads live on the Colorado Plateau. Tadpoles live in wet springtime potholes as well as in streams and seeps. If you're camping in a canyon, you may be lucky enough to be serenaded by a toad chorus.

Bullfrogs are not native to the western United States, but since they were introduced in the early 1900s, they have flourished at the expense of native frogs and toads, whose eggs and tadpoles they eat.

The big round toes of the small spotted canyon tree frog make it easy to identify—that is, if you can see this well-camouflaged frog in the first place. These frogs are most active at night, spending their days on streamside rocks or trees.

Toads present in Utah's parks include the Great Basin spadefoot, red spotted toad, and western woodhouse toad.

Birds

Have you ever seen a bird pant? Believe it or not, that's how desert birds expel heat from their bodies. They allow heat to escape by drooping their wings away from their bodies, exposing thinly feathered areas (sort of like pulling up your shirt and using it to fan your torso).

The various habitats across the Colorado Plateau, such as piñon-juniper, perennial streams, dry washes, and rock cliffs, allow many species of bird to find homes. Birders will find the greatest variety of birds near rivers and streams. Other birds, such as golden eagles, kestrels (small falcons), and peregrine falcons nest high on cliffs and patrol open areas for prey. Common hawks include the red-tailed hawk and northern harrier; late-evening strollers may see great horned owls.

People usually detect the canyon wren by its lovely song; this small long-beaked bird nests in cavities along cliff faces. The related rock wren is—as its name implies—a rock collector: It paves a trail to its nest with pebbles, and the nest itself is lined with rocks. Another canyon bird, the white-throated swift, swoops and calls as it chases insects and mates, rather dramatically, in flight. Swifts are often seen near violet-green swallows (which are equally gymnastic fliers) in Canyonlands and Arches.

Several species of hummingbird (mostly black-chinned, but also broad-tailed and rufous) are often seen in the summer. Woodpeckers are also common, including the northern flicker and red-naped sapsucker, and flycatchers like Say's phoebe, western kingbird, and western wood pewee can be spotted too. Two warblers—the yellow and the yellow-rumped—are common in the summer, and Wilson's warbler stops in during spring and fall migrations. Horned larks are present year-round.

Mountain bluebirds are colorful, easy for a novice to identify, and common in Canyonlands and Arches.

Both the well-known scrub jay and its local cousin, the piñon jay, are noisy visitors to almost every picnic. Other icons of western avian life—the turkey vulture, the raven, and the magpie—are widespread and easily spotted.

Fish

Obviously, deserts aren't particularly known for their aquatic life, and the big rivers of the Colorado Plateau are now dominated by non-native species such as channel catfish and carp. Many of these fish were introduced as game fish. Native fish, like the six-foot, 100-pound Colorado pikeminnow, are now uncommon.

Spiders and Scorpions

Tarantulas, black widow spiders, and scorpions all live across the Colorado Plateau, and all are objects of many a visitor's phobias. Although the black widow spider's venom is toxic, tarantulas deliver only a mildly toxic bite (and they

rarely bite humans), and a scorpion's sting is about like that of a bee.

ENVIRONMENTAL ISSUES

Utah's national parks have generally been shielded from the environmental issues that play out in the rest of the state, which has always been business-oriented, with a heavy emphasis on extractive industries such as mining and logging.

The main environmental threats to the parks are consequences of becoming too popular. During the summer, auto and RV traffic can clog park roads, with particularly bad snarls at viewpoint parking areas.

Hikers also have an impact, especially when they tread on fragile cryptobiotic soil. Killing this living soil crust drastically increases erosion in an already easily eroded environment.

ATV Overkill

Off-road vehicles, or ATVs (all-terrain vehicles), have gone from being the hobby of a small group of off-road enthusiasts to being one of the fastest-growing recreational markets in the country. Although use of ATVs is prohibited in the national parks, these dune buggies on steroids are having a huge impact on public lands adjacent to the parks and on Bureau of Land Management (BLM) lands that are currently under study for designation as wilderness. The scope of the issue is easy to measure. In 1979 there were 9,000 ATVs registered in Utah. In 2010 there were over 120,000. In addition, the power and dexterity of the machines has greatly increased. Now essentially military-style assault machines that can climb near-vertical cliffs and clamber over any kind of terrain, ATVs are the new "extreme sports" toy of choice, and towns like Moab are now seeing more visitors coming to tear up the backcountry on ATVs than to mountain bike. The problem is that ATVs are extremely destructive to the delicate natural environment of the Colorado Plateau deserts and canyon lands, and the more powerful, roaring,

exhaust-belching machines put even the most remote and isolated areas within reach of large numbers of potentially destructive revelers.

Between the two camps—one that would preserve the public land and protect the ancient human artifacts found in remote canyons, the other that sees public land as a playground to be zipped over at high speed—is the BLM. The Moab BLM office has seemed to favor the ATV set, abdicating its role to protect the land and environment for all. Groups like Southern Utah Wilderness Alliance (SUWA, www.suwa.org) are constantly strategizing to force the BLM to comply with its responsibility for environmental stewardship of public land.

Nonnative Species

Nonnative species don't respect park boundaries, and several nonnative animals and plants have established strongholds in Utah's national parks, altering the local ecology by outcompeting native plants and animals.

Particularly invasive plants include tamarisk (salt cedar), cheatgrass, Russian knapweed, and Russian olive. Tamarisk is often seen as the most troublesome invader. This thirsty Mediterranean plant was imported in the 1800s as an ornamental shrub and was later planted by the Department of Agriculture to slow erosion along the banks of the Colorado River in Arizona. It rapidly took hold, spreading upriver at roughly 12 miles per year, and is now firmly established on all of the Colorado's tributaries, where it grows in dense stands. Tamarisk consumes a great deal of water and rarely provides food and shelter necessary for the survival of wildlife. It also outcompetes cottonwoods because tamarisk shade inhibits the growth of cottonwood seedlings.

Courthouse Wash in Arches National Park is one of several sites where the National Park Service has made an effort to control tamarisk. Similar control experiments have been established in nearby areas, mostly in small tributary canyons of the Colorado River.

History

The landscape isn't the only vivid aspect of southeastern Utah. The area's human history is also noteworthy. This part of the West has been inhabited for over 10,000 years, and there are remnants of ancient villages and panels of mysterious rock art in now remote canyons. More recently, colonization by Mormon settlers and the establishment of the national parks have brought human history back to this dramatic corner of the Colorado Plateau.

PREHISTORY

Beginning about 15,000 years ago, nomadic groups of Paleo-Indians traveled across the Colorado Plateau in search of game animals and wild plants, but they left few traces.

Nomadic bands of hunter-gatherers roamed the Colorado Plateau for at least 5,000 years. The climate was probably cooler and wetter when these first people arrived, with both food plants and game animals more abundant than today.

Agriculture was introduced from the south about 2,000 years ago, and it brought about a slow transition to a settled village life. The Fremont culture emerged in the northern part of the region and the Anasazi in the southern part. In some areas, including Arches, both groups lived contemporaneously. Although both

groups made pots, baskets, bowls, and jewelry, only the Anasazi constructed masonry villages. Thousands of stone dwellings, ceremonial kivas, and towers built by the Anasazi still stand. Both groups left behind intriguing rock art, either pecked in (petroglyphs) or painted (pictographs).

The Anasazi and Fremont departed from this region about 800 years ago, perhaps because of drought, warfare, or disease. Some of the Anasazi moved south and joined the Pueblo people of present-day Arizona and New Mexico. The fate of the Fremont people remains a mystery.

After the mid-1200s and until white settlers arrived in the late 1800s, small bands of nomadic Ute and Paiute moved through southern Utah. The Navajo began to enter Utah in the early 1800s. None of the three groups established firm control of the region north of the San Juan River, where the present-day national parks are located.

AGE OF EXPLORATION

The Old Spanish Trail, used 1829-1848, ran through Utah to connect New Mexico with California, crossing the Colorado River near present-day Moab. Fur trappers and mountain men, including Jedediah Smith, also traveled

ANASAZI OR ANCESTRAL PUEBLOAN?

As you travel through the Southwest, you may hear reference to the "Ancestral Puebloans." In this guide, we've chosen to use the more familiar name for these people–the Anasazi. The word *anasazi* is actually a Navajo term that archaeologists chose, thinking it meant "old people." A more literal translation is "enemy ancestors." For this reason, some consider the name inaccurate. The terminology is in flux, and which name you hear depends on whom you're talking to or where you are. The National Park Service now uses the more descriptive term Ancestral Puebloan. These prehistoric people built masonry villages and eventually moved south to Arizona and New Mexico, where their descendants, such as the Acoma, Cochiti, Santa Clara, Taos, and Hopi Mesas, live in modern-day pueblos.

southern Utah's canyons in search of beaver and other animals during the early 1800s; inscriptions carved into the sandstone record their passage. In 1859 the U.S. Army's Macomb Expedition made the first documented description of what is now Canyonlands National Park. Major John Wesley Powell's pioneering river expeditions down the Green and Colorado Rivers in 1869 and 1871-1872 filled in many blank areas on the maps.

MORMON SETTLEMENT

In 1849-1850, Mormon leaders in Salt Lake City took the first steps toward colonizing southern Utah. In 1855 a successful experiment in growing cotton along Santa Clara Creek near present-day St. George aroused considerable interest among the Mormons, and the same year, the Elk Ridge Mission was founded near present-day Moab. It lasted only a few months before skirmishes with the Utes led to the deaths of three Mormon settlers and sent the rest fleeing for their lives. Church members had better success when they returned to the area in 1877.

For sheer effort and endurance, the efforts of the Hole-in-the-Rock Expedition of 1879-1880 are remarkable. Sixty families with 83 wagons and more than 1,000 head of livestock crossed some of the West's most rugged canyon country in an attempt to settle at Montezuma Creek on the San Juan River. They almost didn't make it: A journey expected to take six weeks turned into a six-month ordeal. The exhausted company arrived on the banks of the San Juan River on April 5, 1880. Too tired to continue just 20 easy miles to Montezuma Creek, they stayed and founded the town of Bluff. The Mormons also established other towns in southeastern

Utah, relying on ranching, farming, and mining for their livelihoods. None of the communities in the region ever reached a large size; Moab is the biggest, with a current population of 5,500.

NATIONAL PARK MOVEMENT IN UTAH

In the early 1900s, people other than Native Americans, Mormon settlers, and government explorers began to notice that southern Utah was a remarkably scenic place and that it might be developed for tourism.

In 1909 a presidential Executive Order designated Mukuntuweap (now Zion) National Monument in Zion Canyon. Early homesteaders around Bryce took visiting friends and relatives to see the incredible rock formations, and pretty soon they found themselves in the tourism business. In 1923, when Bryce Canyon National Monument was dedicated, the Union Pacific Railroad took over the fledgling tourist camp and began building Bryce Lodge, and Bryce became a national park in 1928.

Like Bryce and Zion, Arches was also helped along by railroad executives looking to develop their own businesses. In 1929 President Herbert Hoover signed the legislation creating Arches National Monument.

During the 1960s the National Park Service responded to a huge increase in park visitation nationwide by expanding facilities, spurring Congress to change the status of several national monuments to national parks. Canyonlands became a national park in the 1960s, after a spate of uranium prospecting in the nuclear-giddy 1950s. Arches gained national park status in 1971.

The People

One of the oddest statistics about Utah is that it's the most urban of the country's western states. Eighty-five percent of the state's population of 2.8 million live in urban areas, and a full 80 percent reside in the Wasatch Front area. That means that there aren't many people in remote southeastern Utah. With the exception of Moab, there are no sizable communities in this part of the state. Even the undaunted Mormon settlers found this a forbidding place to settle during their 19th-century agrarian colonization of Utah.

Moab is known as a youthful and dynamic town, and its mountain bikers set the civic tone more than the Mormon Church. However, outside Moab, most small ranching communities in southeastern Utah are still deeply Mormon. It's a good idea to develop an understanding of Utah's predominant religion if you plan on spending any time here outside the parks and Moab.

LATTER-DAY SAINTS

One of the first things to know is that the term *Mormon* is rarely used by church members themselves. The church's proper title is the Church of Jesus Christ of Latter-day Saints, and members prefer to be called Latter-day Saints, Saints (usually this term is just used among church members), or LDS. While calling someone a Mormon isn't wrong, it's not quite as respectful.

The religion is based in part on the Book of Mormon, the name given to a text derived from a set of golden plates found by Joseph Smith in 1827 in western New York State. Smith claimed to have been led by an angel to the plates, which were covered with a text written in "reformed Egyptian." A farmer by upbringing, Smith translated the plates and published an English-language version of the Book of Mormon in 1830.

The Book of Mormon tells the story of the lost tribes of Israel, which, according to Mormon teachings, migrated to North America and became the ancestors of today's Native Americans. According to the Book of Mormon, Jesus also journeyed to North America, and the book includes teachings and prophecies that Christ supposedly gave to the ancient Native Americans.

The most stirring and unifying aspect of Mormon history is the incredible westward migration made by the small, fiercely dedicated band of Mormon pioneers in the 1840s. Smith and his followers were persecuted in New York and then in their newly founded utopian communities in Ohio, Missouri, and Illinois. After Smith was murdered near Carthage, Illinois, in 1844, the group decided to press even farther westward toward the frontier, led by church president Brigham Young. The journey across the then very Wild West to the Great Salt Lake basin was made by horse, wagon, or handcart—hundreds of Mormon pioneers pulled their belongings across the Great Plains in small carts. The first group of Mormon pioneers reached what is now the Salt Lake City area in 1847. The bravery and tenacity of the group's two-year migration forms the basis of many Utah residents' fierce pride in their state and their religion.

Most people know that LDS members are clean-living, family-focused people who eschew alcohol, tobacco, and stimulants, including caffeine. This can make it a little tough for visitors to feed their own vices, and indeed, it may make what formerly seemed like a normal habit feel a little more sinister. But Utah has loosened up a lot in the last decade or so, largely thanks to having hosted the 2002 Winter Olympics, and it's really not too hard to find a place to have a beer with dinner, although you may have to make a special request. Towns near the national parks are particularly used to hosting

non-Mormons, and residents attach virtually no stigma to waking up with a cup of coffee or winding down with a glass of wine.

SOUTHERN UTAH'S NATIVE AMERICANS

It's an oddity of history that most visitors to Utah's national parks will see much more evidence of the state's ancient native residents—in the form of eerie rock art, stone pueblos, and storehouses—than they will of today's remaining Native Americans. The prehistoric residents of the canyons of southeastern Utah left their mark on the land but largely moved on. The fate of the ancient Fremont people has been lost to history, and the abandonment of Anasazi, or Ancestral Puebloan, villages is a mystery still being unearthed by archaeologists. When the Mormons arrived in the 1840s, isolated bands of Native Americans lived in the river canyons. Federal reservations were granted to several of these groups.

Ute

Several bands of Utes, or Núuci, ranged over large areas of central and eastern Utah and adjacent Colorado. Originally hunter-gatherers, they acquired horses around 1800 and became skilled raiders. Customs adopted from Plains people included the use of rawhide, tepees, and the travois, a sled used to carry goods. The discovery of gold in southern Colorado and the pressures of farmers there and in Utah forced the Utes to move and renegotiate treaties many times. They now have the large Uintah and Ouray Indian Reservation in northeast Utah, the small White Mesa Indian Reservation in southeast Utah, and the Ute Mountain Indian Reservation in southwest Colorado and northwest New Mexico.

Navajo

Calling themselves Diné, the Navajo moved into the San Juan River area around 1600. The Navajo have proved exceptionally adaptable in learning new skills from other cultures: Many Navajo crafts, clothing, and religious practices have come from Native American, Spanish, and Anglo neighbors. The Navajo were the first in the area to move away from hunting and gathering lifestyles, relying instead on the farming and shepherding techniques they had learned from the Spanish. The Navajo are one of the largest Native American groups in the country, with 16 million acres of exceptionally scenic land in southeast Utah and adjacent Arizona and New Mexico. The Navajo Nation's headquarters is at Window Rock, Arizona.

ESSENTIALS

Getting There

If you're driving from other points in North America, Utah is easy to reach. The parks are east of I-15, which runs parallel to the Rocky Mountains from Montana to Southern California. And they're south of I-70, which links Denver to I-15.

International travelers flying into the region have numerous options. Salt Lake City is convenient as a terminus for travelers who want to make a road-trip loop tour through all of Utah's parks. For other travelers, Utah's national parks may be best seen as part of a longer U.S. road trip. Many European travelers fly into Denver, rent vehicles or RVs, cross the Rocky Mountains, and explore the parks of southern Utah and perhaps the Grand Canyon on the way to Las Vegas, whence they return.

Also note that there are no scheduled flights from Salt Lake City to Moab, the only airport in southeastern Utah with commuter flights. If you want to fly into Moab, you have to fly from Denver on Great Lakes Airlines (800/554-5111, www.flygreatlakes.com).

Public transportation, like regularly scheduled flights, is almost nonexistent in southeastern

4 WHEELERS/MOTORCYCLIST ONLY

Utah and the parks; you'll need your own vehicle to explore this corner of the state.

FROM SALT LAKE CITY
Many tours of Utah's national parks begin in Salt Lake City. Its busy airport and plethora of hotels make it an easy place to begin and end a trip.

Airport
Salt Lake City is a hub for Delta Airlines, and the other major domestic airlines have regular flights into **Salt Lake City International Airport** (SLC, 776 N. Terminal Dr., 801/575-2400, www.slcairport.com). The airport is an easy seven miles west of downtown; reach it via I-80 or North Temple Boulevard.

You can't fly from Salt Lake City to Moab, at the heart of southeastern Utah's national parks; you have to drive.

The Salt Lake City airport has three terminals; in each you'll find a ground transportation information desk, restaurants, motel and hotel courtesy phones, and car rentals (all the major companies are either on-site or a short shuttle ride away). Terminal 2 houses Zion's First National Bank for currency exchange. Terminal 3 is dedicated to international arrivals and departures.

Train
The only passenger train through Salt Lake City is Amtrak's *California Zephyr,* which heads west to Reno and Oakland and east to Denver and Chicago four times a week. **Amtrak** (station 340 S. 600 W., 800/872-7245, www.amtrak.com) prices tickets as airlines do, with discounts for advance booking, special seasonal fares, and other discounts available. Amtrak office hours are irregular and timed to meet the trains, so call first.

Long-Distance Bus
Salt Lake City is at a crossroads of several major highways and has good bus service from **Greyhound** (160 W. South Temple,

801/355-9579 or 800/231-2222, www.greyhound.com). Generally speaking, buses run north and south along I-15 and east and west along I-80; you won't be able to take the bus to any of Utah's national parks.

Car
From Salt Lake City, it's a long 238-mile drive to Moab, the center for exploring Arches and Canyonlands National Parks. The fastest route takes you south from Salt Lake City on I-15, cutting east at Spanish Fork on U.S. 6/89 to Price, south to Green River and I-70, and then to Moab on U.S. 191. Dramatic scenery highlights the entire length of this four-hour drive.

You'll find all of the major car rental companies at the Salt Lake City airport (www.slcairport.com).

RV and Motorcycle Rentals
Expect to pay $1,000-1,800 per week to rent an RV, depending on the season and the size of the vehicle; small travel trailers are less expensive.

Access RV Rental (2240 S. State St., Salt Lake City, 801/936-1200 or 800/327-6910, http://rent-motorhome.com) is a local company with relatively good rates on RV rentals. **Cruise America** (4125 S. State St., Salt Lake City, 801/288-0930, www.cruiseamerica.com) is a larger company with RV rentals available. **El Monte RV** (250 U.S. 89, North Salt Lake City, 888/337-2214, www.elmonterv.com) also provides rentals.

Rent a BMW motorcycle ($110-200 per day) from Salt Lake City-area **Street Eagle** (339 W. 9000 S., Sandy, 801/658-7368 or 800/717-7970, www.streeteagle.com).

Accommodations
Salt Lake City has many hotel rooms across all price categories. We've included a few of our favorites here. Although most aren't airport hotels, the airport is pretty easy to get to from all of them.

If you're driving into town and just want to find a hotel room fast, head south and west of downtown, where chain hotels proliferate.

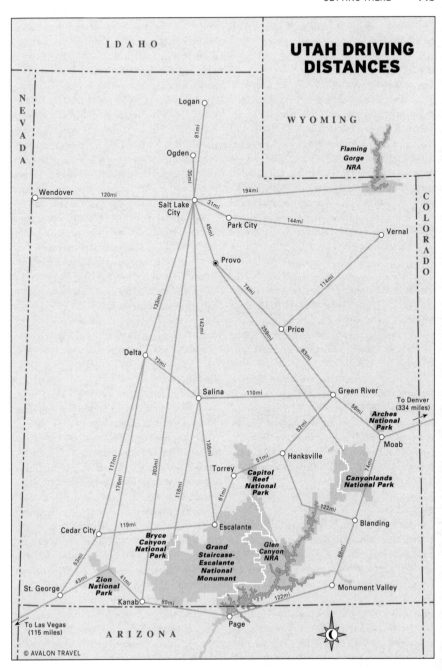

UTAH DRIVING DISTANCES

IDAHO

WYOMING

NEVADA

COLORADO

Flaming Gorge NRA

Logan

Ogden

81mi

35mi

Wendover

120mi

Salt Lake City

31mi

194mi

Park City

144mi

Vernal

45mi

Provo

74mi

114mi

133mi

142mi

Price

259mi

63mi

Delta

72mi

Salina

110mi

Green River

56mi

To Denver (334 miles)

Arches National Park

52mi

Moab

51mi

Hanksville

74mi

117mi

303mi

136mi

Torrey

Capitol Reef National Park

Canyonlands National Park

61mi

118mi

122mi

Cedar City

119mi

Escalante

Blanding

Bryce Canyon National Park

Grand Staircase-Escalante National Monumant

Glen Canyon NRA

88mi

53mi

St. George

43mi

Zion National Park

41mi

Kanab

80mi

122mi

Monument Valley

To Las Vegas (115 miles)

Page

ARIZONA

© AVALON TRAVEL

The area around 600 South and 200 West is especially fertile ground for mid-priced hotels.

UNDER $50

The Avenues Hostel (107 F St., 801/363-3855, www.saltlakehostel.com, $18 dorm, $40 d, only half have private baths), one mile east of Temple Square, offers lodging with the use of a kitchen, a TV room, and laundry. Information-packed bulletin boards list city sights and goings-on, and you'll meet travelers from all over the world. Reservations (with first night's deposit) are advised in the busy summer travel and winter ski seasons. From downtown, head east on South Temple Street to F Street, then turn north and go two blocks.

$50-100

The **Howard Johnson Express Inn** (121 N. 300 W., 801/521-3450 or 800/541-7639, www.hojo.com, from $64) is an older but well-maintained motor-court motel near Temple Square with a pool, complimentary continental breakfast, and free HBO.

Just east of Temple Square is the pleasant, well-maintained **Carlton Hotel** (140 E. South Temple, 801/355-3418 or 800/633-3500, www.carltonhotel-slc.com, from $74). The Carlton is an older hotel in a great location and offers guest laundry, an exercise room, a sauna, a hot tub, and in-room VCRs with free movies; there are also five suites.

$100-150

On the campus of the University of Utah, the **University Guest House and Conference Center** (110 S. Ft. Douglas Blvd., 801/587-1000 or 888/416-4075, www.universityguesthouse.com, from $95) is a good choice if you want a comfortable room, free parking, and nice walks nearby (check out the Red Butte Garden). Good restaurants are nearby, and downtown is a short drive or light-rail trip away.

Comfortable guest rooms, an outdoor pool, and a better-than-average included continental breakfast make the **Comfort Inn Airport** (200 N. Admiral Byrd Rd., 801/537-7444 or 800/535-8742, www.comfortinn.com, $129 and up) an appealing place to spend a night.

The **Radisson Hotel Salt Lake City Airport** (2177 W. North Temple, 801/364-5800 or 800/967-9033, www.radisson.com, $112 and up) is an attractive lodge-like building with nicely furnished guest rooms. Guests receive a complimentary continental breakfast and newspaper, and in the evenings there's a manager's reception with free beverages. Facilities include a pool, a spa, and a fitness room. Suites come with a loft bedroom area. There's quite a range in room rates, and package rates and promotions can bring the rates down dramatically. At the **Airport Hilton** (5151 Wiley Post Way, 801/539-1515 or 800/999-3736, www1.hilton.com, from $135), guest rooms are spacious and nicely furnished, and facilities include two pools, a putting green, a sports court, and an exercise room and whirlpool. The hotel even has its own lake.

OVER $150

If you really want to do Salt Lake City in style, two downtown hotels are good places to splurge. **Hotel Monaco** (15 W. 200 S., 801/595-0000 or 877/294-9710, www.monaco-saltlakecity.com, from $219) occupies a grandly renovated historic office building in a convenient spot in the middle of downtown; on the main floor is Bambara, one of the most sophisticated restaurants in Utah. Guest rooms are sumptuously furnished with real élan: This is no anonymous upscale hotel in beige and mauve. Expect wild colors and contrasting fabrics, lots of flowers, and excellent service. Facilities include an on-site fitness center, meeting rooms, and concierge and valet services. Pets are welcome, and if you forgot your own pet, the hotel will deliver a companion goldfish to your room. Room rates vary greatly; check the website to discover unexpected bargains.

The gigantic **Grand America Hotel and Suites** (75 E. 600 S., 800/533-3525, www.grandamerica.com, $309 and up), is Salt Lake City's take on the Vegas fantasy hotel. A block square (that's 10 acres in this land of long blocks), its 24 stories contain 775 guest rooms, more than half of them suites. Guest rooms have luxury-level amenities; expect all the perks and niceties that modern hotels can offer.

Camping

Of the several commercial campgrounds around the periphery of Salt Lake City, **Camp VIP/Salt Lake City KOA** (1350 W. North Temple, 801/328-0224, www.koa.com) is the most convenient, located between downtown and the airport. It offers tent sites (from $27) and RV sites (from $47) year-round with showers, a swimming pool, a game room, a playground, a store, and laundry. From I-15 northbound, take exit 308 onto I-80; go west 1.3 miles on I-80, exit north on Redwood Road (Hwy. 68) and go 0.5 miles, then turn right and continue another 0.5 miles on North Temple. From I-15 southbound, take exit 310 and go south 1.5 miles on 900 West, then turn right and drive less than one mile on North Temple. From I-80 take either the North Temple exit or Redwood Road (Hwy. 68), and go 0.5 miles, then turn right and continue another 0.5 miles on North Temple.

There are two good Forest Service campgrounds in Big Cottonwood Canyon, about 15 miles southeast of downtown Salt Lake City, and another two up Little Cottonwood Canyon, about 19 miles southeast of town. All have drinking water, and all prohibit pets because of local watershed regulations; sites range $19-22, and some can be reserved (877/444-6777, www.recreation.gov, $10 reservation fee). **Spruces Campground** (elevation 7,400 feet, early June-mid-Oct.) is 9.1 miles up Big Cottonwood Canyon. **Redman Campground** (elevation 8,300 feet, no reservations,

mid-June-early Oct.) is between Solitude and Brighton, 14 miles up Big Cottonwood Canyon.

Tanners Flat Campground (elevation 7,200 feet, no reservations, mid-May-mid-Oct.) is 4.3 miles up Little Cottonwood Canyon. **Albion Basin Campground** (elevation 9,500 feet, no reservations, early July-late Sept.) is high in the mountains a few miles past Alta Ski Area; go 11 miles up the canyon, the last 2.5 miles on gravel.

Food

If you're going to be camping on your trip through southeastern Utah's national parks, you may want to pick up some provisions in Salt Lake City before hitting the road south. Just east of I-15, off I-80 in the Sugar House district, **Whole Foods Market** (1131 E. Wilmington Ave., 801/359-7913) has a good deli, lots of organic produce, bulk foods, and good bread (likely the last you'll see for a while). It's in a complex that also contains some good restaurants, a camping supply store, and the brightest, shiniest tattoo parlor you'll ever lay eyes on.

Downtown, stop at **Tony Caputo Market & Deli** (308 W. Broadway, 801/531-8669, www.caputosdeli.com, 9am-7pm Mon., 9am-9pm Tues.-Sat., 10am-5pm Sun.), an old-style Italian deli brimming with delicious sausages, cheeses, and olives. Don't forget to get a sandwich to go.

For Salt Lake City's best restaurants, you have to head downtown. **Lamb's** (169 S. Main St., 801/364-7166, www.lambsgrill.com, 7am-9pm Mon.-Fri., 8am-9pm Sat., $13-15) claims to be Utah's oldest restaurant. You can still enjoy the classic 1930s diner atmosphere as well as the tasty food. Lamb's is an especially good place for breakfast.

Red Iguana (736 W. North Temple, 801/322-1489, www.rediguana.com, 11am-10pm Mon.-Thurs., 11am-11pm Fri., 10am-11pm Sat., 10am-9pm Sun., $8-22), on the way in from the airport, is one of the city's favorite Mexican restaurants and offers excellent south-of-the-border cooking with a specialty

in Mayan and regional foods. Best of all, the flavors are crisp, fresh, and earthy. The Red Iguana is very popular, so arrive early—especially at lunch—to avoid the lines.

For fine dining, the **Metropolitan** (173 W. Broadway, 801/362-3472, www.themetropolitan.com, 11:30am-2pm and 6pm-9pm Mon.-Thurs., 11:30am-2pm and 6pm-9:30pm Fri., 6pm-9:30pm Sat., 6pm-9pm Sun., $25-35) is easily Salt Lake City's most ambitious restaurant, taking "fusion cuisine" to new lengths. In this high-design dining room (reserve tables near the fireplace and water sculpture), the foods of the world meet and mingle on your plate in preparations that are sometimes unexpected but always stylish.

In the Hotel Monaco, **Bambara** (202 S. Main St., 801/363-5454, www.bambara-slc.com, 7am-10am, 11am-2pm, and 5:30pm-10pm Mon.-Thurs., 7am-10am, 11am-2pm, and 5:30am-10:30pm Fri., 8am-11am and 5:30pm-10:30pm Sat., 8am-noon and 5:30pm-9pm Sun., $20-25) has a menu that emphasizes the freshest and most flavorful local meats and produce, with preparations in a wide-awake New American style that is equal parts tradition and innovation.

Utah's oldest brewpub is **Squatters Pub Brewery** (147 W. Broadway, 801/363-2739, www.squatters.com, 11am-midnight Mon.-Thurs., 11am-1am Fri., 10:30am-1am Sat., 10:30am-midnight Sun., $8-18). In addition to fine beers and ales, the pub serves sandwiches, burgers, and other light entrées in a handsome old warehouse. In summer there's seating on the back deck. Another popular brewpub is the **Red Rock Brewing Company** (254 S. 200 W., 801/521-7446, www.redrockbrewing.com, 11am-midnight Sun.-Thurs., 11am-1am Fri.-Sat., $10-20), offering pasta, salads, and sandwiches, including an excellent variation on the hamburger, baked in a wood-fired oven inside a bread pocket. There's often a wait to get in the door, but the food and brews are worth it.

FROM DENVER

Although it may not seem intuitive to start your tour of southeastern Utah's national parks in Denver, that's exactly what works best for many folks, especially those who fly from European capital cities to Denver International Airport. From there, it's easy to rent a car or RV and begin a tour that typically includes Rocky Mountain National Park, Utah's five national parks, and the Grand Canyon before terminating at Las Vegas.

Airport

Locals joke that **Denver International Airport** (DEN, 8500 Peña Blvd., 303/342-2000, www.flydenver.com), often referred to as DIA, is in Kansas; it's actually 23 miles northeast of downtown Denver on Highway 470, north of I-70. Major airlines using DIA include American, British Airways, Continental, Delta, and United.

DIA's Jeppesen Terminal has a giant atrium and three concourses connected by a light-rail train. Car-rental counters are in the central terminal atrium between security screening areas.

Car

To drive from Denver to southeastern Utah's national parks, follow I-70 west, up over the Continental Divide along the Rocky Mountains, and down to the Colorado River. Cross into Utah and take I-70 exit 212 at Cisco. From Denver to Cisco is 297 miles, all on the freeway. From Cisco, follow Highway 128 for 37 highly scenic miles through red-rock canyons to Moab. Allow 5.5 hours of driving time between Moab and Denver.

All major car rental agencies have facilities near DIA.

RV Rentals

B&B RV (6960 Smith Rd., Denver, 303/322-6013, www.bb-rv.com) is a local company that rents RVs. **Moturis Inc./Camping World** (4100 Youngfield St., Denver, 800/222-6795, www.moturis.com) is west of downtown Denver.

Regional corporations with offices in Denver include **Cruise America** (8950 N. Federal Blvd., Denver, 303/650-2865, www.cruiseamerica.com) and **El Monte RV** (5989 Main St., Louviers, 303/426-7998 or 888/337-2214, www.elmonterv.com).

Accommodations

Chain hotels have set up shop in the area surrounding DIA. Almost all offer shuttles to and from the airport.

For budget travelers, the **11th Avenue Hotel and Hostel** (1112 N. Broadway, 303/861-7777, http://innkeeperrockies.com, $21 dorm, $29 pp private rooms) is a 1903 hotel on the edge of downtown that's now a blend of hotel and hostel. Facilities include laundry, Internet access, and cable TV. There's no kitchen, but guests have access to a barbecue grill, a microwave, and a toaster oven.

The closest lodgings to DIA are about six miles from the airport. The **DIA Microtel Inn** (18600 E. 63rd Ave., 303/371-8300 or 800/771-7171, www.microtelinn.com, from $79) offers free breakfast. The **Quality Inn** (6890 Tower Rd., 303/371-5300 or 877/424-6423, www.qualityinn.com, from $89) is easy to find north of I-70 exit 286. About 12 miles south of the airport, near the intersection of I-70 and Peña Boulevard, is a cluster of chain motels, including **Comfort Inn** (16921 E. 32nd Ave., 303/367-5000, www.comfortinn.com, from $89).

The **Hilton Garden Inn Denver Airport** (16475 E. 40th Circle, 303/371-9393, www1.hilton.com, from $149) is near the intersection of I-70 and Peña Boulevard, south of the airport. Other comfortable DIA-area hotels include **Comfort Suites** (6210 Tower Rd., 303/371-9300, www.comfortsuites.com, from $109), where all guest rooms are suites, and the **Fairfield Inn Denver Airport** (6851 Tower Rd., 303/576-9640, www.marriott.com, $139). If you're looking for the classic swanky downtown-Denver hotel, try the **Brown Palace**

(321 17th St., 303/297-3111 or 800/321-2599, www.brownpalace.com, from $233), a historic and ornate hotel from Denver's 1890s heyday.

Food

If you're just passing through DIA on your way to Utah, you'll find that there's not a lot of fine dining near the airport; inside the terminals there is a **Wolfgang Puck Express** (Concourse B, 303/342-7611), which is worth knowing about. You'll have to travel into Denver if you want to explore the dining scene.

There's a large Hispanic population, so it's no surprise that Denver has lots of Latin American restaurants, and these are often good and reliable places for inexpensive meals. However, some of Denver's most exciting restaurants are Nuevo Latin American restaurants—where familiar tacos, tortillas, and enchiladas are updated into zippy fine dining. One of the best is **Lola** (1575 Boulder St., 720/570-8686, www.loladenver.com, 4pm-10pm Mon.-Fri., 10am-10pm Sat.-Sun., entrées under $25), a hip and happening restaurant with over 150 tequilas to choose from and main courses like grilled pork with habañero sauce. Guacamole is prepared table-side, like Caesar salad in traditional American steak houses. More upscale is **Tamayo** (1400 Larimer St., 720/946-1433, www.richardsandoval.com, 11:30am-2pm and 5pm-10pm Mon.-Thurs., 11:30am-2pm and 5pm-11pm Fri., 5pm-11pm Sat., 5pm-10pm Sun., entrées $20-28), a hybrid of French refinement and zesty Mexican flavors. Views from this rooftop dining room overlook Larimer Square and the Rockies, making it a top spot for margaritas and appetizers, particularly the excellent shrimp tacos.

At **Deluxe** (30 S. Broadway, 303/722-1550, http://deluxedenver.com, 5pm-10pm Tues.-Sat., $10-28), the emphasis is on seasonal ingredients and perfect execution of international comfort foods such as spring vegetable risotto and lamb *ragù* with fresh pasta ribbons, along with

delicious cocktails. The **Barolo Grill** (3030 E. 6th Ave., 303/393-1040, www.barologrilldenver.com, 5:30pm-10:30pm Tues.-Sat., $15-30) is a comfortable northern Italian restaurant with good salads and pasta as well as grilled fish, game, and chicken main courses. The wine list is outstanding. Denver is known for its steak houses, and one of the best is the locally owned **Capital Grille** (1450 Larimer St., 303/539-2500, www.thecapitalgrille.com, 11:30am-2:30pm

and 5pm-10pm Mon.-Thurs., 11:30am-2:30pm and 5pm-11pm Fri., 5pm-11pm Sat., 4pm-9pm Sun., $19-40), with swank surroundings, an attentive staff, and excellent steaks, prime rib, and chops. For a lighter meal, go to **Falling Rock Tap House** (1919 Blake St., 303/293-8338, www.fallingrocktaphouse.com, 11am-2am daily, $8-20), one of Denver's top regional beer pubs, with over 75 brews on tap and tasty pub grub.

Getting Around

For most travelers, getting around southeastern Utah requires using some form of automobile. Public transportation is nonexistent in and between the parks, and distances are great—although the parks cover a relatively compact area, the geography of the land is so contorted that there are few roads that connect the dots. For instance, from Moab to the Arizona border, a distance of nearly 130 miles, only one bridge crosses the Colorado River once it drops into its canyon. Cars can easily be rented in Salt Lake City and Denver, and the Moab airport has car rentals, but it's wise to rent well in advance as the quantity is limited. Once you get to Moab, you'll find a plethora of jeep and Humvee rentals as well.

Bicycle touring is certainly an excellent option, but cyclists need to be in good shape and be prepared for intense heat during summer trips. For detailed information on cycling Utah, read the classic *Bicycle Touring in Utah* by Dennis Coello, now out of print but available from libraries and secondhand from online sources.

STREET NUMBERING AND GRID ADDRESSES

Many towns founded by Mormon settlers share a street-numbering scheme that can be confusing to first-time visitors but quickly becomes intuitive. A city's address grid will generally have its temple at the center, with blocks numbered by hundreds out in every direction. For instance, 100 West is one block west of the center of town, then comes 200 West, and so on. In conversation, you may hear the shorthand "4th South," "3rd West," and so on to indicate 400 South or 300 West.

While this street-numbering system is a picture of precision, it's also confusing at first. All addresses have four parts: When you see the address 436 North 100 West, for instance, the system tells you that the address will be found four blocks north of the center of town, on 100 West. One rule of thumb is to remember that the last two segments of an address (300 South, 500 East, 2300 West) are the street's actual name—the equivalent of a single street signifier such as Oak Street or Front Street.

TRAVELING BY RV

Traveling the Southwest's national parks in an RV is a time-honored tradition, and travelers will have no problem finding RV rentals in major cities like Denver and Salt Lake City. The parks have good campgrounds, and towns like Moab have some very spiffy campground options with extras like swimming pools and wireless Internet.

DRIVING THE PARKS

During the summer, patience is key to driving in southeastern Utah's national parks. Roads

VISITOR INFORMATION

General tourism literature and maps are available from the **Utah Travel Council** (Council Hall/Capital Hill, Salt Lake City, UT 84114-7420, 801/538-1030, fax 801/538-1399, www.utah.com). Call or write in advance of your visit to obtain maps and brochures from the parks; all printed material is available for download from the park or visitors center websites.

Arches National Park
P.O. Box 907
Moab, UT 84532
435/719-2299
www.nps.gov/arch

Canyonlands National Park
2282 SW Resource Blvd.
Moab, UT 84532

435/719-2313
www.nps.gov/cany

Hovenweep National Monument
McElmo Route
Cortez, CO 81321
970/562-4282, ext. 10
www.nps.gov/hove

Natural Bridges National Monument
HC-60 Box 1
Lake Powell, UT 84533
435/692-1234, ext. 16
www.nps.gov/nabr

Moab Area Travel Council
P.O. Box 550
Moab, UT 84532
www.discovermoab.com

are often crowded with slow-moving RVs, and traffic jams are not uncommon.

Summer heat in the desert puts an extra strain on both cars and drivers. It's worth double-checking your vehicle's cooling system, engine oil, transmission fluid, fan belts, and tires to make sure they are in top condition. Carry several gallons of water in case of a breakdown or radiator trouble. Never leave children or pets in a parked car during warm weather; temperatures inside can cause fatal heatstroke in minutes.

At times the desert has too much water, when late-summer storms frequently flood low spots in the road. Wait for the water level to subside before crossing. Dust storms can completely block visibility but tend to be short-lived. During such storms, pull completely off the road, stop, and turn off your lights so as not to confuse other drivers. Radio stations carry frequent weather updates when weather hazards exist.

If stranded, stay with your vehicle unless you're positive of where to go for help, then leave a note explaining your route and departure time. Airplanes can easily spot a stranded car (tie a piece of cloth to your antenna), but a person walking is more difficult to see. It's best to carry emergency supplies: blankets or sleeping bags, a first-aid kit, tools, jumper cables, a shovel, traction mats or chains, a flashlight, rain gear, water, food, and a can opener.

Maps

The Utah Department of Transportation prints and distributes a free, regularly updated map of Utah, although its size and quality have declined in recent editions. Ask for it when you call for information or when you stop at a visitor information office. Benchmark Maps' *Utah Road and Recreation Atlas* is loaded with beautiful maps, recreation information, and global positioning system (GPS) grids. If you're planning on extensive backcountry exploration, be sure to ask locally about conditions.

Off-Road Driving

Here are some tips for safely traversing the

backcountry in a vehicle (preferably one with four-wheel drive):

- Drive slowly enough to choose a safe path and avoid obstacles such as rocks or giant potholes, but keep up enough speed to propel yourself through sand or mud.

- Keep an eye on the route ahead of you. If there are obstacles, stop, get out of your vehicle, and survey the situation.

- Reduce the tire pressure if you're driving across sand.

- Drive directly up or down the fall line of a slope. Cutting across diagonally may seem less frightening, but it puts you in a position to slide or roll over.

If you really want to learn to drive your 4WD rig, consider signing up for a class.

TOURS

Bus tours of the southern Utah national parks, often in conjunction with Grand Canyon National Park, are available from several regional tour companies. **Southern Utah Scenic Tours** (P.O. Box 1113, Cedar City, 435/867-8690 or 888/404-8687, www.utahscenictours.com) offers multiday scenic and thematic tours of the Southwest, including the Utah national parks.

For a truly unusual bus tour, consider the **Adventure Bus** (21 E. Kelsey Ave., Salt Lake City, 909/633-7225 or 888/737-5263, www.adventurebus.com), a bus that has had most of its seats removed to make lounge and sleeping areas. Guests live on the bus (some meals are provided) as it makes tours of Utah and other Southwestern hot spots.

Recreation

Southeastern Utah's national parks are home to epic landscapes—red-rock canyons, towering arches, and needles of sandstone that are best explored by foot, by bike, or on the water. Hikers will find a variety of trails, ranging from paved all-abilities paths to remote backcountry tracks. Rafts and jet boats out of Moab provide another means to explore rugged canyons otherwise inaccessible to all but the hardiest trekkers. The sheer rock cliff faces and promontories in the parks provide abundant challenges to experienced rock climbers; be certain to check park regulations before climbing, however, as restrictions may apply.

HIKING

Utah's national parks offer lots of opportunities for hikers and backcountry enthusiasts interested in exploring the scenery on foot. Each of the parks has a variety of well-maintained hiking trails, ranging from easy strolls to multiday backcountry treks. In fact, much of the Needles and Maze districts in Canyonlands are

accessible only on foot; visits to remote Anasazi ruins and petroglyphs are among the rewards for the long-distance hiker.

CAMPING

All of Utah's national parks have campgrounds, with each park keeping at least one campground open year-round. Most campgrounds are first-come, first-served; reservations (877/444-6777, www.recreation.gov, $10 reservation fee) are accepted seasonally at Devils Garden Campground in Arches National Park. During the summer and on holiday weekends during the spring and fall, it's best to arrive at the park early in the day and select a campsite immediately. Don't expect to find hookups or showers at National Park Service campgrounds. For these comforts, look just outside the park entrances, where you'll generally find a full-service commercial campground.

Backcountry Camping

Backcountry campers in national parks must stop by the park visitors center for a

HOW TO CHOOSE AN OUTFITTER

Utah has several outfitters, guides, trail-drive operators, and guest ranches, all of which promise to get you outdoors and into an Old West adventure. But all outfitting and recreational services are not created equal. The most important consideration in choosing an outfitter is safety; the second is comfort. Make sure you feel confident on both counts before signing on.

Here are some points to ponder while you plan your adventure vacation.

All outfitters should be licensed or accredited by the state and be happy to provide you with proof. This means that they are bonded, carry the necessary insurance, and have the money and organizational wherewithal to register with the state. This rules out fly-by-night operations and college students who've decided to set up business for the summer. If you're just starting to plan an excursion, contact the Utah Travel Council (Capitol Hill, Salt Lake City, 801/538-1030 or 800/200-1160, www.utah.com). The council's website contains an extensive network of outfitters and guides.

Many outfitters offer similar trips. When you've narrowed down your choices, call and talk to the outfitters on your short list. Ask lots of questions, and try to get a sense of who the people are; you'll be spending a lot of time with them, so make sure you feel comfortable. If you have special interests, like bird- or wildlife-watching, be sure to mention them to your potential outfitter. A good outfitter will take your interests into account when planning a trip.

If there's a wide disparity in prices among outfitters for the same trip, find out what makes up the difference. The cheapest trip may not be the best choice for you. Food is one of the most common areas to economize in. If you don't mind having cold cuts each meal for your five-day pack trip, then maybe the cheapest outfitter is OK. If you prefer a cooked meal, or alcoholic beverages, or a choice of entrées, then be prepared to pay more. On a long trip, it might be worth it. Also be sure you know what kinds of accommodations are included in multiday trips. You may pay more to have a tent or cabin to yourself, but again, it may be worth it.

Ask how many years an outfitter has been in business and how long your particular escort has guided this trip. Although a start-up outfitting service can be perfectly fine, you should know what level of experience you are buying. If you have questions, especially for longer or more dangerous trips, ask for referrals.

Most outfitters will demand that you pay a portion (usually half) of your fee well in advance to secure your place, so be sure to ask about cancellation policies. Some lengthy float trips can cost thousands of dollars; if cancellation means the forfeiture of the deposit, you need to know that. Also, find out what the tipping or gratuity policy is for your outfitter. Sometimes 15 or 20 percent extra is added to your bill as a tip for the "hands." Although this is undoubtedly nice for the help, you should be aware that your gratuities for a week's stay can run into the hundreds of dollars.

---

backcountry permit. Backcountry camping may be limited to specific sites in order to spread people out a bit; if so, a park ranger will consult with you and assign you a campground.

Before heading into the backcountry, check with a ranger about weather, water sources, fire danger, trail conditions, and regulations. Backpacking stores are also good sources of information. Here are some tips for traveling safely and respectfully in the backcountry:

- Tell rangers or other reliable people where you are going and when you expect to return; they'll alert rescuers if you go missing.
- Travel in small groups for the best experience (group size may also be regulated).
- Avoid stepping on—or camping on—fragile cryptobiotic soils.
- Use a portable stove to avoid leaving fire scars.
- Resist the temptation to shortcut switchbacks; this causes erosion and can be dangerous.

- Avoid digging tent trenches or cutting vegetation.
- Help preserve old Native American and other historic ruins.
- Camp at least 300 feet away from springs, creeks, and trails. Camp at least 0.25 miles from a lone water source to avoid scaring away wildlife and livestock.
- Avoid camping in washes at any time; be alert to thunderstorms.
- Take care not to throw or kick rocks off trails—someone might be below you.
- Don't drink water directly from streams or lakes, no matter how clean the water appears; it may contain the parasitic protozoan *Giardia lamblia,* which causes giardiasis. Boiling water for several minutes will kill giardia as well as most other bacterial or viral pathogens. Chemical treatments and water filters usually work too, although they're not as reliable as boiling (giardia spends part of its life in a hard shell that protects it from most chemicals).
- Bathe and wash dishes away from lakes, streams, and springs. Use biodegradable soap, and scatter your wash water.
- Bring a trowel for personal sanitation. Dig 6-8 inches deep and cover your waste; in some areas, you'll be required to carry portable human waste disposal systems.
- Pack out all your trash, including toilet paper and feminine hygiene items.
- Bring plenty of feed for your horses and mules.
- Leave dogs at home; they're not permitted on national park trails.
- If you realize you're lost, find shelter. If you're sure of a way to civilization and plan to walk out, leave a note with your departure time and planned route.
- Visit the Leave No Trace website (www.lnt.org) for more details on responsible backcountry travel.

CLIMBING

Most visitors to Utah's national parks enjoy spotting rock climbers scaling canyon walls and sandstone pillars, but for a few, the whole reason to visit southeastern Utah is to climb. These folks need a climbing guide, either the classic and rather hard-to-find *Desert Rock* by Eric Bjørnstad or *Rock Climbing Utah* by Stewart M. Green.

Prospective climbers should take note: Just because you're the star of the local rock gym, don't think that climbing the remote sandstone towers in Canyonlands is going to be simple. Sandstone poses its own set of challenges; it weakens when wet, so it's wise to avoid climbing in damp areas or after rain. The Entrada sandstone in Arches is particularly tough to climb.

Climbers in the national parks should take care to use clean climbing techniques. Approach climbs via established trails to prevent further erosion of slopes. Camp in park campgrounds, or on multiday climbs, get a backcountry permit. Because white chalk leaves unsightly marks on canyon walls, add red pigment to your chalk. Do not disturb vegetation growing in cracks along your route. Tube or bag human waste and carry it out. Remove all old worn rope and equipment, but do not remove fixed pins. Make sure your climb is adequately protected by visually inspecting any preexisting bolts or fixed pins. It is illegal to use a power drill to place bolts. Never climb directly above trails, where hikers may be hit by dislodged rocks.

In Canyonlands, even stricter regulations are in place. Here, no new climbing hardware may be left in a fixed location; protection may not be placed with the use of a hammer except to replace existing belay and rappel anchors and bolts on existing routes (or for emergency self-rescue); and unsafe slings must be replaced with earth-colored slings.

Plan to climb in the spring or fall. During the summer, the walls become extremely hot. Some climbing areas may be closed during the spring to protect nesting raptors. Check at the visitors centers for current closures.

Tips for Travelers

Southeastern Utah may seem a remote, uninhabited, and even hostile destination, but it sees hundreds of thousands of travelers each year and has sufficient facilities to ensure that visitors have a pleasant vacation. Before you visit, here are a few tips to ensure that your Utah vacation goes well.

FOREIGN VISITORS
Entering the United States
Citizens of Canada must provide a passport to enter the United States, but a visa is not required for Canadian citizens.

Citizens of 28 other countries can enter the United States under a reciprocal visa-waiver program. These citizens can enter for up to 90 days for tourism or business with a valid passport, and no visa is required. These countries include most of Western Europe plus Japan, Australia, New Zealand, and Singapore. For a full list of reciprocal visa-waiver countries (along with other late-breaking news for travelers to the United States), check out www.travel.state.gov. Visitors on this program who arrive by sea or air must show round-trip tickets out of the United States dated within 90 days, and they must present proof of financial solvency (credit cards are usually sufficient). If citizens of these countries are staying longer than 90 days, they must apply for and present a visa.

Citizens of countries not covered by the reciprocal visa-waiver program are required to present both a valid passport and a visa to enter the United States. These are obtained from U.S. embassies and consulates. These travelers are also required to offer proof of financial solvency and show a round-trip ticket out of the United States dated within the timeline of the visa.

Once in the United States, foreign visitors can travel freely among states without restrictions.

Customs
U.S. Customs allows each person over the age of 21 to bring one liter of liquor and 200 cigarettes into the country duty-free. Non-U.S. citizens can bring in $100 worth of gifts without paying duty. If you are carrying more than $10,000 in cash or traveler's checks, you are required to declare it.

Money and Currency Exchange
Except in Salt Lake City, there are few opportunities to exchange foreign currency or traveler's checks in non-U.S. funds at Utah banks or exchanges. Traveler's checks in U.S. dollars are accepted at face value in most businesses without additional transaction fees.

By far the best way to keep yourself in cash is by using bank, debit, or cash cards at ATMs (automated teller machines). Not only does withdrawing funds from your own home account save on fees, but you also often get a better rate of exchange. Nearly every town in Utah has an ATM. Most ATMs at banks require a small fee to dispense cash. Most grocery stores allow you to use a debit or cash card to purchase food, with the option of a cash withdrawal. These transactions are free to the withdrawer.

Credit cards are accepted nearly everywhere in Utah. The most common are Visa and MasterCard. American Express, Diners Club, and Discover are also used, although these aren't as ubiquitous.

Electricity
As in all of the United States, electricity is 110 volts, 60 hertz. Plugs have either two flat prongs or two flat prongs plus one round prong. Older homes and hotels may have outlets that only have two-prong outlets. If you're traveling with computers or appliances that have three-prong plugs, ask your hotel or motel manager for an adapter. You may need to buy a three-prong adapter, but the cost is small.

ACCESS FOR TRAVELERS WITH DISABILITIES

Travelers with disabilities will find Utah progressive when it comes to accessibility. Both Arches and Canyonlands have all-abilities trails and services. Visitors centers are all accessible, and at least a couple of trails in each park are paved or smooth enough for a wheelchair user to navigate with some assistance. Each park has a few accessible campsites.

Most hotels also offer some form of barrier-free lodging. It's best to call ahead and inquire what these accommodations are, however, because these services can vary quite a bit from one establishment to another.

TRAVELING WITH CHILDREN

The parks of southeastern Utah are filled with dramatic vistas and exciting recreation. The parks provide lots of opportunities for adventures, whether it's rafting the Colorado River or hiking to ancient Anasazi ruins, and most children will have the time of their young lives in Utah.

Utah is a family-vacation type of place, and no special planning is required to make a national park holiday exciting for children. Children do receive discounts on a number of things, ranging from motel rooms (where they often stay for free, but inquire about age restrictions, which vary) to museum admissions. One exception to this family-friendly rule is B&Bs, which frequently don't allow children at all.

Utah law requires all children age four or younger to be restrained in a child safety seat. Child seats can be rented from car-rental agencies—ask when making a car reservation.

SENIOR TRAVELERS

The parks and Utah in general are hospitable for senior travelers. The long-standing National Park Service-issued Golden Age Passport has been replaced by the America the Beautiful-National Parks and Federal Recreational Lands Senior Pass. This is a lifetime pass for U.S. citizens or permanent residents age 62 or over. The pass provides access to, and use of, federal parks and recreation sites that charge an entrance fee or standard amenity. The pass admits the pass holder and passengers in a noncommercial vehicle at per-vehicle fee areas, not to exceed four adults. The pass costs $10 and can only be obtained in person at the park. There is a similar discount program at Utah state parks.

GAY AND LESBIAN TRAVELERS

Utah is not the most enlightened place in the world when it comes to equality issues, but that shouldn't be an issue for travelers to the national parks. Needless to say, a little discretion is a good idea in most public situations, and don't expect to find much of a gay scene anywhere in southeastern Utah. Moab is notably more progressive than anywhere else in this part of the state, but there are no gay bars or gathering places.

PETS

Unless you really have no other option, it's best not to bring your dog (or cat, or bird, or ferret) along on a national park vacation. Although pets are allowed in national parks, they aren't permitted on the trails. This limits you and your dog to leashed walks along the roads, around campground loops, and in parking areas. During much of the year, it's far too hot to leave an animal in a parked car.

Several pet boarding services are available in Moab:

- **Karen's Canine Campground** (2781 S. Roberts Rd., 435/259-7922)
- **Desert Doggie Daycare** (4890 Sunny Acres Lane, 435/259-4841, http://moabdesertdoggiedaycare.com)
- **Moab Veterinary Clinic** (4575 Spanish Valley Dr., 435/259-8710, http://moabvetclinic.com)

When in Moab, visit the **Moab Bark Park** (300 S. 100 E.), a fenced off-leash dog park.

UTAH'S DRINKING LAWS

The state's liquor laws can seem rather confusing and peculiar to outsiders. Changes to Utah's once prohibitive rules have made it easier to buy and consume alcohol. Note that it's no longer necessary to be a member of a private club in order to consume alcohol in a bar—no more buying a temporary membership or signing in on someone else's membership just to enjoy a drink.

Several different kinds of establishments are licensed to sell alcoholic beverages:

Taverns, which include brewpubs, can sell only 3.2 percent beer (beer that is 3.2 percent alcohol by volume). Taverns can't sell wine, which is classed as hard liquor in Utah. Stronger beer is available in Utah, but only in bottles, and this beer is also regulated as hard liquor. You don't need to purchase food to have a beer in a tavern. With the exception of brewpubs, taverns are usually fairly derelict and not especially cheery places to hang out.

Licensed restaurants are able to sell beer, wine, and hard liquor, but only with food orders. In many parts of Utah, you'll need to specifically ask for a drink or the drink menu to begin the process. In Salt Lake City, Moab, and Park City, most restaurants have liquor licenses. In small towns, few eating establishments offer alcohol.

Cocktail bars, lounges, live music venues, and nightclubs, which once operated on the private-club system, can now serve alcohol without asking for membership. However, some continue the income flow by demanding a cover charge for entry. Depending on which county you are in, you may still be required to order some food to have a drink.

Nearly all towns will have a state-owned **liquor store,** though they can be difficult to find, and 3.2 percent beer is available in most grocery stores and gas station minimarts. Many travelers find that carrying a bottle of your favorite beverage to your room is the easiest way to enjoy an evening drink. The state drinking age is 21.

CONDUCT AND CUSTOMS
Alcohol and Nightlife

Observant Mormons don't drink alcoholic beverages, and state laws make purchasing alcohol relatively awkward. If going out for drinks and nightclubbing is part of your idea of entertainment, you'll find that only Moab offers much in the way of nightspots. Most towns have a liquor store; outside Moab, many restaurants don't serve alcohol.

Smoking

Smoking is taboo for observant Mormons, and smoking is prohibited in almost all public places. You're also not allowed to smoke on church grounds. Obviously, take care when smoking in national parks and pick up your own butts. Besides the risk of fire, there's nothing that ruins a natural experience more than windblown piles of cigarette filters.

Small-Town Utah

If you've never traveled in Utah before, you may find that Utahans don't initially seem as welcoming and outgoing as people in other Western states. In many smaller towns, visitors from outside the community are a relatively new phenomenon, and not everyone in the state is anxious to have their towns turned into tourism or recreational meccas. The Mormons are very family- and community-oriented, and if certain individuals initially seem insular and uninterested in travelers, don't take it as unfriendliness.

Mormons are also orderly and socially conservative people. Brash displays of rudeness or use of foul language in public will not make you popular.

Health and Safety

There's nothing inherently dangerous about Utah's national parks, although a few precautions can help minimize what risks do exist. For the most part, using common sense about the dangers of extreme temperatures, remote backcountry exploration, and encounters with wildlife will assure a safe and healthy trip.

HEAT AND WATER

Southeastern Utah in summer is a very hot place. Be sure to use sunscreen, or else you risk having an uncomfortable vacation. Wearing a wide-brimmed hat and good sunglasses, with full UV protection, can shield you from the sun's harmful effects. Heat exhaustion can also be a problem if you're hiking in the hot sun. In midsummer, try to get an early start if you're hiking in full sun. If you're out during the heat of the afternoon, look for a shady spot and rest until the sun begins to drop.

Drink steadily throughout the day, whether you are thirsty or not, rather than gulping huge amounts of water once you feel thirsty. For hikers, one of the best ways to drink enough is to carry water in a hydration pack (the two top brands are Camelbak and Platypus). These collapsible plastic bladders come with a hose and a mouthpiece, so you can carry your water in your pack, threading the hose out the top of the pack and over your shoulder, which keeps the mouthpiece handy for frequent sips of water. One easy way to tell if you're getting enough to drink is to monitor your urine output. If you're only urinating a couple of times a day, and the color and odor of your urine are both strong, it's time to start drinking more water.

HYPOTHERMIA

Don't think that just because you're in the Utah desert that you're immune to hypothermia. This lowering of the body's temperature

below 95°F causes disorientation, uncontrollable shivering, slurred speech, and drowsiness. The victim may not even realize what's wrong. Unless corrective action is taken immediately, hypothermia can lead to death. Hikers should therefore travel with companions and always carry wind and rain protection. Space blankets are lightweight and cheap and offer protection against the cold in emergencies. Remember that temperatures can plummet rapidly in Utah's dry climate—a drop of 40 degrees between day and night is common. Be especially careful at high elevations, where sunshine can quickly change into freezing rain or a blizzard. Simply falling into a mountain stream can also lead to hypothermia and death unless proper action is taken. If you're cold and tired, don't waste time: Seek shelter and build a fire, change into dry clothes, and drink warm liquids. If a victim isn't fully conscious, warm him or her by skin-to-skin contact in a sleeping bag. Try to keep the victim awake and offer plenty of warm liquids.

GIARDIA

Giardia lamblia is a protozoan that has become common in even the most remote mountain streams. It is carried in animal or human waste that is deposited or washed into the water. When ingested, it begins reproducing, causing intense cramping and diarrhea in the host; this can become serious and may require medical attention.

No matter how clear a stream looks, it's best to assume that it is contaminated and to take precautions against giardia by filtering, boiling, or treating water with chemicals before drinking it. A high-quality filter will remove giardia and a host of other things you don't want to be drinking. (Spend a bit extra for one that removes particles down to one micrometer in size.) It's also effective to simply boil your water; 2-5 minutes at a rolling boil

will kill giardia even in the cyst stage. Because water boils at a lower temperature as elevation increases, increase the boiling time to 15 minutes if you're at 9,000 feet. Two drops of bleach left in a quart of water for 30 minutes will remove most giardia, although some microorganisms are resistant to chemicals.

HANTAVIRUS

Hantavirus is an infectious disease agent that was first isolated during the Korean War and then discovered in the Americas in 1993 by a task force of scientists in New Mexico. This disease agent occurs naturally throughout most of North and South America, especially in dry desert conditions. The infectious agent is airborne, and in the absence of prompt medical attention, its infections are usually fatal. This disease is called hantavirus pulmonary syndrome (HPS). It can affect anyone, but given some fundamental knowledge, it can also be easily prevented.

The natural host of the hantavirus appears to be rodents, especially mice and rats. The virus is not usually transmitted directly from rodents to humans; rather, the rodents shed hantavirus particles in their saliva, urine, and droppings. Humans usually contract HPS by inhaling particles that are infected with the hantavirus. The virus becomes airborne when the particles dry out and get stirred into the air (especially from sweeping a floor or shaking a rug). Humans then inhale these particles, which leads to the infection.

HPS is not considered a highly infectious disease, so people usually contract HPS from long-term exposure. Because transmission usually occurs through inhalation, it is easiest for a human being to contract hantavirus within a contained environment, where the virus-infected particles are not thoroughly dispersed. Being in a cabin or barn where rodents can be found poses elevated risks for contracting the infection.

Simply traveling to a place where the hantavirus is known to occur is not considered a risk factor. Camping, hiking, and other outdoor activities also pose low risks, especially if steps are taken to reduce rodent contact. If you happen to stay in a rodent-infested cabin, thoroughly wet any droppings and dead rodents with a chlorine bleach solution (one cup of bleach per gallon of water) and let them stand for a few minutes before cleaning them up. Be sure to wear rubber gloves for this task, and double-bag your garbage.

The first symptoms of HPS can occur anywhere between five days and three weeks after infection. They almost always include fever, fatigue, aching muscles (usually in the back, shoulders, or thighs), and other flu-like symptoms. Other early symptoms may include headaches, dizziness, chills, and abdominal discomfort such as vomiting, nausea, or diarrhea. These symptoms are shortly followed by intense coughing and shortness of breath. If you have these symptoms, seek medical help immediately. Untreated infections of hantavirus are almost always fatal.

THINGS THAT BITE OR STING

Although travelers in Utah's national parks are not going to get attacked by a grizzly bear, and encounters with mountain lions are rare, there are a few animals to watch out for. Snakes, scorpions, and spiders are all present in considerable numbers, and there are a few key things to know about dealing with this phobia-inducing trio.

Snakes

Rattlesnakes, including the particularly venomous midget faded rattlesnake, are present throughout southern Utah. The midget faded snakes live in Arches and Canyonlands, where they frequent burrows and rock crevices and are mostly active at night. Even though their venom is toxic, full venom injections are relatively uncommon, and, like all rattlesnakes, they pose little threat unless they're provoked.

If you see a rattlesnake, observe it at a safe

distance. Be careful where you put your hands when canyoneering or scrambling—it's not a good idea to reach above your head and blindly plant your hands on a sunny rock ledge. Hikers should wear sturdy boots to minimize the chance that a snake's fangs will reach the skin if a bite occurs. Do not walk barefoot outside after dark, as this is when snakes hunt for prey.

First aid for rattlesnake bites is full of conflicting ideas: to suck or not to suck; to apply a constricting bandage or not; to take time treating in the field versus rushing to the hospital. Most people who receive medical treatment after being bitten by a rattlesnake live to tell the story. Prompt administration of antivenin is the most important treatment, and the most important aspect of first aid is to arrange transportation of the victim to a hospital as quickly as possible.

Scorpions

A scorpion's sting isn't as painful as you'd expect (it's about like a bee sting), and the venom is insufficient to cause any real harm. Still, it's not what you'd call pleasant, and experienced desert campers know to shake out their boots every morning, as scorpions and spiders are attracted to warm, moist, dark places.

Spiders

Tarantulas and black widow spiders are present across much of the Colorado Plateau. Believe it or not, a tarantula's bite does not poison humans; the enzymes secreted when they bite do turn the insides of frogs, lizards, and insects to a soft mush, allowing the tarantula to suck the guts from its prey. Another interesting tarantula fact: While males live about as long as you'd expect a spider to live, female tarantulas can live for up to 25 years. Females do sometimes eat the males, which may account for some of this disparity in longevity.

Black widow spiders, on the other hand, have a toxic bite. Although the bite is usually painless, it delivers a potent neurotoxin, which quickly causes pain, nausea, and vomiting. It is important to seek immediate treatment for a black widow bite; although few people actually die from these bites, recovery is helped along considerably by antivenin.

RESOURCES

Suggested Reading

ARCHAEOLOGY

Childs, Craig. *House of Rain: Tracking a Vanished Civilization across the American Southwest.* New York: Back Bay Books, 2006. Only part of this book deals with Utah, but it's a great read about the Anasazi.

Lister, Robert, and Florence Lister. *Those Who Came Before.* Southwest Parks and Monuments, 1983. A well-illustrated guide to the history, artifacts, and ruins of prehistoric Southwestern people. The author also describes parks and monuments containing archaeological sites.

Simms, Steven R. *Traces of Fremont: Society and Rock Art in Ancient Utah.* Salt Lake City: University of Utah Press and Price, UT: College of Eastern Utah Prehistoric Museum, 2010. Great photos accompany the text in this look into Fremont culture.

Slifer, Dennis. *Guide to Rock Art of the Utah Region: Sites with Public Access.* Albuquerque: University of New Mexico Press, 2000. The most complete guide to rock-art sites, with descriptions of more than 50 sites in the Four Corners region. Complete with maps and directions, and with an overview of rock art styles and traditions.

GUIDEBOOKS AND TRAVELOGUES

Benchmark Maps. *Utah Road & Recreation Atlas.* Medford, OR: Benchmark Maps, 2008. Shaded relief maps emphasize landforms, and recreational information is abundant. Use the atlas to locate campgrounds, back roads, and major trailheads, although there's not enough detail to rely on it for hiking.

Huegel, Tony. *Utah Byways: 65 of Utah's Best Backcountry Drives.* Berkeley, CA: Wilderness Press, 2006. If you're looking for off-highway adventure, this is your guide. The spiral-bound book includes detailed directions, human and natural history, outstanding photography, full-page maps for each of the 65 routes, and an extensive how-to chapter for beginners.

Zwinger, Ann. *Wind in the Rock: The Canyonlands of Southeastern Utah.* Tucson: University of Arizona Press, 1986. Well-written accounts of hiking in the Grand Gulch and nearby canyons. The author tells of the area's history, archaeology, wildlife, and plants.

HISTORY AND CURRENT EVENTS

Dellenbaugh, Frederick S. *A Canyon Voyage: The Narrative of the Second Powell Expedition.* Tucson: University of Arizona Press, 1984. A

well-written account of John Wesley Powell's second expedition down the Green and Colorado Rivers, 1871-1872. The members took the first Grand Canyon photographs and obtained much valuable scientific knowledge.

Powell, John Wesley. *The Exploration of the Colorado River and Its Canyons.* Mineola, NY: Dover Publications, reprinted 1997 (first published in 1895). Describes Powell's 1869 and 1871-1872 expeditions down the Green and Colorado Rivers. His was the first group to navigate through the Grand Canyon. A description of the 1879 Uinta Expedition is also included.

Stegner, Wallace. *Beyond the Hundredth Meridian: John Wesley Powell and the Second Opening of the West.* New York: Penguin Books, 1992 (first published in 1954). Stegner's book tells the story of Powell's wild rides down the Colorado River, then goes on to point out why the United States should have listened to what Powell had to say about the U.S. Southwest.

MEMOIRS

Abbey, Edward. *Desert Solitaire.* New York: Ballantine Books, 1991. A meditation on the Red Rock Canyon country of Utah. Abbey brings his fiery prose to the service of the American outback, while excoriating the commercialization of the West.

Childs, Craig. *The Secret Knowledge of Water.* Boston: Back Bay Books, 2001. Childs looks for water in the desert, and finds plenty of it.

Meloy, Ellen. *Raven's Exile.* New York: Henry Holt & Company, 1994. Throughout a summer of Green River raft trips, Meloy reflects on natural and human history of the area.

Zwinger, Ann. *Run, River, Run: A Naturalist's Journey down One of the Great Rivers of the American West.* Tucson: University of Arizona Press, 1984. An excellent description of the author's experiences along the Green River, from its source in the Wind River Range of Wyoming to the Colorado River in southeastern Utah. The author weaves geology, Native American ruins, plants, wildlife, and her personal feelings into the text and drawings.

NATURAL SCIENCES

Chronic, Halka. *Roadside Geology of Utah.* Missoula, MT: Mountain Press Publishing, 1990. This layperson's guide tells the story of the state's fascinating geology as seen by following major roadways.

Fagan, Damian. *Canyon Country Wildflowers.* Helena, MT: Falcon Publishing, 1998. A comprehensive field guide to the diverse flora of the Four Corners area.

Fagan, Damian, and David Williams. *A Naturalist's Guide to the White Rim Trail.* Seattle: Wingate Ink, 2007. Take your time to explore nature on the White Rim Trail.

Williams, David. *A Naturalist's Guide to Canyon Country.* Helena, MT: Falcon Publishing, 2000. If you want to buy just one field guide, this is the one to get. It's well written, beautifully illustrated, and a delight to use.

OUTDOOR ACTIVITIES

Belnap, Bill, and Buzz Belnap. *Canyonlands River Guide.* Evergreen, CO: Westwater Books, 2008. River map guide to the Colorado and Green Rivers, printed on waterproof paper.

Bickers, Jack. *Canyon Country Off-road Vehicle Trails: Maze Area.* Moab, UT: Canyon Country Publications, 1988. Descriptions of backcountry roads and off-road vehicle trails in the Maze area; out of print, but relatively easy to track down.

Bjørnstad, Eric. *Desert Rock: Rock Climbs in the National Parks.* Helena, MT: Falcon

Publishing, 1996. A classic climbing guide by one of Utah's most respected climbers.

Bloom, David. *Indian Creek: A Climbing Guide.* Boulder, CO: Sharp End Publishing, 2011. The definitive guide to the world's best crack climbing.

Crowell, David. *Mountain Biking Moab,* 2nd edition. Guilford, CT: Globe Pequot, 2004. A guide to the many trails around Moab, from the most popular to the little explored, in a handy size—small enough to take on the bike with you.

Day, David. *Utah's Favorite Hiking Trails.* Provo, UT: Rincon Publishing, 2002. Good simple maps and detailed descriptions of trails all over the state, including many in southern Utah's national parks and monuments.

Green, Stewart M. *Rock Climbing Utah.* Helena, MT: Falcon Publishing, 1998. Good

detail on climbs in all of Utah's national parks, including many line drawings and photos with climbing routes highlighted.

Kelsey, Michael R. *Canyon Hiking Guide to the Colorado Plateau.* Provo, UT: Kelsey Publishing, 2006. One of the best guides to hiking in southeastern Utah's canyon country. Geologic cross sections show the formations you'll be walking through.

Schneider, Bill. *Best Easy Day Hikes Canyonlands and Arches.* Helena, MT: Falcon Publishing, 2005. Twenty hikes in this popular vacation area, geared to travelers who are short on time or aren't able to explore the canyons on more difficult trails.

Wells, Charles A. *Guide To Moab, UT Backroads & 4-Wheel Drive Trails.* Monument, CO: Funtreks, 2008. Good descriptions and GPS waypoints for Moab-area four-wheelers.

Internet Resources

Although a virtual visit to Utah cannot replace the real thing, you'll find an enormous amount of helpful information online. Thousands of websites cover everything from ghost towns to the latest community news.

The American Southwest
www.americansouthwest.net/utah
Utah Guide provides an overview of national parks, national recreation areas, and some state parks.

Canyonlands Utah
www.canyonlands-utah.com
Good source for information on Moab and the surrounding areas, including Canyonlands and Arches National Parks.

Desert USA
www.desertusa.com
Desert USA's Utah section discusses places to visit and what plants and animals you might meet there. Here's the best part of this site: you can find out what's in bloom at www.desertusa.com/wildflo/wildupdates.

Moab Area Travel Council
www.discovermoab.com
Upcoming events, mountain bike trails, local restaurants and lodging, and outfitters are all easy to find at this comprehensive site.

National Park Service
www.nps.gov
The National Park Service offers pages for all

its areas at this site. You can also enter this address followed by a slash and the first two letters of the first two words of the place (first four letters if there's just a one-word name); for example, www.nps.gov/brca takes you to Bryce Canyon National Park and www.nps.gov/zion leads to Zion National Park.

Recreation.gov
www.recreation.gov
If a campground is operated by the federal government, this is the place to make a reservation. You can expect to pay close to $10 for this convenience.

Reserve America
www.reserveamerica.com
Use this website to reserve campsites in state campgrounds. It costs a few extra bucks to reserve a campsite, but compare that with the cost of being skunked out of a site and having to resort to a motel room.

State of Utah
www.utah.gov
The official State of Utah website has travel information, agencies, programs, and what the legislature is up to.

U.S. Forest Service
www.fs.fed.us/r4
Utah falls within U.S. Forest Service Region 4. The Manti-La Sal National Forest (www.fs.fed.us/r4/mantilasal) is in southeast Utah around Moab and Monticello.

Utah Mountain Biking
www.utahmountainbiking.com
Details mountain biking routes listed in this book as well as other local trails.

Utah State Parks
www.stateparks.utah.gov
The Utah State Parks site offers details on the large park system, including links to reserve campsites.

Utah Travel Council
www.utah.com
The Utah Travel Council is a one-stop shop for all sorts of information on Utah. It takes you around the state to sights, activities, events, and maps, and offers links to local tourism offices. The accommodations listings are the most up-to-date source for current room rates and options.

Index

List of Maps

Front color maps

Discover Arches & Canyonlands

Arches National Park

Canyonlands National Park

Moab

The Southeastern Corner

Background

Essentials

www.moon.com

MOON.COM is ready to help plan your next trip! Filled with fresh trip ideas and strategies, author interviews, informative travel blogs, a detailed map library, and descriptions of all the Moon guidebooks, Moon.com is all you need to get out and explore the world—or even places in your own backyard. While at Moon.com, sign up for our monthly e-newsletter for updates on new releases, travel tips, and expert advice from our on-the-go Moon authors. As always, when you travel with Moon, expect an experience that is uncommon and truly unique.